THE SURVIVOR'S GUIDE TO
Buying a Freehold

Kat Callo

The Survivor's Guide to Buying a Freehold
by Kat Callo

© 2006 Lawpack Publishing

Lawpack Publishing Limited
76–89 Alscot Road
London SE1 3AW

www.lawpack.co.uk

ISBN: 1-905261-10-1
ISBN: 978-1-905261-10-9

Exclusion of Liability and Disclaimer

While every effort has been made to ensure that this Lawpack publication provides accurate and expert guidance, it is impossible to predict all the circumstances in which it may be used. Accordingly, neither the publisher, author, retailer, nor any other suppliers shall be liable to any person or entity with respect to any loss or damage caused or alleged to be caused by the information contained in or omitted from this Lawpack publication.

For convenience (and for no other reason) 'him', 'he' and 'his' have been used throughout and should be read to include 'her', 'she' and 'her'.

Contents

About the author

Kat Callo is an international strategy consultant, writer and leading expert on leaseholder rights in England and Wales. She is founding director of Rosetta Consulting Ltd (www.rosettaconsulting.com), a strategy consultancy that advises leaseholders, solicitors, surveyors, government bodies and other clients on collective enfranchisement, lease extensions, right to manage and related leasehold subjects. The author of *Making Sense of Leasehold Property*, Kat writes extensively on rights of apartment leaseholders and the shift to resident-owned blocks of flats in the United Kingdom. Before incorporating Rosetta, she worked for 17 years at Reuters, initially as a foreign correspondent and later as a media executive at the international headquarters in London. An Anglo-American born in New York, Kat's journalistic postings with Reuters took her to Belgium, the Philippines, Hong Kong and Vietnam, where she set up Reuters first Hanoi news bureau in 1990. She also did reporting for Reuters from Afghanistan, Cambodia, Guam, New Caledonia and other locations in the Asia-Pacific region. Kat later created a number of new information and news products while working on the commercial side of Reuters in London and served as senior vice president in charge of a global media business. She is a graduate of Columbia University School of Journalism and London Business School. Kat and her husband, Peter Wilson-Smith, and their sons, Henry and Ben, divide their time between London and Suffolk.

Acknowledgements

It is my hope that this book will help many leaseholders and residential property experts, but I would not have been able to write it without having received so much assistance myself over the years from people working in this specialist area. I would like to thank the many readers of my previous book, *Making Sense of Leasehold Property*, who have written or called to tell me how much this layperson's guide has helped them. Many of these readers inspired me to write this latest book.

I am grateful to Siobhan McGrath, Senior President of the Residential Property Tribunal Service, and to her team of experts, especially Yoro Edmond, for his help with RPTS statistics. I am indebted to Peter Haler and his team of tireless advisers at the Leasehold Advisory Service, who have provided enormous and valuable support on an ongoing basis.

I have benefited from the generous assistance of Muriel Guest Smith, Robert Levene and Lord Coleraine at the Federation of Private Residents' Associations. Solicitors and surveyors with deep expertise in collective enfranchisement have helped me along the way, including Jennifer Israel, Alan Edwards, Swita Chandarana, Jonathan Small, Jonathan Harris and Mark Wilson.

Special mention goes to Joan South, a trailblazer who campaigned selflessly for years for leaseholders' rights to secure full ownership of their homes. Her advice to me on the necessity to describe the terrible human cost paid by many leaseholders when trying to enfranchise their block of flats helped me to shape this book.

I am grateful to the journalists who play a crucial role in telling this story and who have provided valuable support to me. They are Lorna Bourke, Jane Barry, Liz Hodgkinson and Chris Partridge. I would also like to thank

Julie Purkiss, Lynne East and Neil Abel for helping to spread the word to leaseholders across the country about their rights.

My thanks go to Charlotte Sewell for the important work done by the Leasehold Reform Division of the Department for Communities and Local Government, and for the sound advice and valuable input provided to me by Justin Downes, Julie Purkiss and Paul Cheng.

This book encapsulates many stories told to me by leaseholders and residential property experts, including tales in which unscrupulous landlords and incompetent professional advisers have effectively denied leaseholders their right to enfranchise. I would like to express my gratitude to Nicola Pharoah, Lesley Fraser, Bob Hrabal, Robert Neil Manning, Emma Jinks and Annabel Cary for sharing their stories with me and to the many other leaseholders, including clients of Rosetta Consulting Ltd, who have helped me to understand the obstacles faced by would-be enfranchisers. The leaseholders of Burnham Court and my fellow directors of Burnham Court Ltd deserve special praise for their strong running legs and single-minded focus throughout the enfranchisement marathon.

I hope that leaseholders and residential property experts will continue to share their stories with me, by emailing me at kat.callo@rosettaconsulting. com.

My editors, Jamie Ross and Jane Perris, at Lawpack Publishing have helped me enormously. It has been a delight to work with them on this book.

My father, Joe Callo, deserves special thanks for teaching me, when I was a skinny teenager, about the mindset of the long-distance runner. 'Run until you taste blood' is not the advice that every daughter expects from her father, but it has stood me in good stead. I would like to thank Sally Callo for her endless support and superb advice, including on communications and how to get over the bumps. I am eternally grateful to my mother, Sue Callo, for being my tireless cheerleader, and for selflessly and graciously stepping in to help when things start to crumble.

I would not have been able to write this book without the love and support of my family. My husband, Peter Wilson-Smith, initially thought his New-York-born wife had gone mad for campaigning for the leaseholder's right to enfranchise. He has been an enormous help to me, including by playing devil's advocate. His support and advice have been invaluable over the years, especially as he has challenged me to transform this complex, technical subject into one that is accessible to the average homeowner. Our sons, Henry and Ben, have become enfranchisement experts in their own right as a result of listening to their mother. I thank them for their cheerful, soul-enriching support.

Foreword

It is generally accepted that the most serious traumas likely to be experienced by the average person are bereavement, divorce and moving house. However, there is another candidate, which for some unfortunate flat owners has eclipsed the others, the horrors of a collective acquisition of the freehold of the building. This book provides a timely guide under the razor wire and through the minefields of the process.

The Leasehold Reform Act 1993 introduced the landmark right for a group of leaseholders to get together and force the freeholder to sell; the right was empowering but the procedures were intimidating. Substantial changes were brought in with the 2002 amending legislation. But, based on experiences to date, it is still a route requiring a clear head and firm guidance.

Firstly, there is the simple matter of getting and holding together a disparate group of leaseholders with only one interest in common. Then there are the legal issues where trapdoors and problems abound; this is a job requiring an experienced specialist solicitor, not something to be put in the hands of the old family lawyer who dealt with your relative's Will and arranged the conveyance of your flat.

Property valuation often provides a shock to the layperson experiencing it for the first time, an arcane process full of references to yields and relativities but ultimately down to a negotiation between the two sides' valuers, not entirely removed from haggling over the price of a carpet in a Turkish bazaar.

The Survivor's Guide to Buying a Freehold by Kat Callo tells you what you need to know to understand the process, identifies where you need professionals and how to instruct them, and provides a simple introduction to the principles of valuation. Thousands of leaseholders have successfully bought their freeholds. This book makes it all a great deal easier.

Peter Haler, Chief Executive, Leasehold Advisory Service

Introduction

How can you own your home while not owning your home? In most of the world's industrialised countries, it is not possible. This riddle simply does not exist. But in England and Wales, the paradox of being a homeowner while not being a homeowner is an everyday reality for millions of flat dwellers because of the leasehold system.

Leaseholders of flats face the worst aspect of ownership, the cost, because they pay for all repairs, maintenance and running costs of their building. Yet they are deprived of the best aspect of ownership, the full control and enjoyment of their homes. Whether a block of flats is located in London, Liverpool or Brighton, it is the landlord or freeholder who enjoys total ownership and control of the building and the way it is managed, but he pays none of the cost year after year of maintaining the structure. Many buyers of London flats are shocked to discover, after paying as hefty a price as would apply for an apartment on Park Avenue in Manhattan, that they have not truly bought their flat. They have simply acquired a piece of paper, a lease, that provides limited rights of residence and that will eventually expire and leave the buyer with nothing.

For those concerned with consumer rights, the good news is that the leaseholders of flats have finally secured a legal right to eliminate this paradox by buying the freehold of their building and thus securing full, permanent ownership of their homes. But, more than a decade since the relevant legislation came into force, few flat owners are aware of this right. Even more discouraging, many leaseholders that have sought to buy their building through the statutory route since the 1990s have failed. Many residents and the lawyers and chartered surveyors that advise them say the law is so complex and filled with loopholes that landlords are often able to foil initiatives by leaseholders to buy the freehold.

This book is a guide for leaseholders of flats on how to buy the freehold of their building **and** survive the process. It is also meant to inform the growing number of solicitors and chartered surveyors who advise leaseholders what it is **really** like for their clients, a group of busy flat owners, to join forces to buy their freehold. This book is an equally essential tool for estate agents, managing agents of residential buildings, property investors and property developers who urgently need to become more knowledgeable about this crucial property issue.

Since 1993, two major laws have been passed that enable leaseholders to compel their landlord to sell to them their freehold and to do so at a fair price within statutory deadlines, a process known as 'collective enfranchisement'. This landmark legislation followed decades of efforts by both Labour Party and Conservative Party governments to reform the leasehold system, the origins of which date back to the Middle Ages. But these two laws are fraught with problems. The Leasehold Reform, Housing and Urban Development Act 1993 and the Commonhold and Leasehold Reform Act 2002 are complex laws, little understood by the average homeowner.

The tips and solutions for homeowners presented in this book draw on the experiences of leaseholders in hundreds of buildings across the country. Over the years, I have heard detailed accounts of efforts by many residents, some successful, some not, to buy their building freehold. Some of these stories have been told to me when I was providing strategy advice to flat owners through my company, Rosetta Company Ltd. Other accounts were gathered during nationwide research that I have carried out on collective enfranchisement. I have also benefited from crucial first-hand lessons learned over many years as chairperson of a residents' association in a large 100-year-old block of flats in central London.

Why do so many efforts to buy one's freehold, to enfranchise one's building, end in failure? Industry experts estimate that there are more than four million flats in England and Wales, and the number is growing quickly as a result of the construction boom in flat developments, yet only a tiny percentage of these buildings has become resident-owned. Why do so many freehold purchase projects never get off the ground? And why have several leaseholders told me that their health was literally destroyed by the long years of hard work and stress involved in attempting to enfranchise their building?

The answers to these questions include not only the unusual complexity of the 1993 Act and the 2002 Act. They also involve the striking mismatch that exists between the two parties, the landlord and the leaseholders' group, that lock horns in what is, by its nature, an adversarial commercial transaction. This book analyses in detail the vastly different organisational structure and resource base of the residents' association and that of the large corporate landlord upon whom the leaseholders are forcing a compulsory sale, and presents workable solutions to overcome some of the worst problems.

This book tells many stories that have previously remained untold. Some of the stories, including those in the case studies at the end, are unsettling. Others are deeply disturbing. Many describe instances in which large landlords have, through one or more actions, sought effectively to deny leaseholders the legal right won in the 1993 Act and the 2002 Act to secure full and permanent ownership of their homes, at a fair price and with a reasonable effort.

Homeowners will be better served by wider news coverage of enfranchisement in the main media in the UK. The trend for flat leaseholders to buy their building freehold is the story of a major, dramatic transfer in ownership of one of the country's biggest asset classes, residential property, from one group, that of large landowners, to another, individual homeowners. It is a change in ownership that has important implications for unlocking consumer spending on and improving the maintenance of billions of pounds' worth of property, an investment that promises a powerful impact on the local economies involved.

The quest to enfranchise is a compelling story about money, people's homes and basic consumer rights, but leading newspapers and broadcasters remain woefully silent on this important subject. This lack of informed media coverage makes it all the more essential for leaseholders to do their homework and acquire the information they need to enfranchise successfully.

In my previous book, *Making Sense of Leasehold Property*, I set out to answer important questions about the way in which the leasehold and freehold system works, and to identify and explain main leaseholder rights. This book digs deeply into one of the hottest questions today for flat owners. How do you transform a group of busy, diverse, often geographically-dispersed flat owners into a united entity that has the motivation, tenacity and organisational efficiency to raise required finance and maintain cohesion long enough to complete a freehold purchase project that can drag on for years?

The flat leaseholders' quest for home ownership

There has been unprecedented interest expressed by flat dwellers in recent years in buying the freehold of their building. It is not difficult to see why. Many suffer from the 'short-lease' problem. As the term of a lease gets shorter, the real market value of the residential unit decreases. If the lease has 999 years left, then the relative annual decrease in market value is so small as to be insignificant. But if the lease has 70 years or less, the shortness of the lease becomes a pressing problem. By the time the term of the lease drops to 60 or 50 years, the owner can have trouble selling the flat. This is because mortgage lenders see that the end of the lease, when the leaseholder must hand over his keys to the landlord because he no longer has any ownership of the flat, is within sight.

Many flat owners seek to resolve the short-lease problem by buying an extension of the lease from the landlord, but many complain about being overcharged for this. Buying the freehold of the building is an important way in which to overcome this obstacle, since leaseholders, after enfranchising, can grant themselves 999-year leases for as little as £1 plus legal fees. Thus, a main driver for buying one's freehold is the understandable desire to protect the value of one's home, which, for most people, represents their most valuable asset.

Another main driver spurring leaseholders to enfranchise is a growing demand for cost accountability and quality control in the management of residential buildings. Numerous government reports since the 1980s have cited decades of abuse by landlords who fail to carry out appropriate maintenance and repairs in buildings where the leaseholders have little say but have to pay all the bills. The increasing focus of consumer rights has prompted a growing number of flat dwellers to challenge this system.

Demographic shifts also explain the rush to buy one's freehold. A growing proportion of residents in London and other cities in the UK are spending time in other countries where they discover that flat owners really **do** own their homes. In the United States, it is the condominium flat or, in New

York, the co-operative or 'co-op'. In France, they call it 'co-propriété'. The concept is simple. Every flat owner owns his flat totally and in perpetuity, and he and others in the building jointly own the entire structure. This flat ownership model is used across Europe, North America and much of the Asia-Pacific region. Within the industrialised world, the leasehold system in England and Wales represents an antiquated anomaly. Indeed, the freehold system in this country was established in the 11th century, after William the Conqueror, victorious at the battle of Hastings, declared all the land in England his and then parcelled it out to his main supporters. These noblemen from Normandy became the 'freeholders' of the King's land because they were freemen and not serfs. To this day, all land in England still technically belongs to the Crown, with landowners actually holding a tenancy in the land, although this tenancy, freehold, equates for practical purposes to ownership.

One businessman in New York told me some time ago that enfranchisement, because it represented a compulsory sale forced on the landlord, sounded like a 'bizarre British socialist idea'. This is far from the truth. The quest for full ownership of one's flat for which one has paid a hefty purchase price represents the capitalist dream of home ownership.

The 2002 Act, in addition to widening the right for leaseholders of flats to enfranchise their building, also introduced the system of commonhold. In a commonhold building, the owners of flats possess the freehold of their individual units permanently and they jointly own all the common parts of the building. In a commonhold building, which is similar to the condominium system in the United States and much of Europe, there are no leases. The commonhold system offers attractive benefits for flat owners compared to the existing leasehold system, but it has been slow to take off since this part of the 2002 Act took effect on 27 September 2004. This has been due partly to restrictions in the law for converting a leasehold-freehold building to commonhold. This book does not address commonhold.

Over the years I have received many calls at my office from leaseholders wanting to buy their freehold. Their questions are often the same. How much will it cost? Do we qualify for the right to enfranchise? How do we get started? How long will it take? Since the 2002 Act, which expanded the leaseholder's right to enfranchise, flat owners have sent a flood of applications to the Leasehold Valuation Tribunal (LVT), the quasi-judicial body that decides on the freehold price. The graph below shows the number of enfranchisement applications received by the LVT since 2000. These figures comprise applications for collective enfranchisement and for lease extensions, since the tribunal describes the latter as 'individual enfranchisement'.

The number of enfranchisement applications made to the LVT

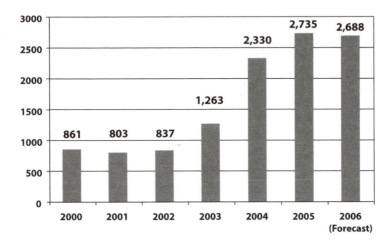

Source: *Residential Property Tribunal Service*

The benefits and risks of collective enfranchisement

Many flat owners make the unrealistic assumption that if they have the legal right to enfranchise, then they will succeed in doing so. They fail to recognise the many operational obstacles in their way and thus fail to get the freehold purchase project off to a sound start. I have heard countless tales of enfranchisement projects that have collapsed after years of hard work, because the main organiser moved away from the building. Again and again leaseholders tell me, 'If we only knew five years ago what we know now, we would have done things differently'.

Then there is the unfortunate scenario of the residents' group that succeeds in buying their building, only to achieve a Pyrrhic victory. Many organisers of enfranchisement initiatives have described to me a terrible personal toll they paid for leading a freehold purchase project that went on for years, forcing them to spend long hours away from family and business, and resulting in almost unbearable stress. I have seen several instances in which a lack of clarity, good governance and strong leadership by enfranchisement organisers helped to create or exacerbate conflicts amongst residents in a building. I have seen blocks of flats where the atmosphere had become so poisoned by the end of a freehold purchase project that some residents yearned for the past when their building had been owned by the absentee corporate landlord.

This book takes a no-nonsense approach to the many risks that plague the collective enfranchisement of a large block of flats. In some cases the obstacle is a landlord who is not willing to sell the freehold and who presents fierce and effective resistance. In other cases the main problem is the residents themselves. The tips and strategies in this book have been developed primarily for the large residents' association in a block of flats, whose membership comprises people living in the building and also absentee leaseholders who live overseas and rent out their UK flat. However, this survivor's guide is equally useful for the smaller building and for advisers and professionals concerned with residential property.

Addressing the David and Goliath mismatch

Leaseholders who consider the two enfranchisement laws passed since 1993 as panacea for the flat owner are mistaken. So are those that consider these laws so complex as to be worthless. The truth is somewhere in the middle. It is difficult, but possible, for a large group of residents to join forces and buy their building freehold. This book aims to help leaseholders to be better equipped and more knowledgeable about common pitfalls, so that they can develop a successful, street-savvy strategy to enfranchisement and still be smiling at the end of the process.

The single biggest mistake made by leaseholders' groups when setting out to buy their freehold is to fail to recognise the major risks inherent in the organisational mismatch between their residents' association and the large corporate landlord. The residents' association is a hierarchically flat organisation, the leaders of which have little if any formal authority over fellow committee members or association members. It is a qualitatively different environment from that of the salaried working world. While there is a strong deterrent to failing to do one's paid job at the office, because one might lose one's job and salary, there is no such 'killer deterrent' on the committee of a residents' association. Most residents' association committee members do this work on a volunteer part-time basis, driven by a sense of communitarianism amongst neighbours. The head of the residents' association and committee members, in order to be effective, often get things done by inspiring and motivating association members, rather than by ordering members around. An effective consensus-driven management style is required.

The organisational chart below illustrates the flat structure of the residents' association, with a dotted line rather than a formal solid reporting line of responsibility, between the committee and association members. Although the chart shows an organisation loosely held together, even this loose organisation tends to overstate the degree of cohesion, since it portrays the committee as a solid entity. In reality, there are few if any formal organisational constraints that bind together the committee members of a residents' association. The rules of a residents' association ideally are defined within a written constitution, although many such groups have no such document. It is unusual to find a residents' association constitution that contains a description of formal legal or commercial responsibilities amongst committee members or between the committee and association members.

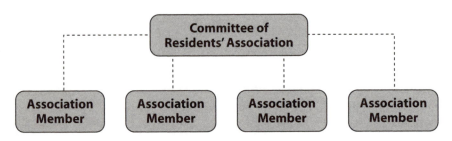

The hierarchical structure and management style of the large corporate landlord is dramatically different. Those within the organisation are paid employees, normally working on a full-time basis. There is more of a command-and-control hierarchy in which a board of directors establishes strategy and delegates the work to employees with specialist knowledge and experience. Importantly, the maximisation of the value of property assets is the full-time business-critical function of the landlord company. People risk losing their jobs if they fail to contribute to this corporate goal.

The organisational chart below illustrates just one section of one of the many corporate structures that one might find within a large corporate landlord. The difference between the formal reporting lines, amount of human resource and organisational clout of the large landlord company, and that of the residents' association is striking.

While the committee members of most residents' associations do this work on a part-time, unpaid basis, the large corporate landlord is filled with full-time employees whose jobs depend, day after day, on property assets owned by the company. While most residents' association committee members spend most of their day working at the 'day job', the corporate landlord is fully engaged in maximising the value of the company's property.

These two vastly different organisational structures help to explain why the corporate culture in most large landlord companies bears no resemblance to that of the residents' association. While senior executives within a company that owns many blocks of flats can delegate work to subordinates and expect for the work to be done, committee members of residents' associations must get things done by using moral authority, rather than formal commercial or legal authority, to persuade association members to do work, or else the committee members must do the work themselves.

I began studying the difference between the residents' association and the large corporate landlord many years ago, but this analysis deepened while I was studying for a business degree in the 1990s at London Business School. As part of the business course, I and fellow students examined in depth hundreds of companies and other organisations to understand why some were successful and others failed. I began to apply these models of organisational study to the area of enfranchise, to understand why so many residents' associations fell apart after a few years of trying to tackle as difficult a project as buying the freehold of a large block of flats.

What I discovered was an absurdly-imbalanced David and Goliath contest. While many large corporate landlords have deep pockets, strong organisational cohesion and clout, and a far-sighted strategy for their residential property assets, the typical residents' association lacks organisational structure, focus, and financial and human resource.

While a landlord with hundreds of buildings has large corporate scope to develop deep experience and expertise in enfranchisement, including ways to avoid being 'enfranchised out' of a building, I have seen many residents' associations waste years seeking to become experts in enfranchisement rather than hire experienced advisers that can help speed up the transfer of knowledge on this highly technical subject.

In many blocks of flats, the leaseholders themselves present the greatest obstacle to a successful collective enfranchisement. Because so many residents fail to understand the enormity of the mismatch between their own organisational clout and that of the landlord, many flat owners set unrealistic goals and try to achieve too much, only to see the residents' association collapse after a few years.

I have often heard worrying complaints about the way in which many residents' associations function. While this book does not encourage leaseholders to create a corporate entity as soon as they begin to explore the option of buying their freehold, it is essential to make clear to flat owners that the purchase of a freehold is a serious commercial transaction that is entered into collectively by people in the building. A residents' association that is focused on enfranchising a large building must not become a friends' club or a neighbours' complaint forum. Many leaseholders have told me that they have despaired after attending residents' association meetings, because these meetings were chaotic, unfocused and not chaired properly. Leaseholders who could have contributed valuable expertise in organisational, legal or commercial matters simply refused to be involved in residents' meetings in which there was no agreed agenda, no time keeping and no decisions taken on actions that would be carried out by a specific person by an identified deadline.

This book provides many sobering messages for residents' associations about how to get their act together, how to achieve an optimum degree of organisation, focus and purpose to survive the process of buying one's freehold. Many of the chapters are designed to assist leaseholders in avoiding a common situation in which the leaseholders become their own worst enemy, and where their own actions, rather than the landlord's actions, lead to the collapse of an enfranchisement initiative.

In order to organise, project manage and complete the freehold purchase of a large block of flats successfully, leaseholders must take care not to fight too many battles on too many fronts. Early in the project committee members must make clear their commitment to association members, but they must also secure a strong commitment from all members to this complex endeavour in which the adversary can often outpunch the residents' group in many ways.

It is understandable for leaseholders to become emotional when they feel threatened about the security with which they own their homes or their ability to protect the value of that home. One can see why leaseholders of flats become upset when they feel that they are being overcharged for their building service charges or being asked by the landlord to pay too high a price for a lease extension or the building freehold. But this book recommends a calm approach to what is often an emotive subject. Residents need to approach the project of buying their freehold in a dispassionate, business-like manner in order to succeed.

The long-distance race

This book presents an analogy of the freehold purchase project as the long-distance race. When I was growing up in a suburban town 30 miles north of New York City, my two brothers, two sisters and I were passionate about competitive running. Our enthusiasm for athletics was encouraged by our father, Joseph Callo, who, as a university student, had run for the Yale track team, and by our mother, Sue Callo, who was also very active and sporty. As a skinny, sports-mad teenager, I became disillusioned by the uninspired athletics coaching at the girls' school I attended as a day student in the next town. I asked my father if he would coach me in running and help me win races.

I have thought back many times to the lessons he taught me in those early-morning coaching sessions. 'The long-distance is completely different from the 50-metre sprint,' he said. To win a long-distance race, or indeed, even to finish it, it is not enough to have strong legs. It is not enough to have powerful lungs and a well-conditioned heart. You have to have the **mind** to run the long-distance race, my father explained to his young athlete. You have to have the tenacity to stick with it, the mental willingness to keep going when your legs tell you to stop. And you have to become familiar with pain and be able to overcome a fear of the pain that you will experience. 'Run until you taste blood' was his familiar coaching advice when I headed out to run a few miles in the morning, an hour before my school bus came and two weeks before a major athletic competition.

Having examined the existing legislation on collective enfranchisement and having studied hundreds of residential buildings, I have concluded that the process of buying the freehold of a large block of flats is like running a long-distance race. It requires more than the legal right to enfranchise in order to succeed. It requires more than a bit of enthusiasm by a handful of leaseholders who are upset about a large service charge bill. It requires single-minded focus and discipline, and patience and endurance, coupled with solid strategy and carefully-laid plans for business-like implementation.

Chapter 1 aims to help leaseholders avoid the common problem of the stuttering start, the situation in which residents spend years talking about buying their freehold without ever formally starting the process. Practical advice on how to come to grips with the critical documentation involved in collective enfranchisement without getting buried in paperwork is covered in chapter 2. Because so many flat owners are frightened away from enfranchisement because of what they see as impenetrable principles of valuing the freehold of a building, I have dedicated chapter 3 to demystifying the valuation process.

The long-distance runner spends many hours training for just one race. Similarly, chapter 4 focuses on the most important work in buying one's freehold, the preparation that is required before one can begin the formal process of enfranchising. Chapter 5 presents the runner at the starting line, when the leaseholders begin the official collective enfranchisement by serving notice on the landlord. Given the speed with which people come and go in a large block of flats, chapter 6 presents practical solutions for ensuring that the number of participants of an enfranchisement project does not dwindle before the freehold purchase has been concluded.

I have been surprised over the years to see how many enfranchisements have been foiled or seriously delayed not by the landlord, but by a small vocal group of opponents amongst the residents. For this reason, I have mapped out in chapter 7 how residents' associations should address this well-known problem. Because a vast majority of enfranchisements are concluded in a negotiated agreement between the residents and the landlord, rather than going all the way to a hearing at the LVT, chapter 8 covers the subject of negotiations in a freehold purchase project.

Chapter 9 is about crossing the finish line and surviving the process. Many residents' associations open the champagne bottles too soon after an LVT decision has been communicated or a negotiated settlement has been reached with the landlord, only to find the project in chaos when the landlord appeals the LVT decision or project participants fail to pay their share of the freehold cost. Because I have seen a large number of residents' associations collapse when the main organiser on the committee leaves the building or declares that he is stepping down, I have dedicated chapter 10 to the many ways in which committee members can avoid burnout.

I have included seven case studies that describe real people in real buildings, to illustrate how things can go well or disastrously wrong in an enfranchisement. The first four case studies describe problems experienced by enfranchisers as a result of difficult landlords and/or poor advice or service provided by professional advisers. The fifth and sixth case studies describe instances in which one or more leaseholders in the building represented the main obstacle to a smooth enfranchisement and post-enfranchisement management of the building. Case Study 7 describes a success story from beginning to end, as a result of quick-thinking enfranchisers who planned their freehold purchase carefully and were able to respond effectively to an unexpected offer by the landlord to sell the freehold. I am not suggesting with these case studies that six out of seven enfranchisements end badly. Rather, I have chosen case studies with powerful messages that should help leaseholders avoid some of the worst pitfalls.

Because of the complexity of the 1993 Act and the 2002 Act, enfranchisers are strongly advised to get help from an external project manager who has strong experience and expertise in enfranchisement, and who will ensure that a solicitor and a chartered surveyor with a solid track record in this specialist area are used. This book does not recommend that leaseholders pursue a do-it-yourself enfranchisement, because of the risks involved. However, the advice throughout the book and the essential documents provided in the Appendices will help residents understand the process and reap the greatest benefit from qualified advisers.

Although it is a misnomer to describe the leaseholder of a flat as a homeowner or the owner of the flat, because a leaseholder only really owns his lease, I use these definitions throughout this book for the sake of brevity.

Leasehold ownership is, strictly speaking, a form of tenancy and leaseholders are, by law, tenants. I avoid using the term 'tenant' in this book when describing leaseholders, however, because of the pejorative connotation for many homeowners, including the association with the tenement building. The legally-accurate term 'tenant' illustrates all too well the antiquated nature of the leasehold and freehold system, and the degree to which today's flat leaseholder is not the empowered homeowner that one encounters in other industrialised countries.

The information provided in this book relates to England and Wales, which have one system of residential property law. It does not relate to Scotland or Northern Ireland, which have different residential property systems.

Many people have asked me how I became an advocate of leaseholder rights and an enfranchisement expert, given my earlier career at Reuters that spanned two continents and nearly two decades. In my early years at Reuters, I worked as a foreign correspondent in London, Brussels, Manila, Hong Kong and Hanoi. Later I was promoted to the corporate side of the company, where I worked in strategy, marketing, product development, business development and as a line manager. I completed my time at Reuters as senior vice president, running a multi-million-pound global business.

My work at Reuters was varied and exciting, whether as a journalist covering attempted coups d'état in the Philippines, civil war in Afghanistan or political and economic reform in Vietnam, or later, when, as a media executive, I established new strategies and products, and raised finance to build new international businesses.

I have brought much of the training and experience developed at Reuters to my enfranchisement work, where I help leaseholders analyse large amounts of complex information and transform this quickly into simple, clearly-identified goals. The skills that enable an executive or manager of a fast-moving knowledge-based business like Reuters to build effective project teams amongst diverse individuals across corporate departments and national boundaries, and to initiate and complete difficult projects are, in many ways, similar to the skills required to build a strong residents' association amongst leaseholders living around the world and to buy one's building freehold.

It is my hope that this book will save leaseholders time, money and effort when they set out to enfranchise their building. Whether a resident reads the book from cover to cover, or simply skims the '100 top tips' in this book, he is likely to avoid many of the pitfalls that have foiled so many attempts to buy a building freehold. While many leaseholders in large blocks of flats have described to me their enfranchisement as a long and gruelling project, it is possible to cross the finish line with a smile on one's face. And it is very often worth the effort. A main goal of this book is to help leaseholders of flats not only to survive the long-distance race that is the collective enfranchisement process, but also to enjoy the journey.

CHAPTER 1

Avoiding the stuttering start

Leaseholders of flats have gained the important new right to force their landlord to sell to them the freehold of their building, but many residents have failed in their attempts to exercise this right. Indeed, in many buildings, owners of flats have spent years discussing amongst themselves the need to collectively enfranchise their building, only to see the initiative collapse before the formal process ever begins.

It is easy to see what happens when we compare the large residents' association that wishes to buy the freehold to the long-distance runner. For the runner to win the long-distance race or even to finish the race, it is not enough to have a right to take part. It is not enough for the runner to identify the intention to compete in the race, to have good muscle tone or to identify plans to begin training. The runner must make a real start towards the realisation of his goal by actually **beginning** the training. This chapter is about starting the training process, to ensure that the goal to buy one's freehold becomes realisable and does not simply remain the subject of discussion year after year at residents' association meetings.

How to get started on a collective enfranchisement

The challenge of jump-starting a freehold purchase project in a large residential building is considerable and multi-faceted. It is unusual for busy leaseholders to dedicate the time, money and effort required to enfranchise their building when they are happy with the status quo, when they have 999-year leases and are delighted by the quality and cost of the building management provided by their landlord. It is typically troubled buildings that enfranchise. The impetus to pursue this complex joint project amongst neighbours becomes greatest when there is a multitude of problems, including short leases, poor management of the building and a perception of unreasonably high service charges.

Leaseholders who are most highly motivated to buy their freehold are often angry and frustrated at the situation in their building. The catalyst for action might be a lift in the building that breaks down repeatedly or a letter from the landlord demanding that leaseholders pay a large sum of money for major repairs. Disgruntled residents start talking to one another and eventually a meeting of residents is organised one evening in someone's flat.

I have seen many buildings in which a residents' association in this troubled environment convenes a series of meetings that drag on and on, as leaseholders voice unhappiness about the ownership of the building. It is essential to recognise and be aware of the important paradox of the troubled building. The outburst of anger and emotion that is often required to initiate a freehold purchase project can also prevent the project from getting off the ground. This happens because residents' associations become bogged down in complaining about the past and the present situation, rather than dedicating the association's scarce resources on implementing solutions for the future.

Leaseholders who wish to organise a successful collective enfranchisement must remember that the flat hierarchical structure of the residents' association, in which the committee has little if any formal authority over association members, makes it extremely difficult to organise and see through a complex project such as a freehold purchase. One of the first steps, therefore, is for the association to identify and agree on the single-minded goal of collective enfranchisement, and to agree to avoid other labour-intensive tasks until this major project has been completed.

One of the greatest drains I have seen on the limited attention span of the average residents' association is the service charge dispute. It is understandable for leaseholders to be unhappy about service charges that they consider to be unreasonably high, but the association committee must warn against the well-known trap of engaging in endless fights with the landlord over such charges. Leaseholders have a legal right to challenge what they consider unreasonable service charges. But landlords also have a legal right to take action against leaseholders who violate their lease by failing to pay service charges. Residents' associations that get mired in lawsuits and counter lawsuits that are typical of service charge disputes rarely succeed in applying the required focus to buy their freehold.

The right to challenge the reasonableness of service charges does not mean that this is the most effective use of the residents' association's limited resources and capability. Ironically, it is frequently the residents in a building who offer to do the least amount of work and who make the loudest demands that the association committee fight endless battles with the landlord over service charges.

Service charge disputes cause damage to an enfranchisement that goes beyond distracting organisers. When leaseholders reach the end of the process, when they buy the freehold from the landlord, they must normally pay to the landlord any unpaid service charges. This is because they are buying an entity, a building freehold, with all the assets and liabilities on its balance sheet. Debts owed to the freeholder regarding the building, in the form of unpaid service charges owed by leaseholders, appear as assets on the balance sheet. The enfranchisers will have the right, after they have become the new freeholder, to recover these debts. But I have seen enfranchisement projects risk collapse at the end of the process because of a cash flow crisis caused by having to pay for unpaid service charges.

Committee members must take a firm and disciplined approach in helping residents' association members not only to identify the ambitious goal of buying the freehold, but also to identify the many things the association will not do during this extremely labour-intensive project, including pursuing service charge disputes.

At the beginning of the enfranchisement project, organisers should state in writing to all participants that the residents' association will not pursue service charge disputes and that each participant will be responsible either for paying his service charges or for resolving on an individual basis within six months of the start of the enfranchisement process any formal challenge pursued over service charges.

Leaseholders who are determined to challenge their service charges on an individual basis without causing disruption to a collective enfranchisement need to complete an Application Form S27A Landlord and Tenant Act 1985 and send the application, with a copy of the lease and an application fee that ranges from £50 to £350, to the Residential Property Tribunal Service (RPTS). The RPTS is the umbrella body for Leasehold Valuation Tribunals, which decide on freehold prices in enfranchisements, reasonableness of service charges and other disputes between leaseholders and landlords. The S27A form can be downloaded at www.rpts.gov.uk. More information on service charge disputes is provided in my book *Making Sense of Leasehold Property*, also published by Lawpack.

 Identify the purchase of the freehold as the single most important goal of the residents' association and identify other time-consuming activities, such as challenging service charges, as activities the residents' association will **not** pursue.

Once the leaseholders have reached sufficient consensus to investigate the possibility of buying the freehold, the residents' association must determine whether the building qualifies for collective enfranchisement and whether each would-be participant qualifies to take part. Appendix 3 provides a list of qualification elements.

Although there are exceptions, most flat owners with a lease that had more than 21 years at the start qualify to join an enfranchisement. In order for a building to qualify, a minimum of 50 per cent of all the flats in the building must take part. It does not matter whether some of the flats are owned by leaseholders and others by the landlord, such as a porter's flat. Fifty per cent of the **total** number of flats must participate. Also, a building will not qualify for enfranchisement if more than 25 per cent of the floor space in the building is for commercial use.

In order for a leaseholder to qualify to take part, it does not matter whether he lives in the building or on the other side of the world, or whether the leaseholder is a person or company. While there used to be restrictions against participation in an enfranchisement by absentee leaseholders and leaseholders that were companies under the 1993 Act, these restrictions were eliminated in the 2002 Act. It is important to remember, however, that no leaseholder owning more than two flats in the building can take part in the enfranchisement.

How long will the enfranchisement take?

The formal process involved in enfranchising a building, which begins the moment the leaseholders serve the required written notice on the landlord and ends when they buy the freehold, normally takes about one year. The timeline below illustrates the milestones in the formal process and the time required, if leaseholders move as quickly as the law allows from one stage to the next.

Typical timeline of a collective enfranchisement

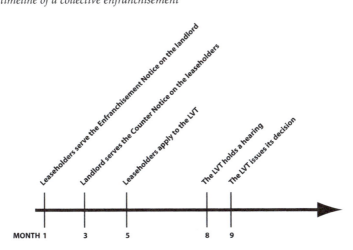

There are five main stages in the statutory enfranchisement process, with strict deadlines applying to the second and third stages. Appendix 4 provides details of the main stages of the typical enfranchisement.

Stage one of the formal process is the serving of an Enfranchisement Notice, also referred to as the Initial Notice, by participating leaseholders on the landlord. In fact, the notice is served by an entity called a 'nominee purchaser', which is the company created by the participating leaseholders to buy the freehold. While it is not required by law for leaseholders to set up a company limited by shares for this purpose, it is best practice to do so. The steps involved in creating this company are detailed in chapter 4. The Enfranchisement Notice informs the landlord that the participating leaseholders are compelling him to sell to them the freehold and it contains an offer price. The landlord has a maximum of two months to reply to the Enfranchisement Notice. If he fails to do so within the two months, the enfranchisers get to buy at their offer price.

Stage two begins when the landlord serves the Counter Notice on the enfranchisers. In the Counter Notice, the landlord must either acknowledge that the participants qualify to enfranchise or else claim that they do not qualify and state the reason. If the landlord accepts that the leaseholders qualify to enfranchise, in the Counter Notice he must accept the offer price or propose a 'counter offer' price. It is typical for large corporate landlords to propose a counter offer price that is higher than the leaseholders' offer price.

If a landlord proposes a counter offer price in his Counter Notice, the two sides can then begin negotiations. In a large block of flats, it is normally the chartered surveyor hired by the enfranchisers who negotiates with the landlord's surveyor. The issues that they debate regarding freehold valuation are described in chapter 3.

If the leaseholders and landlord fail to agree on the freehold price, the leaseholders can submit an application to the LVT to decide on the price. This application to the LVT represents stage three in the formal enfranchisement process. If the enfranchisers wish to apply to the LVT, they must do so no sooner than two months and no later than six months after the date by which the Counter Notice was due. If the leaseholders miss this crucial four-month window, there is considered to be a 'deemed withdrawal' of their Enfranchisement Notice, that is, they are considered to have dropped the claim. If there is a 'deemed withdrawal' or if the leaseholders purposely withdraw their claim, they must wait one year before they are allowed to start a new enfranchisement process.

Stage four takes place when an LVT hearing is held. Timings vary, but it often takes about three months from the time an application is sent to the LVT until the time that the hearing is held. For a small residential building with three or four flats, an LVT hearing can last as little as half a day. For a large block of flats, leaseholders should expect a two-day hearing. In complicated cases, the hearing might go on for three days. At an LVT hearing, there is a panel of two or three people which hears arguments and examines evidence presented by both sides. Panels of three people comprise a lawyer, a valuer and a layperson knowledgeable about enfranchisement. A two-person panel will comprise a lawyer and a valuer.

Stage five of the formal enfranchisement process begins when the LVT panel sends its written decision to both parties. Again, the length of time required for an LVT panel to send its written decision varies, but leaseholders should expect it to take about six weeks. The decision includes the price at which the landlord must sell the freehold to the enfranchisers.

Things usually move quickly after the LVT decision has been sent to both parties. The landlord must prepare a contract of sale and must give this to the nominee purchaser within 21 days of the LVT decision. The landlord can require a ten per cent deposit when the contract is provided to the nominee purchaser.

After both parties have received the written decision of the LVT panel, it is possible for either party to appeal the tribunal's decision to the higher-level Lands Tribunal, but written permission to do so must first be obtained from the LVT or the Lands Tribunal. The implications for enfranchisers of an appeal and ways they can minimise the risk that the landlord will appeal are covered in chapter 9.

Some enfranchisements take less than a year, if the landlord says in his Counter Notice that he accepts the offer price in the Enfranchisement Notice or if a negotiated settlement is reached in the weeks following the Counter Notice. The formal process, from stages one to five, can take well over a year. If the landlord presents tough and effective resistance, the process can drag on for two or more years. In chapter 4, we identify ways in which leaseholders can decrease the risk of this kind of protracted enfranchisement.

While a year-long enfranchisement, through all five stages, seems a long time, many enfranchisers find the time goes quickly, because of the deadlines laid down by law. The most time-consuming aspect of a freehold purchase initiative is not the formal process, but rather the early phase in which one or more proponents in the building seeks to build consensus and to organise the project.

If there is strong consensus amongst residents, the initial organising can take just a few weeks. But in a large block of flats where many leaseholders live outside the UK, reaching the stage when leaseholders are ready to begin the formal enfranchisement process usually takes months and often takes years. Hiring an outside project manager can speed up the process by clarifying issues quickly and eliminating the common pitfall for residents' associations to hold numerous meetings at which the same questions are raised again and again.

In order to get a freehold purchase project off the ground, proponents should first determine that the building qualifies for collective enfranchisement and then they should send a formal written invitation to all the leaseholders to join the project by a specific deadline date. The invitation should require that a deposit be paid in order to join. It is important that the invitation be sent to the confirmed leaseholder(s) of every flat, not the person or people **believed** by the residents' association committee to be the leaseholder(s). To draw up a confirmed list, the organisers should download a leasehold title for every flat in the building from the HM Land Registry website. This costs £4 per leasehold title and plan (or £2 for a leasehold title or a plan only). The website is at www.landregisteronline.gov.uk. The visitor to the site needs to click on 'Property Enquiry', then fill in the leasehold title number or address of the property and click 'Search'. Alternatively, copies of leasehold titles can be obtained by completing an OC1 Form with payment to the appropriate regional Land Registry office. Appendix 5 shows what the OC1 Form looks like. The form can be downloaded from the Land Registry's main website at www.landregistry.gov.uk. Chapter 2 provides a template for this invitation document.

It is important to make the process of inviting participation as fair and transparent as possible, to reduce the risk of failure for an enfranchisement and to preserve social harmony in the building. The same written invitation should be sent by the residents' association committee on the same date to all the leaseholders. Although it is not required by law to invite all the leaseholders to participate, it is best practice to do so. By sending the same invitation to all flat owners, the organisers also diminish the likelihood that non-participants will claim later that they did not know about the project or did not realise there was a deadline for joining.

Organisers can find the task of initiating, project managing and concluding a large enfranchisement as difficult as juggling ten screaming cats for a year. It is essential to get the project off to a sound start by managing expectations and making clear project milestones. The document that invites leaseholders to join the enfranchisement should state clearly that the project will not proceed if fewer than 50 per cent of all flats sign up and pay their deposit by the deadline date.

Some residents' groups create unnecessary delays of months, even years, by insisting on 100 per cent participation in an enfranchisement by all qualifying leaseholders. It is unusual to achieve unanimity about a freehold purchase project in a large building. Organisers must remember the '80–20 rule', which applies in many ways to the enfranchisement of a large block of flats. My investigations into hundreds of residential buildings have revealed that efforts by organisers to secure the participation in an enfranchisement of the last 20 per cent of residents requires far more time and effort than is required to get the first 80 per cent signed up. Getting the last 20 per cent of hesitant residents on board is simply not worth the cost to the project and should not be pursued beyond a reasonable point. Chapter 3 explains why the cost to each participant should not increase significantly, whether 50 per cent or 100 per cent of all the leaseholders take part.

 Identify in writing a deadline for leaseholders to join the enfranchisement project and require payment of a deposit for joining.

How much will the enfranchisement cost?

The question most often asked by leaseholders when considering whether to enfranchise their building is 'How much will the freehold cost?' This is obviously a crucial question, but often an unreasonable amount of time and effort is wasted in search of a definitive figure. Leaseholders must understand that there is **no** definitive figure to be found at the beginning of the process. Just as one cannot guarantee the price at which one will sell one's flat until the transaction has been completed, there cannot be certainty about the cost of the freehold until the end of the enfranchisement process.

Leaseholders can, however, make reasonable estimates about costs and they should present these estimates to fellow residents when trying to decide whether to begin an enfranchisement process. The easiest ways to establish an informal 'back-of-the-envelope' cost estimate for a building freehold are described in chapter 3. The main cost components in a freehold purchase that follows the statutory route through all five stages are as follows:

- The cost of the freehold.

- The stamp duty to be paid on the cost of the freehold (see Appendix 6 for the amounts due).

- The project manager working for leaseholders, whose cost includes solicitor and surveyor fees, or alternatively the cost of a solicitor and surveyor if the residents project manage the enfranchisement themselves.

- The landlord's 'reasonable' solicitor and surveyor fees up to and excluding an LVT hearing.

- The Land Registry fee for registering the new freehold title.

- The conveyancing fee.

By law, enfranchisers must pay to the landlord at the end of the process the reasonable fees he has incurred in dealing with the Enfranchisement Notice, and preparing and serving the Counter Notice. The landlord must hire a solicitor and also a surveyor to carry out his own valuation. If leaseholders feel at the end of the process that the landlord has demanded an unreasonably large amount for legal and surveyor fees, they can challenge the amount by applying to the LVT. The LVT will then decide on the reasonable amount.

It is important for organisers, every time they provide cost estimates to participants, to state clearly that these are only estimates and that the figures do not represent a guarantee of the final freehold cost. I am amazed at how many organisers have to deal with the unnecessary stress, after spending years project managing a large enfranchisement in a very professional manner, of being told by some participants, 'I can't pay my share of the freehold cost. You promised me that the cost would be half of that.'

A crucial cost element that must be considered at the beginning of the process is one that rarely gets quantified in a large building and that is normally not shared amongst participants. This is the personal cost to the main organiser of taking ownership of the enfranchisement project. I have seen buildings in which the main organiser spends the equivalent of hundreds of thousands of pounds of his money in the form of time and effort donated to a freehold purchase project that lasts for years. I have met organisers who said that the workload and stress involved in running such a complex endeavour involving fellow residents had damaged their career and marriage, and even destroyed their health.

Because of the heavy personal cost of a large enfranchisement for the main organiser, the option of hiring a professional project manager should be seriously considered. Also, understanding the hidden costs involved in running an enfranchisement project should prompt organisers to demand early on the commitment and co-operation that is needed from all participants to reach the end of the race.

One of the most helpful pieces of information about cost that can be provided to leaseholders considering whether to enfranchise their building is the fact that a 90-year lease extension costs essentially the same as the share of the cost of the freehold. By law, leaseholders have the right not only to compel their landlord to sell to them their building freehold, but each leaseholder also has the individual right to force the landlord to sell to him a 90-year lease extension at a fair price within the deadlines established by law. The law defines the process of compelling the landlord to sell a 90-year lease extension to the leaseholder as an individual enfranchisement. The stages and deadlines involved in getting a 90-year lease extension, in which the 90 years are added on to the number of years presently left on the lease, are similar to those in a collective enfranchisement. Importantly, the statutory formula for calculating the value of a 90-year lease extension is the same as that used for the value of the freehold for each participating flat.

 Explain before the enfranchisement project begins that a share of the freehold will cost each participant roughly the same as a 90-year lease extension.

Avoiding the chicken-and-egg dilemma about money

Many enfranchisement projects fail to get off the ground because leaseholders get caught in a vicious cycle in the early organising stage when discussing possible costs. The cycle involves the following discussion between leaseholders:

Organiser: 'Will you join the enfranchisement? We've provided this informal cost estimate.'

Hesitant leaseholder: 'No, I won't join until I see a **formal** valuation that has been carried out by a chartered surveyor and I need to be given a **guarantee** of what the final price will be.'

Organiser: 'But we have already explained that the final price will only be known at the end of the process. We've also explained that the project will not progress to the point where we spend any money on hiring a chartered surveyor to do a valuation unless at least 50 per cent of all flats first sign up and pay their deposit.'

Hesitant leaseholder: 'Well, I won't pay my deposit until you have a valuation done.'

The organiser who is caught in this exasperating chicken-and-egg debate should not spend too much time trying to persuade this leaseholder to join the project. If a majority of leaseholders in the building insist on following this cyclical reasoning, then proponents of enfranchisement have the answer to their question. This is not a building in which they will succeed in buying the freehold.

 Provide an informal cost estimate at the start of the project, but only get a paid freehold valuation carried out once a minimum of 50 per cent of all the flats have signed up for the enfranchisement and paid their deposit, and the project's joining deadline has passed.

The fencesitter and the latecomer

A large number of enfranchisements are delayed at the early stage by the fencesitter who says that he will join the project only if the required minimum of 50 per cent of all flats have signed up. Again, organisers must refuse to be drawn into this kind of cyclical reasoning. If each leaseholder waits until the required 50 per cent of all flats have signed up, then no one will sign up. The organisers need to demonstrate their commitment to the project and demand an appropriate level of commitment from others in the building who want to buy the freehold.

The 80–20 rule applies to fencesitters. Organisers should not spend an inordinate amount of time trying to coax them off the fence. It must be clearly communicated to fencesitters that those wishing to buy a share of the freehold after the enfranchisement has ended will not be able to do so. They will also not get the 999-year lease that participants in the project will get.

Organisers should never harangue leaseholders into joining the project. Every resident in a building has his priorities and available budget. While a 30-year-old professional who is earning a large salary might wish desperately to buy the freehold and get a 999-year lease in order to increase the value of his flat for a profitable sale in the near future, a 90-year-old resident who is on a fixed pension and has no living relatives is likely to have other priorities and a different budget. Organisers of an enfranchisement should respect all the residents' issues and priorities, whether these include short leases, poor management of the building or skyrocketing service charges.

Hiring a professional project manager can make it easier in the early planning stage to communicate to residents that project deadlines are real. The outside professional can often get hesitant leaseholders to understand more quickly that latecomers will have to buy any lease extension after the enfranchisement has ended from a new freeholder company that will be owned by their fellow leaseholders. The opportunity to collectively enfranchise one's building is a one-off legal right. Once a building has been enfranchised, non-participants do not have the right to do it again.

 Address the issue of latecomers **before** the enfranchisement project begins. Use an outside project manager to convey the seriousness of project deadlines.

Leaseholders who only want a lease extension

I hear frequent accounts from organisers of large blocks of flats about the non-participant who applies to the landlord for a lease extension after the formal enfranchisement process has begun. The non-participant is then surprised to discover that the landlord is not allowed to sell or otherwise grant any lease extensions from the time that an Enfranchisement Notice has been served until the end of the freehold purchase process.

This situation illustrates a serious miscalculation made by many leaseholders in deciding not to join a collective enfranchisement in their building. Firstly, they fail to recognise that the cost of a 90-year lease extension is essentially the same as the cost of their share of the freehold. Secondly, by refusing to join the enfranchisement, they are forced to wait until the freehold purchase process has ended before they can get a lease extension. Finally, by opting not to take part in the enfranchisement, they lose the right to get a 999-year lease extension and must be satisfied instead with the legal right after the freehold acquisition has concluded of demanding a 90-year lease extension. It is essential for organisers to explain these issues clearly to leaseholders who are trying to decide whether to join a freehold purchase project.

 Explain before the project begins that the landlord will not be allowed to sell any lease extensions after the enfranchisement formally starts, and that any non-participant will have to buy a lease extension after the freehold purchase has been completed from the new landlord, the company owned by the participating leaseholders.

Selling a flat before the enfranchisement has concluded

Sometimes a leaseholder will decline to join a collective enfranchisement because he plans to sell his flat in a few months and does not wish to place the sale at risk. This is another example of a leaseholder who fails to understand the situation. In a well-run enfranchisement, all participants sign a Participation Agreement before the formal freehold purchase process begins. This agreement, which is described in chapter 2, obliges each participant to pay for his share of the freehold at the end of the process and, in the event of selling the flat before the enfranchisement has concluded, to sell to a buyer who will take his place in the project.

It is important for organisers to explain at the early stage that taking part in a collective enfranchisement does not prevent any participant from selling his flat. Indeed, participation makes the flat being sold more attractive than a non-participating flat because the buyer will get a share of the freehold and a 999-year lease at the end of the enfranchisement.

 Explain that any participant can sell his flat before the enfranchisement has been concluded and that the Participation Agreement obliges him to sell to a buyer who will take his place in the enfranchisement project.

The landlord who offers to sell the freehold

There are occasions when leaseholders create unnecessary delays when organising an enfranchisement because they believe that the landlord is a willing seller and that there is no need to pursue the statutory route for buying the freehold. These leaseholders insist that it will be quicker to agree on a negotiated acquisition with the landlord, and they claim that residents will save themselves the cost of having to pay the landlord's legal and surveyor fees.

What these leaseholders fail to realise is that large corporate landlords sometimes say that they are willing sellers in order to delay or foil efforts to organise a collective enfranchisement. I have seen residents' associations that have been delayed for years in their efforts to enfranchise because they believed the landlord was a willing seller. Yet they were never able to obtain a contract of sale from the landlord at a price they considered reasonable. Finally, after years of this waiting game, they realised the landlord had been employing an effective delaying tactic. The value of the freehold, which is linked to the market value of flats in the building, had gone up significantly and the leaseholders were back at square one in organising a formal enfranchisement.

If leaseholders believe that the landlord is truly willing to sell the freehold at a reasonable price, they should require in writing that he send a contract of sale within a defined period of time, such as one month. If one or more leaseholders receive a written offer from the landlord to sell the freehold and this offer has not been sent to all leaseholders, it is possible that the landlord is committing a crime by failing to follow the required procedure of offering the right of first refusal to leaseholders to buy the freehold. The process involved in the right of first refusal is explained in chapter 9. An entire chapter is also dedicated to the right-of-first-refusal process in my book *Making Sense of Leasehold Property*.

 If the landlord says that he is a willing seller, make sure that he produces a contract of sale within one month.

Confidentiality issues once the project begins

The process of buying a building freehold by collective enfranchisement is a complex commercial transaction entered into by a group of residents in a building. It is essential for organisers to advise leaseholders at the earliest stage that all aspects of the enfranchisement, including its existence, are to be kept absolutely confidential. The freehold purchase should not be discussed with anyone inside or outside the building who is not involved in the project, especially the landlord or any person employed by or representing the landlord. Because enfranchisement involves a compulsory sale being forced on the landlord, any information the landlord can obtain regarding the price to be offered, the advisers being used or the timeframe involved can weaken the enfranchisers' position.

Early on in the process, once the deadline for joining the enfranchisement project has passed, the organisers and participants should not communicate in any way about the freehold purchase with leaseholders who have decided not to join. I have seen evidence of large corporate landlords doing deals with non-participants in a building, including forgiving unpaid service charges in exchange for information about an enfranchisement initiative. The participants in a freehold purchase should maintain normal neighbourly relations with non-participants, but must not discuss with them any aspect of the confidential project that the non-participants opted not to join.

 Keep all aspects of the enfranchisement confidential to participants as soon as the deadline date for joining has passed.

When to drop plans to enfranchise

Leaseholders that wish to organise an enfranchisement in a large building need to have a lot of energy, enthusiasm and perseverance to see the project through. But they also need to understand at the beginning that it is not always possible to get such a project off the ground.

The shorter the leases are in a building, the more difficult can be the organisation of an enfranchisement initiative. This is because the share of the cost of the freehold that each participant will have to pay increases as the length of the lease decreases. Thus, it can cost relatively little for each participant to pay his share of the freehold in a building where the leases have 90 years, but that cost can be exorbitantly high in a block of flats where leases have only 20 years left. In a building with such an extreme short-lease problem, it often makes more sense for interested leaseholders to join forces and pursue the statutory route for getting 90-year lease extensions. There is a chapter in my book *Making Sense of Leasehold Property* on how to get a lease extension.

Organisers of a large enfranchisement also need to remind themselves that their residents' group is at a severe organisational disadvantage vis-à-vis the large corporate landlord. Even with a high level of commitment and co-operation from participants, the residents' association can easily be out-manoeuvred and worn down over time by the large corporate landlord that chooses to resist the enfranchisement.

Because of the flat hierarchical structure of the residents' association, where the committee has little if any formal authority over association members, the organisers of an enfranchisement must secure a strong commitment of support at the early stage from participants. They need to remember that the 80–20 rule in this case means that the small number of participants who fail to co-operate will cost the organisers more time and effort than all of the other participants combined. Organisers need to be clear about these organisational challenges and, in some cases, need to be ready and willing to drop an initiative to collectively enfranchise a building.

 Make it clear to the enfranchisement participants that the organisers are committed **and** demand that the participants show their commitment, too.

CHAPTER 2

Dealing with documentation

This chapter examines the ten most important documents with which leaseholders must be familiar in order to organise and see through a successful enfranchisement. This overview spans the entire freehold purchase process, from the earliest preparatory stage, when an invitation to participate is sent by organisers to residents in the building, through to the period after the freehold purchase, when shareholder certificates of participating flats get updated following the sale and purchase of participant flats.

Some leaseholders ask why they should be familiar with detailed operational issues, such as documents that need to be served, since they expect this to be the responsibility of the project manager or solicitor they have hired to take charge of their enfranchisement. This chapter does not recommend that leaseholders personally serve each of the documents described. In a large block of flats, flat owners are advised to instruct a project manager or solicitor, rather than to pursue a do-it-yourself approach.

But leaseholders should be familiar with and understand the ten documents described in this chapter for three important reasons. The first is to enable the organisers to understand the entire enfranchisement process, so that they can ensure good quality control at each stage of the project. Many enfranchisement initiatives collapse due to inadequate preparation and a lack of understanding of the process.

A second imperative for knowing these documents is to enable leaseholders to get good value for money from their professional advisers.

This applies whether the enfranchisers hire a project manager to deal with their freehold purchase who instructs a chartered surveyor and a solicitor, or whether they pursue a do-it-yourself option by carrying out their own project management and instructing a surveyor and solicitor directly. Flat owners are best able to secure competent and cost-effective advisers if they equip themselves with a basic understanding of the enfranchisement process. Sadly, since the early 1990s I have received many first-hand accounts of enfranchisement initiatives that failed because a solicitor or surveyor made a crucial mistake and the leaseholders, due to lack of knowledge of the process, were unable to catch the mistake.

A third reason for looking at the documents in this chapter before setting out to buy one's freehold is to help protect against being overwhelmed by paperwork later on. Like the long-distance runner in the months before the big race, the enfranchiser needs to become familiar with the structure of the freehold purchase process early on, to avoid getting caught by surprise once the strict deadlines are triggered by the serving of the formal notice.

There are other documents that leaseholders will need to deal with in an enfranchisement. Many of these are covered elsewhere in this book and are provided in the Appendices. But the ten in this chapter are central to project success, either because they are required by law or because I consider them to be essential for minimising risks in an enfranchisement. The ten documents are:

1. An invitation to join a freehold purchase project

2. A Sign-Up Form

3. A Participation Agreement

4. An Enfranchisement Notice

5. A Counter Notice

6. An application to the Leasehold Valuation Tribunal (LVT)

7. A Right of First Refusal Notice

8. An acceptance to buy a freehold by right of first refusal

9. A form for participation in an enfranchisement by a new buyer

10. A J30 Stock Transfer Form

The timeline below shows the stage in the process at which each of these documents is relevant, starting with the initial preparatory phase and ending after the freehold purchase. The two documents concerning a right-of-first-refusal offer can be relevant at any time before the leaseholders have served the Enfranchisement Notice on the landlord. The document used when the buyer of a flat participating in an enfranchisement becomes the new participant and the J30 Stock Transfer Form used to transfer the relevant company share certificate are shown here after the freehold has been bought, but these two documents can be used any time after the official enfranchisement process has started.

Typical timeline of an enfranchisement including the main documents

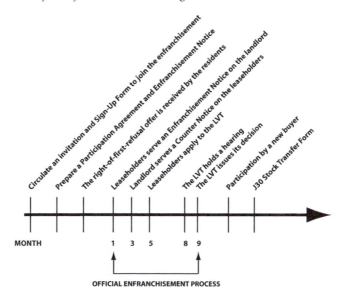

Six of the ten documents in this chapter are required by law. Only one of the six is prescribed by law, with wording that cannot be changed. The four documents that are not required by law, the invitation to join an enfranchisement, the Sign-Up Form, the Participation Agreement and the form for joining an ongoing enfranchisement by the buyer of a participating flat, represent best-practice tools for ensuring that an enfranchisement project does not founder.

By relying on documents in this chapter as template tools, leaseholders can manage their freehold purchase in a professional manner. For instance, the Participation Agreement helps to minimise the risk of participants refusing to pay their share of the freehold cost at the end of the process. I see too many buildings in which organisers donate long hours on behalf of fellow leaseholders over the course of two or three years to bring about a freehold purchase, only to have to chase after two or three difficult neighbours who fail to pay their share in the days before the acquisition is completed. Thoughtful use of these documents can help leaseholders avoid becoming their own worst enemies during the enfranchisement project.

The seventh and eighth documents examined in this chapter, regarding the right of first refusal, are relevant only if a landlord decides voluntarily to sell the freehold. In most residential buildings the landlord must by law offer a right of first refusal to leaseholders to buy the property before he can seek to sell it to a third party. I have included the right of first refusal documents because many leaseholders are unnecessarily caught off guard when they receive the first of these notices, which is also called a Section 5 Notice. Since leaseholders only get two months to reply to an offer by the landlord to buy the freehold, it is essential that enfranchisers be familiar with the process and the documents required.

The invitation to join a freehold purchase project

As soon as a significant number of leaseholders in a block of flats have decided that they want to buy the freehold, organisers should draft and circulate a formal invitation to all the leaseholders asking them to join the project. There is no legal requirement for enfranchisers to send such an invitation, but in large buildings and/or those with absentee leaseholders, this is often an essential first step for creating focus on a freehold purchase project. A template for the invitation document is provided in Appendix 7.

The invitation document should provide a brief description of the enfranchisement project being proposed. It should identify the deposit to be paid and the deadline for joining. If possible, the invitation should provide cost estimates for the project, but it must be stated clearly that these are only estimates and that the final cost of the freehold will only be known at the end of the process.

Enfranchisement organisers are under no legal obligation to circulate the invitation to participate to every resident qualifying to take part in the freehold purchase, but it is best practice to do so, to avoid creating conflict amongst neighbours. There are instances, however, when organisers may decide not to send the invitation to a minority of flats, such as flats owned by relatives or business associates of the freeholder, as this could damage the project by providing the landlord with confidential information.

Although a minimum of 50 per cent of all flats in the block must participate in order for the building to qualify for collective enfranchisement, leaseholders should **not** wait until they have the minimum 50 per cent before circulating the initial invitation to participate. This is because many owners of flats will only make a commitment to join a project and pay the initial deposit once they have received an invitation in writing and once they have understood that there is a deadline for joining.

 The residents' association should send a written communication inviting leaseholders to join the collective enfranchisement project and identifying the date by which each leaseholder needs to send his Sign-Up Form and deposit.

It is possible for organisers of an enfranchisement to outsource the work involved in sending the initial invitation to participate to all leaseholders, by instructing an outside project manager. A project manager will normally send a letter on behalf of the residents' association or the organisers that invites all qualifying leaseholders to join the freehold purchase, and that requires the signing of a contract and payment of a deposit.

The Sign-Up Form

When organisers send the invitation to all leaseholders in the building asking them to join the enfranchisement project, they should attach at the back of the document a Sign-Up Form. This should be brief, with a one-sentence commitment that identifies the leaseholder and his flat and says that the leaseholder wishes to take part in the purchase of the building freehold through the process of collective enfranchisement if and when the project is started. Sample wording for the Sign-Up Form is provided in Appendix 8.

Some leaseholders question the value of the Sign-Up Form, saying that it is not legally binding. This document, however, is not meant legally to tie in the leaseholder. It is the Participation Agreement that is described below that legally binds each participant to the enfranchisement. I have never seen a case in which enfranchisers have sued a leaseholder in court for completing a Sign-up Form, then failing later on to comply with the undertaking made in this form. The Sign-up Form simply formalises a leaseholder's early-stage commitment. If, for instance, a leaseholder completes a Sign-up Form, but subsequently refuses to pay his deposit, then he should be dropped from the project.

Getting a freehold purchase project off the ground requires gathering consensus and creating momentum. Many fencesitters are prompted to join such a project when they are shown Sign-up Forms that have been completed and a list of deposits paid by leaseholders who have agreed to participate.

 Organisers should show Sign-up Forms that have been signed by participants and a list of deposits paid when asking the remaining leaseholders to join the enfranchisement project.

The Participation Agreement

The Participation Agreement is a document that leaseholders are not required by law to use, but it is essential in order to avoid the unravelling of a large collective enfranchisement. Indeed, I consider it so important that I urge leaseholders to steer clear of any project manager or solicitor who does not insist on the use of the Participation Agreement in an enfranchisement. The Participation Agreement binds the leaseholder participants into a consortium for the purpose of buying their building freehold. It says two important things about money and participant responsibility. Firstly, the agreement says that each participant is obliged to pay his share of the freehold cost at the end of the process. Secondly, it says that any participant that sells his flat before the enfranchisement has been concluded must sell to a buyer that will automatically take his place in the process. This second element protects against a situation in which, for instance, 20 people join an enfranchisement, but only five participants are left at the end when the money needs to be paid because the other 15 have sold their flats and dropped out. A sample Participation Agreement is provided in Appendix 9.

By insisting on the use of a Participation Agreement, leaseholders address one of the greatest risks to the enfranchisement, that of participant numbers diminishing. While there may be strong consensus to buy the freehold at the beginning when leaseholders are angry about an issue, such as a large service charge invoice, it can be difficult to hold the group together for the two years often required to organise, prepare and see through a big enfranchisement. It is a fact of urban life that people come and go in a large block of flats. In central London, it is not unusual for one third of the participants in a large block to have sold their flats and moved on by the time an enfranchisement project draws to a conclusion. Advice on how to keep all participants and/or buyers of participant flats within the project until the freehold has been bought is provided in chapter 6.

Some leaseholders believe mistakenly that an enfranchisement process will be rendered invalid and the initiative will immediately collapse if any participant moves from the building before the freehold has been bought. This is not the case. While a minimum of 50 per cent of all flats must take part for a building to qualify for enfranchisement, this minimum number of participants applies only to the moment at which the formal process begins, when the leaseholders serve their Enfranchisement Notice on the landlord. After the notice has been served, it will remain valid whether or not all participants stay on in the building or stay involved in the project. Indeed, the Enfranchisement Notice in the block with 20 participants will remain valid even if there is only **one** remaining participant by the time the freehold is being purchased. The problem is that the one leaseholder is left having to pay for the entire freehold.

The Participation Agreement addresses this well-known problem by locking in the participants from the start of the project. By acknowledging that people come and go in a building, the agreement places a legal obligation on any participant wishing to sell his flat to sell to a buyer who will take the participant's place in the enfranchisement process. It is invaluable to have this formalised in a legally-binding contract. Enfranchisers need to be prepared for the possibility that a neighbour who was initially an enthusiastic participant of the freehold purchase may later announce that he is moving from the building. One sometimes sees the organising team itself depleted during the course of an enfranchisement, when marriage, divorce, a job change or some other event prompts a previous proponent of the project suddenly to leave the building.

Unlike the Sign-Up Form described above, the Participation Agreement is a legally-binding document. Much organising work must be done after the Sign-Up Forms and deposits have been collected and before the Participation Agreement is drafted. The minimum of 50 per cent of all flats will have signed up for the project and a formal valuation of the freehold will have been carried out. Participants will have set up a resident management company for the purpose of buying the freehold, in steps that are described in chapter 4.

The legal term for the resident management company that is set up early in the enfranchisement process is the 'nominee purchaser'. This is because this is the legal entity nominated by the enfranchisers to buy the freehold. While it is not required by law for the nominee purchaser to be a company limited by shares, it is best practice to use this model, with all participants becoming shareholders and thus joint owners of the company. Advice on how best to run the resident management company is provided in chapter 4 and also chapter 10.

The Participation Agreement should be signed personally by every participant. If a flat is jointly owned by four people, say, a husband, wife and two adult children, then all four individuals need to sign the document. The Participation Agreement should be drafted and circulated for signature by all participants at the same time as the Enfranchisement Notice, which is described below. If a significant number of participating leaseholders live outside the UK, the organisers will need to allow for several weeks to send these two crucial documents to each participant. It is advisable to send the documents by an international courier service, to ensure against the documents getting lost.

Directors of the nominee purchaser company need to keep an electronic copy of the Participation Agreement. Organisers are often amazed at how quickly a participating leaseholder who is moving from the building forgets that, according to the Participation Agreement, he is obliged to sell to a buyer who takes the seller's place in the enfranchisement process. This should not present any problem for the seller or buyer since the participating flats are normally more sellable than non-participant flats. This is because participants will get a 999-year lease after the freehold has been bought, while non-participant flats will not. But the directors of the nominee purchaser company need to be prepared to send a no-nonsense reminder of this obligation to any seller and, if required, to the seller's solicitor.

 Enfranchisement organisers should **always** require leaseholders to sign a Participation Agreement that obliges participants to pay their share of the freehold cost at the end of the process and that obliges a participant selling his flat before the freehold purchase concludes to sell to a buyer who automatically takes his place in the project.

The Enfranchisement Notice

The Enfranchisement Notice is the document served by the leaseholders' nominee purchaser on the landlord which notifies the landlord that the leaseholders are collectively enfranchising the building. It is also referred to as the Initial Notice or Section 13 Notice, after the relevant section of the Leasehold Reform, Housing and Urban Development Act 1993. The Enfranchisement Notice contains an offer price for the freehold, provides a list of all the participants and identifies the deadline date by which the landlord must reply.

The serving of the Enfranchisement Notice officially starts the collective enfranchisement process. By law, the landlord must send a written reply to the leaseholders within a maximum of two months of the Enfranchisement Notice. This reply, the Counter Notice, is described below. Since the early 1990s many residents' groups have told me that they were enfranchising their building and had started the process months or even years earlier, when, in fact, they had **not** actually begun since no Enfranchisement Notice had yet been served.

The Enfranchisement Notice and the Participation Agreement described above should be prepared and circulated for signature by all the participants at the same time. As we have seen, this final preparation stage only takes place once the minimum of 50 per cent of the flats in the building have joined the project, a formal valuation of the freehold has been carried out and the nominee purchaser company has been set up.

It is required by law for the nominee purchaser in a collective enfranchisement to serve an Enfranchisement Notice on the landlord, but there is no prescribed form to be used. The law does require, however, for certain information to be included in the notice, including the name and address of the nominee purchaser, a description of the property being enfranchised, the offer price and the name, address and signature of all the participants. The information to be included in the notice is identified in Part 1, Chapter 1, Section 13 of the Leasehold Reform, Housing and Urban Development Act 1993. Appendix 10 provides a sample Enfranchisement Notice.

When we consider the analogy of the long-distance runner, the serving of the Enfranchisement Notice represents the starting gun of the race. If the runner has not trained properly, this lack of preparation will soon become evident. Many enfranchisement initiatives collapse because the landlord declares the Enfranchisement Notice invalid. A landlord has the right to do this if the notice fails to include required information. Some landlords, however, claim the Enfranchisement Notice is invalid even when it has been correctly prepared and served, in order to create delay and distraction for leaseholders and to drive up their costs in an attempt to foil the initiative. One solicitor told me that he saw more than half of all Enfranchisement Notices successfully declared invalid over a period of several years by one of the country's largest landlords, which owns much of central London.

Common mistakes that can result in the Enfranchisement Notice being declared invalid include:

- a failure to have every participant personally sign the notice;

- an inclusion in the notice of an unrealistically low offer price; and

- a failure to provide an offer price for the entire building, including flats owned by the landlord and that do not qualify to participate in the enfranchisement.

There have been a surprisingly large number of cases in which Enfranchisement Notices were successfully declared invalid by the landlord because the notice was not personally signed by every participant. The notice cannot be signed by a Power of Attorney, lawyer or any other representative of the participant. It must be signed by the participant himself.

I have also seen Enfranchisement Notices successfully declared invalid by the landlord because the offer price was so low as to be considered unrealistic, because the enfranchisers and their chartered surveyor forgot to include in the offer price an offer for the **entire** freehold, including any flats owned by the landlord. The proper procedure is to include an offer price for the whole freehold, but for enfranchisers to have ready the lower offer price to be made only for the enfranchisable flats if the landlord exercises his right to keep his flats by getting a 'leaseback'. A leaseback is a 999-year lease with a 'peppercorn rent' or zero ground rent that the landlord has a right to demand of the nominee purchaser for flats in the building owned by the landlord. Leasebacks and their implication on freehold valuations are examined in chapter 3.

If the landlord wishes to claim that the Enfranchisement Notice is invalid, he must file a claim in the County Court against the nominee purchaser in which he asks the court to declare the notice invalid. If the landlord files a claim in the County Court, the formal enfranchisement process is effectively put on hold, since the leaseholders cannot proceed to the third formal phase of the enfranchisement to have their case heard by an LVT until the County Court case has been concluded.

While the legal requirement for enfranchisers to include an offer price that is realistic was originally meant to prevent frivolous offers, such as £1 for a building, there has been much abuse of this legal loophole by some large landlords. There are numerous instances in which enfranchising leaseholders have been dragged into the County Court, through no fault of their own, simply because they have a difficult landlord. The leaseholders have had a proper valuation done, but the landlord has claimed that the offer price is unrealistically low because, according to the landlord's valuation, there are, say, hundreds of thousands of pounds of 'development value' in the building. The real problem for enfranchisers in many of these cases has been that the landlord's Counter Notice has contained an unrealistically high counter offer price. We examine this situation in chapter 3.

Flat owners need to be aware of the risk of County Court litigation, since big corporate landlords can make best use of their David-and-Goliath advantages by dragging enfranchisers into a one- or two-year battle in the County Court. Chapter 4 examines ways in which leaseholders can prevent this kind of derailment or delay in their enfranchisement initiative.

If the landlord is successful in his County Court claim, the court will declare the Enfranchisement Notice invalid and the leaseholders must prepare a new notice and start the process all over again. If the landlord is unsuccessful in his claim, the County Court will declare the notice valid and the leaseholders are free to move on to stage three in the formal enfranchisement process, by applying to the LVT for a hearing to decide on the freehold price.

 Ensure that the Enfranchisement Notice includes an offer price for the entire freehold, not just participating flats, that the offer price can be substantiated by valuation evidence and that the notice is **personally** signed by every participant, not by his representative.

The Counter Notice

The Counter Notice is the document served by the landlord on the enfranchising leaseholders that contains his official reply to the Enfranchisement Notice. The serving of the Counter Notice marks stage two in the formal enfranchisement process. The landlord is under no legal obligation to serve a Counter Notice. However, if he fails to serve the Counter Notice by the identified deadline, then the leaseholders get to buy the freehold at the offer price contained in the Enfranchisement Notice. It is unusual for a large corporate landlord to fail to serve a Counter Notice.

If the landlord wishes to challenge any aspect of the freehold purchase proposed in the Enfranchisement Notice, he must by law serve a Counter Notice on the leaseholders. While there is no prescribed form to be used, the Counter Notice must contain certain information. Appendix 11 provides a sample Counter Notice. The information that must be included in the Counter Notice is identified in Part 1, Chapter 1, Section 21 of the Leasehold Reform, Housing and Urban Development Act 1993.

In the Counter Notice, the landlord must state whether or not he accepts that the participating leaseholders qualify to enfranchise the building. If he accepts that they qualify to enfranchise the building, he must either accept or reject the offer price contained in the Enfranchisement Notice. If the landlord accepts the price, then the nominee purchaser can proceed in buying the freehold at this price. If the landlord rejects the offer price, then he must state his 'counter offer' price in the Counter Notice. Most large corporate landlords state a counter offer price in the Counter Notice that is higher than the offer price in the Enfranchisement Notice.

In theory, leaseholders enjoy the same protection by law as landlords against an unrealistic asking price. We have seen that the landlord has a right to challenge in the County Court an unrealistically low offer price contained in the Enfranchisement Notice. In theory, leaseholders have a similar right to challenge an unrealistically high counter offer price contained in the Counter Notice. But enfranchisers must beware. This right exists for leaseholders in theory, but **not** in practice, as is described in Case Study 4.

If the enfranchisers feel that the counter offer price that is demanded by the landlord in the Counter Notice is so high as to be unrealistic, they should **not** file a claim about this in the County Court. They should **not** seek to have the Counter Notice declared invalid. Instead, they should file an application at the LVT and ask for a hearing on this to be held. Enfranchisers need to remember that it is the LVT that decides on the price at which the freehold will be sold by the landlord to the enfranchisers, not the County Court. The County Court only decides in highly-disputed instances whether or not an Enfranchisement Notice or Counter Notice is valid. Because of this, and the fact that the leaseholders are at an extreme organisational disadvantage to the landlord when they are dragged into the County Court, enfranchisers should only engage in battle in this unfriendly terrain if they are prepared to add an additional year or two to their enfranchisement project and to pay significantly higher legal and surveyor fees.

 Enfranchisers should **not** seek to have a Counter Notice from a large corporate landlord declared invalid, unless they are prepared to spend an additional one or two years and significantly increased legal and surveyor fees pursuing this issue in the County Court.

Application to the Leasehold Valuation Tribunal

Once the landlord serves his Counter Notice, if the notice contains a counter offer price that is higher than the initial offer price, then the leaseholders should prepare to proceed to stage three of the formal enfranchisement process. This is the phase at which the flat owners apply to the LVT to decide on the freehold price.

But the leaseholders can also seek at this time to reach a negotiated settlement with the landlord on the freehold price. If the leaseholders wish to negotiate, they normally instruct their chartered surveyor to spend an identified amount of time trying to reach agreement on the price with the landlord's surveyor. Chapter 3 examines the various issues over which surveyors wrangle in a collective enfranchisement. Chapter 8 analyses the negotiation process and explains why a large majority of enfranchisement initiatives are concluded with a negotiated settlement.

If the enfranchiser and landlord fail to reach a negotiated agreement on price, the enfranchisers should file an application to the LVT.

There are strict deadlines regarding this application to the LVT. If enfranchisers wish for an LVT hearing to be held, they must apply to the tribunal no sooner than two months and no later than six months from the date on which the Counter Notice was due. It is essential that the leaseholders not miss this four-month window of opportunity. If they do, there is considered to be a 'deemed withdrawal' of their Enfranchisement Notice. As we saw earlier, this means the leaseholders must wait one year before they are allowed to serve another Enfranchisement Notice on the landlord.

When leaseholders apply to the LVT for a hearing, there is no prescribed form to be used. Appendix 12 provides a sample application to the LVT.

The reason that leaseholders have until six months from the deadline date of the Counter Notice to apply to the LVT is to give them and the landlord time to reach a negotiated agreement. Many corporate landlords only begin to negotiate with enfranchisers in the weeks, days, even minutes before a scheduled LVT hearing. For this reason, it is important for leaseholders to file their application to the LVT at the earliest opportunity, that is, two months after the date by which the Counter Notice was due. The experience of hundreds of residents' groups since the 1990s has shown that many large landlords only engage in constructive negotiations once they see concrete evidence, in the form of an LVT hearing date, that a compulsory sale of the freehold is imminent. Even if leaseholders are confident that they can reach a negotiated settlement with the landlord after the Counter Notice has been received, they should always file the application to the LVT as soon as possible. This serves as a kind of insurance policy against any deemed withdrawal that would result if leaseholders miss the six-month LVT application deadline.

 Enfranchisers should ensure that their application is sent to the LVT just over two months from the date by which the Counter Notice was due and no later than six months after this date, even if the leaseholders expect to reach a negotiated settlement on the freehold price with the freeholder.

The Right of First Refusal Notice

Sometimes leaseholders spend months preparing to enfranchise their building, only to be caught off guard when they receive a written offer by the landlord to sell. In most residential blocks of flats, if the landlord wishes to sell the freehold, he must by law offer a right of first refusal to qualifying residents in the building. If he fails to do so, he commits a criminal offence. The law that initially provided this right of first refusal to leaseholders was the Landlord and Tenant Act 1987. The Housing Act 1996 amended the right.

The document that must be served on leaseholders in the building by a landlord wishing to sell the freehold is a Section 5 Notice. This is because it is based on Section 5 of the Landlord and Tenant Act 1987. There is no prescribed form to use, but the notice must identify the building, the asking price and the deadline date by which the residents must reply. A sample Section 5 Notice is provided in Appendix 13.

The notice must be served on a minimum of 90 per cent of 'qualifying tenants' in the building or a minimum of all qualifying tenants less one if there are fewer than ten qualifying tenants. In order to be a qualifying tenant, a resident must own a maximum of two 'long leases' in the building, that is, leases that had more than 21 years when they started, or the resident must be a regulated tenant. A regulated tenant, also known as a protected tenant, is a person who rents his flat directly from the landlord under a scheme that protects against eviction and certain rent increases. Rent-protected tenancies date back mostly to the Rent Act 1977, with most regulated tenancy agreements having been reached before January 1989. Regulated tenancies are no longer being created. Those that do exist apply to long-standing residents who are typically senior citizens.

Any leaseholder owning more than two flats in the building does not qualify to take part in a right-of-first-refusal purchase of the freehold. To be a qualifying tenant, a resident must not be a protected shorthold tenant, assured tenant, business or agricultural-occupancy tenant or sub-lessee. A list of elements regarding the qualification of a resident and of a building for a right-of-first-refusal process is contained in Appendix 14.

Some enfranchisement projects collapse before they formally start because leaseholders fail to prepare for a possible Section 5 Notice. When a Section 5 Notice arrives, it is the landlord who determines the buying price and deadlines. If the residents wish to buy their freehold at the asking price contained in the Section 5 Notice, they must confirm this in writing to the landlord within a maximum of two months. Their reply, the Section 6 Notice, is described below. Residents can only buy in this right-of-first-refusal process if more than 50 per cent of the qualifying tenants participate in the process.

Buying a freehold through the right-of-first-refusal process presents advantages and disadvantages for the leaseholder. One disadvantage is that residents have no legal right to challenge the landlord's asking price. If they do not wish to buy at the price stated in the Section 5 Notice, the landlord can sell at this price to a third party during the subsequent 12-month period. The landlord is not allowed to sell at a lower price without first offering the freehold to the qualifying tenants at this lower price. On the other hand, if the asking price for the freehold is reasonable, residents can save themselves time, money and effort by forgoing the enfranchisement process. This is because they will not have to pay the landlord's legal or surveyor fees and they avoid going to the LVT.

Leaseholders need to prepare, therefore, in two main ways for a possible right-of-first-refusal offer. Firstly, they need to know what a Section 5 Notice is and not to panic if this legal-looking document arrives in the post. Secondly, they need to have a rough idea of the value of their freehold and/or have the ability to get a valuation done quickly, to determine whether the asking price is reasonable.

 Enfranchisers need to be prepared to receive a Section 5 Notice in which the landlord offers to sell them a right of first refusal to buy the freehold at a specified price and the leaseholders need to be prepared to reply to this by the statutory two-month deadline.

Accepting to buy a freehold by the right of first refusal

If more than 50 per cent of the qualifying tenants in a building wish to buy the freehold through the right-of-first-refusal process, they need to send a Residents' Notice of Acceptance to the landlord within a maximum two months of the Section 5 Notice. The notice of acceptance is called a Section 6 Notice. There is no prescribed form to be used, but the notice must contain certain information. It must identify the property and qualifying participating tenants, and it must agree to the asking price. Appendix 15 provides a sample Section 6 Notice.

If the residents feel that the asking price contained in a Section 5 Notice is unreasonably high, they can choose to ignore the right-of-first-refusal offer and instead pursue their plan to buy the freehold through collective enfranchisement. Even if the landlord sells the freehold to a third party after residents forgo the right of first refusal, the leaseholders still have the right to enfranchise. They will simply need to serve the Enfranchisement Notice on the new landlord.

Chapter 9 provides more information on what leaseholders need to do if they receive a right-of-first-refusal offer from their landlord.

 If enfranchisers receive a Section 5 Notice in which the landlord offers them a right of first refusal to buy their freehold, they should send the required Section 6 Notice accepting the offer if their chartered surveyor says that the selling price is reasonable.

Participation in an enfranchisement by a new buyer

It is important for leaseholders not to become swamped by paperwork once the process is under way. One event that can unsettle and distract organisers of a large freehold purchase project is the sale of one or more participating flats before the enfranchisement has been concluded. As we have seen earlier, organisers should not be surprised by such sales or be unduly worried they will derail the project. As long as the organisers insist at the beginning on a Participation Agreement amongst leaseholders taking part, the sale of a participant flat should neither threaten the success of the project nor require a large amount of work.

As soon as a participant informs the organisers about plans to sell his flat in the building, the organisers need to remind the participant in writing of his legal obligation, according to the Participation Agreement, to sell to a buyer who will automatically take the seller's place in the enfranchisement. A one-sentence email to remind the seller of this obligation should suffice. The seller will need to inform any prospective buyer that this is a participating flat and will also need to provide relevant information to the buyer about the enfranchisement project. It is helpful if the organisers email to the seller a copy of the Participation Agreement, the Enfranchisement Notice and the Memorandum and Articles of Association of the nominee purchaser company, a document we will examine in chapter 4.

It is best practice to require that the buyer of a participating flat sign a brief written undertaking to take part in the enfranchisement and to be bound by the Participation Agreement. This written undertaking can also state that the buyer understands that the nominee purchaser company will transfer to the buyer's name the company share certificate for the flat being purchased. A sample form to be signed by the buyer of a participating flat in an enfranchising building is provided in Appendix 16.

 The nominee purchaser company formed by enfranchisers to buy the freehold should require that any person buying a participating flat before the enfranchisement has ended sign a one- or two-sentence document in which the buyer agrees to comply with the Participation Agreement that was signed earlier by the vendor of the flat.

The J30 Stock Transfer Form

When a participant sells his flat in an enfranchising building, the project organisers need to get the participant to sign a special form to enable the transfer of the share certificate of the resident management company (the 'nominee purchaser') for this flat from the name of the present leaseholder to the name of the buyer. This is called a J30 Stock Transfer Form, which is shown in Appendix 17. Once a J30 Form has been completed, including the signature of the seller, this form must be filed with Companies House, the government department that maintains a register of companies in the country. Chapter 6 and chapter 10 provide tips on how enfranchisers can outsource much of this paperwork in order to minimise the time and effort required to run a resident management company.

Organisers should get a J30 Form signed by the seller of the participating flat as soon as he makes known his intention to sell the flat and before the flat has been sold. The section of the form that identifies the name and address of the seller, as present shareholder, should be completed and the seller should sign, but not date, the form. The section that identifies the name and address of the person to whom the share certificate is being transferred should be left blank.

A failure to get a signed J30 Form before the outgoing participant sells his flat can result in months of delay in transferring the share certificate to the name of the buyer. This is especially the case when the person selling the flat lives outside the UK. The organisers need to remember that even the most enthusiastic participant in an enfranchisement can become unwilling to take the time to sign a J30 Form once he no longer lives in the building and has no personal stake in the success of the freehold purchase project.

 As soon as an enfranchisement participant begins the process to sell his flat, the board of directors of the nominee purchaser company should get the seller to sign a J30 Stock Transfer Form, since the board will need this in order to transfer the seller's share certificate in the nominee purchaser company to the buyer after the flat has been sold.

When organisers become familiar with the ten documents covered in this chapter, they will have completed an essential first stage in the training process before beginning the long-distance race that is the collective enfranchisement. Because of the relative newness of enfranchisement legislation and the shortage of project managers, solicitors and chartered surveyors with deep expertise and experience in this area, leaseholders should not hesitate to discuss these documents, especially the Participation Agreement and Enfranchisement Notice, with their advisers and to check that the documents being used have been correctly prepared. Although this can cause awkwardness if an adviser feels he is being second-guessed, it is awkwardness worth risking if it can prevent an Enfranchisement Notice from being declared invalid or a freehold purchase project from collapsing.

CHAPTER 3

Demystifying the valuation process

This chapter addresses the question most frequently asked by leaseholders when they are considering whether to buy their freehold, 'How much will it cost?' The formula that must be followed when calculating the value of a freehold in a collective enfranchisement was set out in law in the 1993 Act and amended in the 2002 Act. Our examination of valuation principles represents a crucial part of the training regime for the long-distance race that is the freehold purchase process.

Not every flat owner will have the stomach to work his way through the relevant legislation. The freehold valuation formula that we review here is contained in Schedule 6 of the Leasehold Reform, Housing and Urban Development Act 1993 and in Part 2, Chapter 2, Sections 126 through 128 of the Commonhold and Leasehold Reform Act 2002.

Many leaseholders bemoan the complexity of the enfranchisement laws, saying that this legislation can appear impenetrable to the average flat owner. Some complain that the statutory formula for calculating freehold value is unfair to leaseholders and unreasonably favours landlords. While the formula may not be perfect, it should be welcomed that a legislated formula does exist, as this aims to ensure that leaseholders get to buy their freehold at a fair price and the landlord gets to receive a fair price, and leaseholders can seek some transparency in the valuation process.

This chapter is meant to equip the homeowner with a solid layperson's understanding of the formula. It also provides important tips on how to arrive at a rough estimate of the freehold cost early in the process, before the required minimum 50 per cent of all flats have signed up for an enfranchisement and before project participants are ready to spend money on getting a formal valuation done. In this way, leaseholders can escape the 'chicken-and-egg' dilemma that we described in chapter 1 in which residents in a building demand to see a formal valuation before joining an enfranchisement project, only to be told by organisers that no formal valuation will be carried out until after the required 50 per cent of all flats have joined and the deadline for joining the project has passed.

The homeowner should not seek to become a chartered surveyor as part of the enfranchisement process, nor should enfranchisement organisers feel an obligation to be able to explain in fine detail precisely how the valuation has been calculated. While this chapter will provide an organiser with a basic understanding of the issues, this information does not replace the need for leaseholders to have a formal valuation carried out by a chartered surveyor with solid expertise in enfranchisement.

We saw in chapter 1 that the cost borne by an individual leaseholder when buying a 90-year lease extension is effectively the same as his share of the cost of buying the freehold of the building with fellow residents. This is because the same statutory formula applies to valuations in both of these procedures. When a leaseholder compels the landlord to sell him a 90-year lease extension, the resident is carrying out an individual enfranchisement, while the collective enfranchisement relates to the purchase of the entire freehold by all the participants. The diagram below shows how the leaseholder's proportional ownership of the flat decreases and the freeholder's ownership increases year by year as the term on the lease diminishes.

Leaseholder versus freeholder interest in a flat

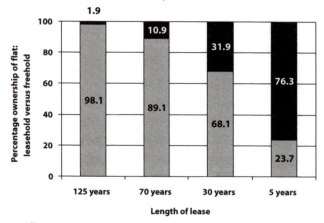

Source: Savills Research 2003 (Savills research stated in 2006 that important Lands Tribunal decisions might require a revision of these figures.)

When leaseholders enfranchise, they are buying from the landlord the area shaded in black in the diagram above. This area is sometimes called the 'landlord's interest' in a flat. As a lease gets shorter, the landlord's ownership interest in the flat increases and so does the value of this ownership. As the diagram shows, Savills Research estimated in 2003 that a leaseholder owned 98.1 per cent of the total value of the flat when there were 125 years on the lease, while the landlord owned just 1.9 per cent of this combined 'long lease' value. Worded differently, the leaseholder is estimated to own a flat that would increase in value by 1.9 per cent of its present market value if the leaseholder got a 90-year lease extension or bought the building freehold with fellow residents and extended the lease to 999 years. By the time this lease has only five years left, however, the leaseholder owns a mere estimated 23.7 per cent of the total value of the flat, while the landlord's ownership stake has increased to 76.3 per cent of the total. This chapter explains how surveyors value the freehold element that is shaded in black in the diagram above, which is what enfranchisers are buying in a freehold purchase.

One of the greatest challenges for enfranchisers in seeking to understand freehold valuation principles is to acquire knowledge of the many issues that can crop up beyond the straightforward valuation formula. These include what to do in an enfranchisement regarding flats in the building that belong to the landlord, such as a porter's flat, whether leaseholders have the right to enfranchise garages and what to do if there is a head lease. This chapter examines the following ten important elements for enfranchisers:

1. Valuation formula

2. Lease length and marriage value

3. Development value

4. Hope value

5. Discount rate

6. Leasebacks

7. Garages, gardens and surrounding property

8. Head lease

9. Informal and formal valuation

10. Hiring a project manager

The above list could easily be tripled in length given the complexity of legislation on enfranchisement, but I urge leaseholders not to spend too much time at the beginning of the process on understanding valuation issues. In the same way that we hire an accountant to prepare our tax return rather than seeking to become accountants ourselves for this task, leaseholders need to arm themselves with basic knowledge and literacy about freehold valuation principles so they can come up with an initial back-of-the-envelope cost estimate and then they need to make best use of a qualified chartered surveyor when the formal valuation is to be done.

The valuation formula

There are three main cost elements in the statutory formula for valuing a building freehold in an enfranchisement. The participating leaseholders must fully or partly compensate the landlord for these elements, which are:

1. the ground rent that the landlord will lose over the term of the lease;

2. full ownership that the landlord would have secured of all the flats when their leases expired. This is called the 'reversion' because full ownership of a flat reverts to the landlord when the lease expires. For this reason, the landlord is sometimes called the 'reversioner'; and

3. the anticipated increase in value of the participating flats once the enfranchisers buy the freehold and grant themselves 999-year leases. The anticipated increase in value is called 'marriage value', since it is value produced when the leasehold ownership and freehold ownership are 'married' or combined when leaseholders buy the freehold.

As part of the freehold cost, enfranchisers must compensate or pay the landlord for:

1. all of the loss regarding the ground rent;

2. all of the loss regarding the reversion; and

3. half of the marriage value for the participating flats.

Taking each of these elements in turn, the ground rent component is valued by calculating the net present value of this income stream over the course of the term of the lease. In other words, if the ground rent for a flat is £50 per year and there are 70 years left on the lease, how much money would one need to have in cash today to produce a 70-year income stream at £50 per year? To calculate this figure, that is, to capitalise the ground rent, one must apply a discount rate. The discount rate acts as a compound interest rate. Appendix 18 provides a present value table, which shows how much £1 at the present time is worth over a number of years when discount rates, or yields, ranging from five per cent to 10.5 per cent are applied.

Next, one must calculate the value of the reversion. Consider the flat that has 70 years left on the lease and a market value of £500,000. The value of the reversion is the amount of money one would need to have in cash today, to be invested at a defined yield that would produce the £500,000 in 70 years' time. Again, one calculates the value that £500,000 in 70 years would have today.

The third valuation element is the marriage value, which is described in detail in the next section. Considering marriage value is a good moment to warn flat owners about valuers' jargon. The subject of enfranchisement, like many specialist areas, is filled with obtuse-sounding terms, but leaseholders should not be put off by this. When reading a valuation report, one will see references such as the 'reversioner's interest'. This means the landlord's interest or his ownership stake in a leasehold flat or in the entire building. In terms of valuation calculations, the 'landlord's interest' normally refers to the compensation that he is demanding for lost ground rent and lost reversion. The 'tenant's interest' usually refers to the market value of the leaseholder's flat, since leasehold is a form of tenancy and thus the flat owner is, legally speaking, a tenant. The glossary at the end of the book is useful for deciphering jargon used by many surveyors and solicitors in an enfranchisement.

 The statutory formula for valuing a building freehold says that enfranchisers must compensate the landlord for the ground rent income stream he will lose; the net present value of the full ownership he would have secured of the flats when the leases expired; and half of the expected increase in the value of participating flats once these flats get lease extensions.

Lease length and marriage value

Many leaseholders become unnecessarily muddled when trying to understand marriage value. They should not. Marriage value, as we have seen, can be described roughly as the expected rise in value of a flat in a building that is participating in an enfranchisement once the leaseholders have collectively bought the freehold and granted themselves 999-year leases. The formula for calculating marriage value is provided below. The reason a flat is worth more after an enfranchisement is because it will get a longer lease and this is worth more than the same flat with a shorter lease.

As we saw in the diagram 'Leaseholder versus freeholder interest in a flat' earlier in this chapter, the leaseholder owns proportionally less and less of the flat as the length of the lease diminishes and the freeholder owns proportionally more and more. Valuers call tables that record these estimated proportional values 'relativity tables'. Different valuers present different estimates. The relativity table prepared by Savills Research, which is provided in Appendix 19, estimates that a leasehold flat with 90 years on the lease is worth 95.3 per cent of what the flat would be worth if 90 years or more were added onto the existing lease. However, once the lease has only 50 years left, the flat is worth just 80.7 per cent of the 'long lease value'. By the time the lease has shrunk to ten years, the leaseholder is holding property that is worth only an estimated 40.9 per cent what it would be worth with a long lease. The relativity table of Savills Research is represented below in graph form and shows how the value of a flat begins to drop off sharply once the lease has fewer than 80 years.

Relativity: Leasehold value as a proportion of combined freehold/leasehold value

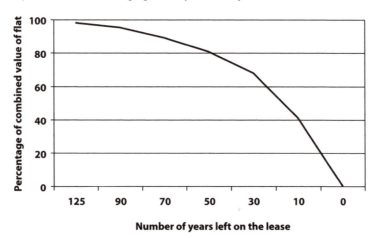

As the length of the lease decreases, the marriage value increases. This is because the shorter the lease gets, the greater will be the relative increase in the value of the flat if 90 years or more are added to the existing term.

By law, enfranchisers must pay to the landlord half of the applicable marriage value. But marriage value **only** applies to participating flats and **only** to those flats that have fewer than 80 years left on the lease. So, any participating flat that has 80 years or more on the lease does not pay any marriage value. There is growing awareness amongst flat owners of this '80-year' rule. While, a few years ago, leaseholders tended to wait until the length of leases had dipped to 70 or 60 years or less before organising to buy their freehold, a growing number of residents' groups are taking steps to buy their freehold while they still have 90 years or more to run and, therefore, before there is any marriage value payable on these flats. In such a building, enfranchisers must compensate the landlord just for the capitalised ground rent and reversion, and not for marriage value.

The formula for establishing the marriage value of an enfranchising flat, in valuer's terminology, is 'future value of the flat minus present value of the flat'. The first step is to calculate the following:

Present value

(a) The 'leaseholder's interest', i.e. the market value of the flat today.

(b) The 'landlord's interest', i.e. the capitalised ground rent and reversion.

Future value

(c) The 'leaseholder's interest', i.e. the estimated value of the flat with an extended lease.

(d) The 'landlord's interest', which is zero once he has sold the freehold.

Once the value of the four components above has been quantified, the next step in calculating the marriage value is to add the leaseholder's and landlord's interest in the flat after the freehold purchase, then subtract from this the sum of the leaseholder's and landlord's interest today. So, the formula for marriage value is:

$$MV = (c+d) - (a+b)$$

The enfranchisers must pay the landlord one half of this marriage value and all of the present value of the landlord's interest, that is:

Freehold value = ½ MV + (b)

A sample valuation of a 90-year lease extension for a flat valued at £44,000, with 70 years left on the lease, is provided in Appendix 20. The valuation, provided by Mark Wilson MRICS of myleasehold.com, also illustrates the expected approximate cost of the share of the building freehold.

Some enfranchisers seek to limit the number of leaseholders participating in the freehold purchase, to avoid paying marriage value on the non-participating flats. This course of action can backfire badly and it is to be avoided. This is because Section 18 of the 1993 Act requires the nominee purchaser to inform the landlord of any agreements reached with non-participants about the freehold purchase. If the nominee purchaser does reach an agreement, behind closed doors, in which one or more non-participants are promised, for instance, a 999-year lease and a share of the freehold after the enfranchisement, the landlord has a right to demand that this payment be included in the freehold cost. A landlord can also seek to have an enfranchisement declared invalid by serving a Section 18 Notice that claims the nominee purchaser has made a deal or had discussions about such a deal behind closed doors without notifying the landlord.

 Enfranchisers should remember that marriage value is the biggest cost component in most enfranchisements and marriage value increases as lease length diminishes, but that marriage value only applies to participating flats and only to flats with fewer than 80 years on their lease.

Development value

Some leaseholders are stunned to see their landlord demand a price for the freehold that is far higher than the offer price recommended by their valuer, including instances when the freeholder is demanding a price that is hundreds of times greater than the offer price. This type of huge valuation discrepancy is often the result of a demand by the landlord for what is called 'development value' in a building.

Development value refers to value that the landlord claims to be losing as a result of being forced to sell the freehold, because the compulsory sale denies the landlord the ability to develop further the property. A freeholder might claim, for instance, that he had planned to build an additional storey on the roof of the building, to add several new flats and to sell these flats. In this case, he might demand that enfranchisers pay him money that he claims he would have made by selling these flats.

In other cases, a landlord might demand compensation on the grounds that he was going to earn money by agreeing to place a mobile telecommunications dish on the roof. In one case years ago in London, enfranchisers of a small residential building had a formal valuation done and then offered the landlord £2,000 for their freehold. They were shocked subsequently to receive a Counter Notice in which the landlord demanded £540,000. The landlord said that this figure mostly represented the development value he was being denied, as he had taken steps to have a telecommunications dish installed on the roof and to be paid for this by the telecommunications company. When the leaseholders took the case to the Leasehold Valuation Tribunal (LVT), the LVT decided that the landlord must sell the freehold to the enfranchisers at £4,135.

Leaseholders should not panic if the landlord demands what appears to be an outrageously large amount of money for the freehold, but they do need to take precautionary steps to guard against having to pay an unfairly high price for the building. One important step is to get to know the planning authority officials at one's local council. I have seen instances in which a landlord demanded an enormous amount of development value for what he described as plans to build an additional storey on the roof of an enfranchising building, only for it to be revealed later that the building was in a conservation area and that the local planning authority was highly unlikely to approve any such proposed construction. If the enfranchisers are able to obtain a letter from the local planning authority saying it is unlikely to approve such a construction, they should do so. This is the kind of written information that the LVT will consider when deciding on the fair price of a freehold.

If leaseholders feel that they are being asked by a landlord in a Counter Notice to pay an unreasonably large amount of development value, they should not seek redress on this issue in the County Court. While some large landlords have succeeded over the years in persuading a County Court to declare an Enfranchisement Notice invalid on the grounds that the offer price was so low as to be unrealistic, enfranchisers have not been successful in persuading a County Court to declare a Counter Notice invalid on the grounds that the counter offer price was so high as to be unrealistic. Case Study 4 on 9 Cornwall Crescent illustrates this point. Leaseholders should take their case to the LVT, whose responsibility is to decide on the fair freehold price.

 Leaseholders can challenge a demand by the landlord for development value of an additional storey on the building by securing a planning rejection from the local council to any such proposed construction.

Hope value

While the formula for valuing a freehold in an enfranchisement says that there is no marriage value counted for non-participating flats, some landlords have fought successfully to be paid some marriage value for non-participating flats. This is called 'hope value', because the landlord says the enfranchisers will have the hope of selling lease extensions to non-participants after they have bought the freehold and the landlord says that he should get a cut of this future expected payment. While leaseholders argue that this demand represents a violation of their right to buy their freehold according to the valuation formula laid down by law, some landlords have succeeded in creating a precedent for receiving around ten or 15 per cent of the marriage value of non-participating flats.

Leaseholders can seek to limit the risk of having to pay hope value to a landlord by inviting in writing all qualifying leaseholders in the building to participate in the freehold purchase project and by repeating this written invitation several times before the deadline for joining the project has passed. If the residents in the building decline repeated invitations to join a freehold purchase project, enfranchisers can use this information to bolster their claim that there is no indication that non-participants will want to buy lease extensions in the foreseeable future.

Enfranchisers should limit the amount of hope value they will have to pay to the landlord by inviting in writing all leaseholders in the building to join the freehold purchase.

The discount rate

The discount rate that is used to calculate the ground rent and reversion of a freehold represents a crucial aspect of valuation and one that is often misunderstood by leaseholders. Because the discount rate serves the same purpose as a compound interest rate, even a small change in the rate can have an enormous effect in increasing or decreasing a freehold valuation.

Let us consider the estimated cost of the share of a freehold for a leaseholder with a flat that has 70 years on the lease, pays £50 per year in ground rent and has an estimated market value of £500,000. The figures below show how the estimated freehold value varies, depending on whether one applies a discount rate of six, seven, eight or nine per cent.

Discount rate	Estimated cost of share of freehold
6%	£25,072
7%	£22,705
8%	£21,473
9%	£20,822

Leaseholders need to remember that the discount rate is meant to reflect the risk profile of the building as an investment asset. The higher the risk of the asset, the higher the discount rate. The lower the risk, the lower the discount rate. For this reason, investors expect to earn a low percentage return on a low-risk investment, such as cash in the bank or the bond market, but they expect to earn more from the higher-risk stock market. At the height of the dotcom boom, investors expected a double-digit return or higher from the riskier stocks, such as technology shares.

Some chartered surveyors appear uncomfortable with the concept that they must justify the discount rate that they apply by describing the risk profile of the building. Enfranchisers should not shy away from this important area of valuation. A well-maintained luxury house in an expensive central London neighbourhood should carry a lower discount rate than a poorly-maintained block of flats not situated in a prime location. This is because, amongst other things, the enfranchisement of the block of flats represents a riskier investment, one that is less likely to produce a profitable return for enfranchisers. If it is a troubled building in which major repairs are needed and many leaseholders have refused for years to pay their service charges, the discount rate applied should be even higher.

A chartered surveyor acting for enfranchisers will sometimes apply a different discount rate when valuing a freehold than will the surveyor acting for the landlord. Normally, if there is a difference, the landlord is applying a lower discount rate, which results in a higher freehold price, while the enfranchisers argue for a higher discount rate, which results in a lower freehold price. If there is disagreement on this point, the LVT will decide on the discount rate to be used. Appendix 21 shows discount rates used in some recent LVT cases.

 The lower the discount rate that is applied in the valuation calculation to ground rent paid by flats in the building and 'reversion', the net present value of the scheduled reversion to the landlord of full ownership of the flats when their leases expire, the higher the resulting freehold price, while a higher discount rate will produce a lower freehold price.

Leasebacks

Another enfranchisement term with which leaseholders need to be familiar is the 'leaseback'. As we saw in chapter 2, this applies to the situation in which one or more flats in the building being enfranchised belong to the landlord and have no long lease. This can include, for instance, a porter's flat. If such flats exist, then the landlord, as part of the freehold purchase process, has the right either to compel the enfranchisers to buy some or all of his flats or to keep the flats himself. If the landlord opts to keep his flats, he gets what is called a 'leaseback' from the nominee purchaser. This means the nominee purchaser, in becoming the new freeholder, grants a 999-year lease for a 'peppercorn rent', which means zero ground rent, to the old freeholder.

Some leaseholders become so worried about possibly having to buy the landlord's flats in a building that they indefinitely postpone their enfranchisement project. But flat owners should be aware that many large landlords opt to get leasebacks on any flats they own in a building that is being enfranchised, rather than force the enfranchisers to buy them out. This is because landlords usually stand to make a greater profit by selling these 999-year leasehold flats after the enfranchisement is over than they would by forcing the enfranchisers to buy the flats when they are still freehold.

When the leaseholders are preparing the Enfranchisement Notice that they will serve on the landlord, they must ensure that the offer price included covers the entire building and all of its flats, even if the building contains some flats that are owned by the landlord and are thus not enfranchisable. They must also have prepared the lower figure that they plan to offer for the freehold of only those flats in the building that are enfranchisable, in case the landlord says that he wishes to keep his flats by getting leasebacks on these.

If the landlord owns any flats in the building, he must state in the Counter Notice whether he wishes to get a leaseback on any of these flats.

 Enfranchisers need to offer a leaseback on any flats owned by the landlord, but they must also be ready to buy these flats and they **must** include in the Enfranchisement Notice an offer price that includes these flats.

Garages, gardens and other surrounding property

When leaseholders buy their freehold through the process of collective enfranchisement, they often have the opportunity to purchase not only the building but also related property around or near the building that makes up the freehold. This other property, which includes things like gardens, garages, pathways, parking area and forecourt, is called the 'appurtenant property'. Enfranchisers need to be sure that all appurtenant property has been properly identified in the Enfranchisement Notice.

If the lease of a flat in a building being enfranchised also provides for a garage, then the enfranchisers have a right to force the landlord to sell them the garage as part of the freehold purchase. If the lease for the garage is held separately from that of any flat in the building, but the garage lease is held by a leaseholder in the building who qualifies to take part in the enfranchisement, then the garage is enfranchisable. It is not necessary for the leaseholder of the garage to be a participant in the enfranchisement in order for the garage to be enfranchisable.

To identify the leaseholder of all flats and all garages, enfranchisers or their project manager or solicitor need to carry out a search of all leasehold titles and to obtain certified copies of all the leases at HM Land Registry. The process for doing this is described in chapter 4. As we saw in chapter 1, this can be done by downloading each leasehold title from the HM Land Registry website or by sending an OC1 Form to the Land Registry in order to obtain the titles by post.

The offer price for the freehold that is included in the Enfranchisement Notice is presented in two figures. The first figure covers the building itself, while the second figure covers the appurtenant property.

 Leaseholders should include in their Enfranchisement Notice any garages held by qualifying leaseholders, and gardens, pathways and other areas included in the freehold.

The head lease

Some residential buildings have not one, but two or more landlords. This occurs in a hierarchical manner, with the freeholder at the top and the next landlord one level down. At the bottom of the ownership structure is the leaseholder. The lower-level landlord is called the 'head leaseholder'. He is also sometimes called the intermediate leaseholder or the leaseholder's superior landlord.

In the same way that the freeholder has an ownership stake in each leaseholder's flat, and this ownership stake grows as the lease gets shorter, the head leaseholder also has an ownership stake. The diagram below shows how crowded the ownership elements can be in one's flat.

Ownership structure of a flat with a head leaseholder

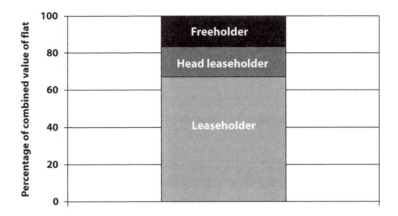

Although the existence of both a freeholder and head leaseholder can complicate an enfranchisement, leaseholders should not be overly alarmed. By law, they have the right to enfranchise their building in a one-step process, by serving one Enfranchisement Notice containing one offer price for the freehold and head lease. The notice gets served on the freeholder, with a copy to the head leaseholder. When the enfranchisement is completed, the nominee purchaser pays one price to the freeholder and the head leaseholder gets a portion of this, as agreed with the enfranchisers or as decided by the LVT.

If the leaseholders have already purchased the head lease of the building, they have taken an important step towards acquiring full and permanent ownership of the building. The only remaining step is to buy the freehold.

 If there is a head lease for the building, leaseholders get to buy the head lease **and** the freehold in the same enfranchisement process, by serving just one Enfranchisement Notice and offering one overall price.

Informal and formal valuations

Leaseholders should come up with a rough estimate of the value of their freehold before they decide whether to go down the road of enfranchising their building. To do this, they can use one of the following methods for reaching an informal valuation estimate:

- Calculate the freehold value themselves.

- Use input from a project manager or local estate agents.

- Use input from chartered surveyors.

To use the first method above, the leaseholders will need to gather a copy of all the leasehold titles from HM Land Registry. This will provide information on the ground rents payable and the length of leases for the leasehold flats in the building. With this information in hand and equipped with a calculator that does net present values, many leaseholders are able to come up with a reasonable rough estimate. Various discount rates, ranging from nine per cent as best case to five per cent as worst case, can be used.

The second method involves asking local estate agents to visit flats in the building to provide free valuations. During each visit, the leaseholder should ask the estate agent how much the flat would increase in value if it got a 90-year lease extension. This figure equates roughly to the marriage value, so half of this value can be used as a rough-and-ready estimate of the cost of the share of the freehold for this flat.

To use the third method, leaseholders can invite one or more chartered surveyors to the building, to discuss possibly having a formal valuation of the freehold carried out. During this 'beauty parade' process, the leaseholders can ask for a rough estimate of the value of the freehold and some surveyors will provide such a figure.

After apartment owners have secured the participation of the required minimum 50 per cent of all flats to enfranchise their building, a chartered surveyor with deep experience in enfranchisement should be instructed to carry out a formal valuation. The resulting valuation report should advise the leaseholders of the fair price of the freehold and also the figure that should be included as the offer price in the Enfranchisement Notice. It is essential, as we have seen, for the offer price to be a realistic one which can be substantiated by valuation evidence.

Some enfranchisers are put off by the fact that lease lengths in a building vary. This should not cause undue concern. If some flats have, for instance, 70 years left on the lease, while others have 125 years, this means that the 125-year leaseholders have effectively already bought their share of the freehold. Because these flats have more than 80 years on the lease, there is zero marriage value to pay for these flats. In a building such as this, the leaseholders with very long leases end up having to pay a smaller share of the cost of the freehold. This is good news for enfranchisers, since the very long leaseholders have to pay only a nominal amount and this often increases the level of participation in the building.

 Organisers of an enfranchisement can provide fellow residents with a rough informal cost estimate of the freehold by calculating half of the expected increase in the value of the participating flats if these flats secured a 90-year lease extension.

Hiring a project manager

Flat owners that want to buy their building freehold need to strike the right balance between, on the one hand, learning about the complex subject of enfranchisement and, on the other hand, avoiding carrying out too much unpaid work on the project. For this reason, many leaseholders decide to outsource to a project manager the task of selecting and working with a solicitor and chartered surveyor who have the required level of expertise and experience in enfranchisement. Instructing a competent project manager can save leaseholders an enormous amount of time and effort, and can often save them a lot of money when buying their freehold. A project manager should be able, for instance, to provide an informal valuation of the freehold. He will instruct and liaise with the surveyor and solicitor, and provide a valuable single point of contact for the leaseholders.

The value of having a professional project manager who oversees all aspects of the enfranchisement should not be underestimated. Many residents have told me nightmare stories over the years of enfranchisement projects in which the solicitor and surveyor did not speak with one another or share information or documents, and the leaseholders had to serve as a communication channel between the two advisers.

 Enfranchisers can outsource the selection of a chartered surveyor with experience in collective enfranchisement and the work involved in liaising with the surveyor by instructing an outside project manager.

This chapter has provided information and tools to enable leaseholders to build literacy in the main principles of valuing a freehold in an enfranchisement. Flat owners should be able to arrive at an informal cost estimate of their freehold in the early stages of the project. The advice in this chapter is aimed at helping leaseholders to even out the odds when they are engaged in a David-and-Goliath encounter with a large corporate landlord. While most enfranchisers go through a freehold purchase only once, the largest landlords have gone through it many times and have developed deep in-house expertise on how to foil an enfranchisement initiative.

Flat owners are encouraged to outsource the labour-intensive tasks of enfranchisement to a project manager, who, in turn, instructs a chartered surveyor and solicitor. But enfranchisers still need to be familiar with the freehold purchase process and they should be ready to raise the alarm if they believe an adviser has made a mistake. Leaseholders who succeed in running the enfranchisement race without collapsing before crossing the finish line are often those that delegate the project management, while keeping an overview to ensure quality control.

CHAPTER 4

Preparation, preparation, preparation

Most of the enfranchisement initiatives that fail do so because of a lack of preparation. This chapter guides the leaseholder through the crucial preparatory steps that must be taken to ensure that the freehold purchase gets off to a good start and can be efficiently managed by the organisers. For our long-distance runner, the advice provided in this chapter represents the essential checklist for training in the months, weeks and days before the big race.

It is not always easy for enfranchisers to focus on long-term strategy and tactics, and to dedicate the time required for adequate preparation. Typically, leaseholders in a troubled building are upset with short-lease problems and/or poor building management, and they are impatient to get the freehold purchase process started. However, organisers must be prudent in managing the significant risks faced by enfranchisers in a large block of flats and must resist the temptation to skip any of the preparatory steps outlined below.

Setting up and running the resident management company

We have seen that the entity that buys a building freehold in an enfranchisement is called the 'nominee purchaser'. By law, the nominee purchaser can be a person, a small group of people, a company or other legal entity. As I have explained, it is best practice for the nominee purchaser to be a company limited by shares. While this is not required by law, my research into enfranchising buildings has revealed that the use of other models, such as the nominee purchaser that is an individual in the building, can lead to disaster. Case Study 6 describes the leaseholder who became the nominee purchaser for his fellow leaseholders in London and then used this status to defraud the enfranchisement participants.

A company limited by shares, or a limited company, is owned by its shareholders. The shareholders appoint directors to run the company. In England and Wales, a limited company must have a minimum of one director and a company secretary, and these cannot be the same person. In a collective enfranchisement, it is best practice for each participant of the project to be made a shareholder of the nominee purchaser company.

 Enfranchisers should set up a resident management company as nominee purchaser which is a company limited by shares.

Corporate governance of the resident management company

The directors that run the resident management company, which starts life as the nominee purchaser company, must put in place sound systems from the start. The board of directors need to establish processes and procedures that provide for good corporate governance, that is, management of the business that complies with good practice and that protects the interests of shareholders and other stakeholders. The directors should also create processes that are efficient and time-saving since they are normally doing this work on a volunteer unpaid basis.

Enfranchisers need to be careful to avoid problems that exist in many residential buildings as a result of poor corporate governance of residents' associations. I have heard horrendous accounts over the years of abuse of power by some residents' association committee members, ranging from improper representation of members to embezzlement of tens of thousands of pounds of association funds. If the enfranchisers fail to put in place a resident management company that is run by a competent, efficient and honest board of directors, the leaseholders can end up getting rid of one landlord only to be saddled with a worse landlord – themselves.

While the Companies Act requires a limited company in England or Wales to have a minimum of one director, it is best practice to have at least two directors in a small residential building and four to six directors in a large building. Having more than six directors can make for an unwieldy board of directors. Enfranchisers in large buildings with dozens of flats should never make every shareholder of the resident management company a director, as this creates organisational paralysis. I strongly recommend outsourcing the company secretary work to a company specialising in this work, such as Jordans Limited. Contact details for Jordans are provided in the section on 'Useful contacts' at the back of the book. The issue of outsourcing non-strategic work is addressed in chapter 10.

When the resident management company is being set up, enfranchisers need to agree on which participants will serve as directors. These individuals need to be appointed by the shareholders in a first instance and then to stand for election at the first Annual General Meeting (AGM). It is best practice in a large residential building for the board of directors to hold a board meeting once every quarter, although the board may decide to hold board meetings more or less frequently. Each board meeting must be minuted, with these minutes making up part of the board's company records.

It is the Memorandum and Articles of Association, also known as the 'MemArts', that contain the rules and regulations of the company. Enfranchisers should buy a set of MemArts specially designed for the resident management company. These can be purchased from Jordans Limited, as mentioned above. The directors need to remember, and to remind shareholders from time to time, that the resident management company is not the same as a residents' association. Directors are bound by the Companies Act and they have legal responsibilities to run the company properly which go far beyond any formal legal constraints on committee members of a residents' association.

The MemArts will specify when the AGM must be held each year and how far in advance AGM documentation must be sent to the shareholders. It will also describe the way in which directors or shareholders can call an Extraordinary General Meeting (EGM). It is best practice for directors of a resident management company, like any other limited company, to have directors' insurance and to have the company pay for this. This is insurance that protects the directors against being sued by a shareholder or someone else in connection with their directorship.

Directors of the resident management company need to be aware of the 80–20 rule as it applies to shareholders that make unreasonable requests of the board. Input I have gathered from many residential buildings suggests that the 20 per cent most difficult shareholders in most buildings require more time and effort by the board of directors than the other 80 per cent of shareholders. It is a painful paradox that some shareholders will bombard directors of a resident management company, who do their work on a volunteer unpaid basis, with unreasonable requests that they would not dream of sending to the paid directors of a commercial company.

For this reason, enfranchisers need to ensure that the board of directors comprises people with integrity and backbone, including the ability to say no. Ideally, board members should have as much commercial, legal, operational and communications skills as possible. Importantly, these individuals need to be doers.

 The resident management company should assemble a board of directors whose members have integrity and backbone, who bring a diversity of commercial, legal, financial and communication skills to the company, and who are skilled at implementation.

Getting an Enfranchisement Notice and Participation Agreement signed

Once the leaseholders have set up their nominee purchaser company and have had the formal valuation done of their building freehold, they are ready to carry out the final preparatory work. This includes preparing the Enfranchisement Notice and the Participation Agreement, which we described in chapter 2. Appendices 9 and 10 provide sample versions of the Participation Agreement and an Enfranchisement Notice respectively.

As we have seen, it is essential for each participant **personally** to sign these two documents. It is **not** acceptable for a Power of Attorney, lawyer or other representative to sign these documents. A failure to secure the personal signature of every participant can result in a landlord seeking to have an Enfranchisement Notice declared invalid in the County Court, as we explained in chapter 2. If a flat is owned by more than one person, then each individual must sign the two documents. The enfranchisement organisers should advise participants **not** to date the documents when they sign them.

Before circulating the original printed Enfranchisement Notice and Participation Agreement for signing, the organisers can email these two documents to the participants, remind the participants in a cover note what the documents are and offer to answer questions. Organisers need to make clear that these documents cannot be altered once they have been sent to all participants for their signature. It is advisable to send these documents within the UK by receipted express mail and by international courier when sent overseas. One of the organisers should track the progress of the documents as they are sent from one participant to the next. The Enfranchisement Notice and Participation Agreement should **always** be sent together.

Enfranchisers need to understand that the process of gathering signatures on these two crucial documents will progress as quickly as the slowest participant. In a building, for instance, with dozens of flats, whose leaseholders live in various countries around the world, enfranchisement organisers should set aside approximately three months in order to gather participants' signatures.

 Enfranchisers in a large block of flats with many absentee leaseholders should allocate about three months to gather signatures on the Enfranchisement Notice and the Participation Agreement.

Gathering the original leases and keys before serving an Enfranchisement Notice

After the leaseholders have gathered all the participants' signatures on the Enfranchisement Notice and Participation Agreement, and before they serve the Enfranchisement Notice on the landlord, they need to take two important precautionary measures. Because the landlord, upon being served an Enfranchisement Notice, has the right to inspect the original deeds of the participants or certified copies and to inspect their flats, the organisers need to gather these documents together and arrange for quick access, if needed, to these flats. The original Deeds of Participants refers to the original lease and any important related document, such as a Deed of Variation.

If the landlord does demand to inspect the participants' original deeds, he has the right to provide the nominee purchaser with as little as ten days' written notice. If the enfranchisers are unable to provide the original leases or certified copies within this timeframe, the landlord can seek to declare this a 'deemed withdrawal' of the Enfranchisement Notice by the leaseholders. It can take months in a large building to gather all the original leases of the participants, so this work needs to be carried out well in advance of serving the Enfranchisement Notice. Original leases, which are normally held by a leaseholder's mortgage lender or solicitor, should be held by the solicitor handling the enfranchisement. Gathering all the participants' leases also saves time at the end of the freehold purchase process, when the participants will need to surrender the existing leases in order to get new 999-year leases. Alternatively, organisers can get certified copies of leases from HM Land Registry, as explained below.

The landlord has the right to inspect the participating flats, after being served with an Enfranchisement Notice, because he has the right to have these flats valued by his own chartered surveyor. He does not have the right to use this inspection for any other purpose. If the landlord does demand the right to inspect the participating flats, he is allowed to provide the nominee purchaser as little as ten days' written notice. If the enfranchisers are unable to provide such access within this timeframe, the landlord can seek to declare this a 'deemed withdrawal' of the Enfranchisement Notice by the leaseholders.

 Before serving the Enfranchisement Notice, organisers should have the original deeds of all the participants or certified copies held by the solicitor and they should arrange quick access to the participants' flats for inspection by the landlord, in case this is needed.

Gathering the certified copies of leases from the Land Registry

As part of the due diligence process in the preparation stage, enfranchisers should gather for their own records copies of all the leases in the building. An easy way to do this is to complete and send to HM Land Registry an OC2 Form and a payment of £4 for each lease. Appendix 22 shows the OC2 Form, which can be downloaded from the Land Registry website at www.landreg.gov.uk. The Land Registry will then send a certified copy of the leases by post. However, the Land Registry does not always have a copy on record of every lease in a building. In such a case, leaseholders need to make a copy of an original lease as provided by an enfranchisement participant.

Organisers harness crucial information by holding a copy of all the leases, including the percentage of total annual service charges in the building that is payable by each leaseholder. By keeping a copy of the leases, the organisers are also able to ensure an efficient sharing of information within the project team. Many leaseholders have complained to me about solicitors and surveyors they had instructed for an enfranchisement, who subsequently refused to share information and documentation with one another and to work together as a team. I have seen lawyers working for enfranchisers fail to give a surveyor access to information contained in the original leases held by the lawyer. If the enfranchisers hold a copy of the leases, they can, at a reasonable photocopying expense, ensure that the solicitor and surveyor each has the required information. If the enfranchisers have hired a project manager, the problem regarding sharing of information should not arise, since the project manager serves as the single point of contact for and provides much of the information to the solicitor and surveyor.

 Enfranchisers should obtain from HM Land Registry, as part of their due diligence and to help their chartered surveyor, a certified copy of all the leases in the building.

Avoiding the County Court

Before the leaseholders serve the Enfranchisement Notice on the landlord, they must run through a checklist to ensure that they have minimised all risks that the landlord will seek to have the notice declared invalid. As we have seen, the organisers need to make sure that every leaseholder of every participating flat has personally signed the notice. One of the most common mistakes made by enfranchisers is that they fail to have every participant sign the notice. If a participating leaseholder is a company, the enfranchisers need to identify the authorised signatories of the company. Often the person living in the flat, who considers it to be his flat, is not an authorised signatory of the company.

The organisers also need to double check, before circulating the Enfranchisement Notice to participants for their signature, that the notice correctly identifies every leaseholder in the building. They can do this by carrying out a quick search of leaseholder titles at the HM Land Registry website at www.landregisteronline.gov.uk. In this way, they can identify whether any leaseholder titles have changed since they last checked.

Another important step in risk management is for the organisers to ensure that the offer price contained in the Enfranchisement Notice is realistic and can be substantiated by valuation evidence. They do not need to become chartered surveyors to do this, but they do need to be ready to query their valuer, or their project manager, if they have outsourced the project management. Enfranchisers are urged to resist the temptation to present as low an offer price as possible in an Enfranchisement Notice, unless they want to encourage the landlord to file a claim in the County Court in which the court is asked to declare the notice invalid for containing an unrealistically low offer price.

If the building being enfranchised contains some leasehold flats and some flats that are owned by the landlord, the organisers must ensure that the offer price contained in the Enfranchisement Notice covers the entire building and all of its flats. As we have seen, they will also have to have in mind a lower offer price figure, supplied by their valuer, that covers the leasehold flats and excludes the landlord-owned flats, in the event that the landlord wants the kind of leaseback on his flats that we addressed in chapter 3.

Enfranchisers should minimise the risk that the landlord will seek to get the County Court to declare the Enfranchisement Notice invalid, by ensuring that the notice has been signed **personally** by all the participants and that it contains a realistic offer price.

Receiving a Right of First Refusal Notice

Leaseholders need to take some simple steps to ensure that they do not get caught off guard if the landlord offers to sell the freehold before the leaseholders have served their Enfranchisement Notice. As we saw in chapter 2, a landlord wishing to sell the freehold must provide a right of first refusal to leaseholders in the building by sending them a Section 5 Notice. To avoid unnecessary panic amongst leaseholders, enfranchisement organisers need to be aware of what a Section 5 Notice looks like and to be clear about the steps to be taken after receiving this type of notice. Appendix 13 provides a sample Section 5 Notice.

The good news is that, the closer that the leaseholders get to the moment of serving an Enfranchisement Notice on their landlord, the less will be the disruption caused by a Section 5 Notice. This is because the enfranchisers will know, once they have had their formal valuation done and have prepared their Enfranchisement Notice, whether the asking price contained in a Section 5 Notice is reasonable.

If the valuer acting for the enfranchisers says that the asking price presented by the landlord in the Section 5 Notice is reasonable, the leaseholders may proceed to buy the freehold through the right of first refusal. If the valuer believes, on the other hand, that the leaseholders have a chance of securing a significantly lower freehold price by going to the Leasehold Valuation Tribunal (LVT), the flat owners may carry on with their plans to serve the Enfranchisement Notice. Residents must remember that a surveyor has no ability to guarantee the price that they will pay for the freehold, as this is only determined at the end of the process. The surveyor can only advise on the fair price of the freehold, according to his valuation.

As we saw in chapter 2, one disadvantage for leaseholders when being served a Section 5 Notice is that they have no legal right to negotiate on the freehold price. They must take or leave the asking price that is presented by the landlord. But there are advantages to buying a freehold through the right-of-first-refusal process, namely, to shorten the freehold purchase process, eliminate possible legal and surveyor fees, and avoid having to go to the LVT. Appendix 15 provides a sample of the Section 6 Notice, which leaseholders need to serve on the landlord if they wish to accept a right-of-first-refusal offer.

 The closer that leaseholders get to serving the Enfranchisement Notice, the greater will be their level of preparedness if the landlord sends them a Right of First Refusal Notice, also known as a Section 5 Notice.

Steering clear of professional advisers without the required expertise

A question posed by many leaseholders is how to find a project manager or, alternatively, a solicitor and chartered surveyor who offer the required level of technical expertise in enfranchisement in a manner that is cost effective and client-friendly. Flat owners have told me many worrying stories about enfranchisement initiatives that have collapsed because a solicitor or surveyor made one or more crucial errors. I have heard numerous accounts of solicitors or surveyors who have claimed to have expertise in enfranchisement, only for the client to discover, too late in the process, that this expertise was lacking.

Leaseholders need to remember that enfranchisement law is still new, since the Commonhold and Leasehold Reform Act 2002 introduced important changes to the Leasehold Reform, Housing and Urban Development Act 1993. There is a small number of solicitors and chartered surveyors with deep expertise and experience in this highly specialised area of property law, and even fewer project managers.

Flat owners are at an additional disadvantage when searching for skilled and affordable advisers since London's largest landlords have hired several of the lawyers and surveyors most experienced in enfranchisement, and they pay top rates for this work, including approximately £400 per hour for some solicitors. We are faced again with the David-and-Goliath equation. While the largest landlords in the country become more and more proficient in how to foil enfranchisements, including by hiring some of the best, most expensive lawyers to work on this, leaseholders are left scrambling to find advisers with the required expertise and that are affordable.

Some residents prefer the do-it-yourself approach to freehold purchase in which they instruct a solicitor and a chartered surveyor, and the residents carry out the project management work themselves. In this scenario, leaseholders need to ensure that the solicitor and surveyor will provide the co-operation needed to hold the project team together.

Where leaseholders are able to instruct a project manager, they should do so. Hiring an outside project manager significantly decreases the amount of work, normally all of it unpaid, that organisers inside the residential building have to carry out. It also helps overcome the lack of co-ordination and co-operation that we discussed earlier between a solicitor and a surveyor, since the project manager controls the information flow.

 Enfranchisers should hire a project manager to select and serve as a single point of contact with a chartered surveyor and a solicitor that have solid expertise in enfranchisement.

Having Plan B ready: lease extensions and/or right to manage

Some flat owners despair if their efforts to organise an enfranchisement are not successful. They feel like failures if they are unable to get to the stage when an Enfranchisement Notice and Participation Agreement are prepared. These organisers should not despair. It is difficult, particularly in a large block of flats with many absentee leaseholders, to get this type of complex project off the ground. In some cases, it is simply impossible.

If leases are too short in a building, for instance, down to 20 years, flat owners might find it too expensive to buy the freehold. Or leaseholders might be too fragmented and unwilling to work together on such an ambitious joint commercial undertaking as an enfranchisement. Finally, if many leaseholders in a building plan to sell their flat within the subsequent year or two, this can create a short-term approach that makes enfranchisement unworkable. In this type of building, it often makes more sense for leaseholders to buy individual 90-year lease extensions. If more than one leaseholder seeks a lease extension, it is sometimes possible to get a group discount from a project manager, or a solicitor and surveyor. My book *Making Sense of Leasehold Property* provides a step-by-step guide on how to obtain the 90-year lease extension to which most leaseholders of flats are legally entitled.

Residents that are seeking to organise the purchase of their freehold sometimes discover that too few leaseholders are willing to spend any money on such a project. Flat owners need to remember that enfranchisement represents the purchase of a piece of property, the freehold, and there is always a cost. If the real problem is poor building management, leaseholders might wish instead to secure the right to manage. This process is also described in my book *Making Sense of Leasehold Property*.

Organisers need to remember that there is no one-size-fits-all solution for every residential building. Each group of leaseholders has its own issues, priorities, budget and dynamics. Leaseholders that are proposing enfranchisement should seek to build the consensus needed to get the project off the ground, but they should not force the issue on unwilling residents. Many enfranchisement initiatives have crumbled because of weak commitment by participants at the start.

 Leaseholders should pursue lease extensions if the leases are too short and the residents too disorganised for a freehold purchase, or right to manage if management is the one pressing problem in the building, and they should only seek to enfranchise if there is sufficient support amongst leaseholders for this 'big bang' solution.

A phased approach to collective enfranchisement

Sometimes residents become unsettled if they set out to buy their freehold, but then discover the length of leases in the building varies widely because some leaseholders have already bought 90-year or longer lease extensions from the landlord. Organisers of an enfranchisement should not allow varying lease lengths to throw them off. The chartered surveyor who carries out the formal valuation of the freehold should provide a breakdown of the share of the cost of the freehold that is to be borne by each participant, which factors in the length of each lease.

Flat owners can also use the right to manage process as a springboard for later starting a freehold purchase project. When residents acquire the official right to manage their building by following the statutory route, they decrease the landlord's incentive to continue on as freeholder. This is because many landlords earn hidden commissions by providing building management and related services, such as insurance, to the buildings they own. Once leaseholders have prised the right to manage away from the landlord, he often has little interest in continuing to own the building.

Leaseholders can also gain valuable experience in setting up and running a resident-owned company by securing the right to manage. This is because they need to establish a right to manage (or RTM) company, the members or shareholders of which are participants in the project. By the time the directors of the RTM company have held one or two AGMs, and the company has successfully managed the building during this period, they have gathered valuable experience that can be transferred easily to a freehold purchase project.

 Leaseholders can pursue collective enfranchisement with a phased approach, after they have secured the right to manage the building and/or one or more residents have bought lease extensions.

Organisers will be in good shape to start their long-distance race of collective enfranchisement after working through the preparatory steps described in this chapter. This preparation work can take weeks or months, depending on the building, but can often save a freehold purchase project from collapsing later on.

Many leaseholders are ready to celebrate the success of their freehold purchase project when they have in fact only succeeded in reaching the point of getting a minimum of 50 per cent of all flats signed up. This is the equivalent of the long-distance runner celebrating victory a year before the big race, because he has simply completed a successful training session.

I have described in this chapter the importance for the nominee purchaser company to be run by directors that have integrity and backbone. They will also need to have enormous patience, as they are likely to be required to explain many times to enfranchisement participants, the shareholders of the company, the main stages and other aspects of the freehold purchase process before the project has ended. Even if the leaseholders hire an outside project manager to enfranchise their building, the directors of the nominee purchaser company will need to understand each project milestone and to be firm with any participant that threatens to slow down or otherwise jeopardise the process.

The tone of a freehold purchase project in a large building changes significantly from the earliest stage, when residents are analysing the issues in and options for a building, to the later preparatory stage, just before the collective enfranchisement officially begins. While the earliest stage is about including all residents in a dialogue, to develop consensus and momentum, the final preparatory phase is marked by sharp focus, concentration and risk management measures. Enfranchisement organisers must not allow themselves to be distracted at this crucial point by the small number of participants who will continue to ask the same questions over and over, and they must certainly not get bogged down in issues raised by non-participants. Indeed, organisers must make clear to all participants that, once the period for joining the project has ended, the enfranchisement project is strictly confidential. If non-participants ask questions about the process, the organisers should explain briefly and firmly that any questions by non-participants will have to be answered after the project has been concluded.

CHAPTER 5

Ready, steady, go!

By the time the leaseholders have completed their preparations and are ready to start the formal process of enfranchisement, the freehold purchase project will have taken on a new look. What may have started years earlier as a free-flowing discussion amongst neighbours about options for the building should by now have evolved into a tightly-organised project plan.

To get the project this far, organisers will have already presented leaseholders in the building with one or more deadlines, including a deadline for joining the enfranchisement initiative and for paying their deposit. The first deadlines that are laid down by law, however, rather than being self-imposed, begin with the serving of the Enfranchisement Notice by the leaseholders on the landlord. Residents need to be clear that the enfranchisement process officially starts only when they serve this notice.

Our runner is now walking to the starting line of the race and will benefit from the intensive training that has taken place in recent months. But the athlete must remember this race is not a sprint requiring a brief burst of energy. It is a long-distance haul that will require pacing, patience and tenacity.

Statutory deadlines in enfranchisement

The strict deadlines established by law for enfranchisements are meant to protect the right of leaseholders to buy their building freehold within a reasonable timeframe while also ensuring that the landlord has adequate time to respond to this compulsory sale situation. If the enfranchisers fail to prepare for these deadlines, they can easily be caught out, with the result that the freehold purchase initiative collapses shortly after launch.

When the leaseholders serve the Enfranchisement Notice on the landlord, the clock begins ticking. The landlord now has a maximum of two months to reply to the Enfranchisement Notice by sending a Counter Notice to the leaseholders. As we saw in chapter 2, it is actually the nominee purchaser company that serves the Enfranchisement Notice and that receives the landlord's Counter Notice.

When the landlord serves the Counter Notice on the enfranchisers, if the two sides do not agree on the price of the freehold, the enfranchisers can apply to the Leasehold Valuation Tribunal (LVT) to decide. However, they can only apply to the LVT during the four-month period that starts two months after the date of the Counter Notice and that ends six months after the date of the Counter Notice.

 Leaseholders need to be prepared for the strict deadlines that apply as soon as they serve the Enfranchisement Notice on the landlord, as a missed deadline can result in failure of the enfranchisement initiative.

Serving the Enfranchisement Notice

When the leaseholders are ready to serve their Enfranchisement Notice on the landlord, they will already have gathered all their personal signatures on the notice. Just before serving the notice, the organisers need to check one last time that no leasehold flats in the building have changed hands since the notice was prepared by visiting the HM Land Registry site at www.landregisteronline.gov.uk. It is essential for flat owners to guard against the landlord making any claim that their Enfranchisement Notice is invalid on the grounds that it incorrectly identifies qualifying leaseholders in the building.

We have seen that the Enfranchisement Notice contains an offer price for the freehold that is presented in the notice in two parts, for the freehold of the building and for the 'appurtenant property', such as pathways, driveways, garages and gardens. The notice must have attached a plan, like an ordnance survey map, that shows the outline of the property and identifies with colour coding the building and appurtenant property being acquired.

The Enfranchisement Notice is normally served on the landlord by the enfranchisers' project manager or solicitor. While the landlord is allowed a maximum of two months from the date of the Enfranchisement Notice to send his Counter Notice, it is advisable for the enfranchisers to add about four business days to the two months. This is to avoid any possibility that the landlord will challenge the validity of the notice on the grounds that it did not provide the required two-month period for the Counter Notice. The deadline date by which the landlord must send his Counter Notice must be identified in the Enfranchisement Notice.

Once the notice has been served on the landlord, the nominee purchaser must advise HM Land Registry of this in writing, to protect leaseholders against the possibility that the landlord will seek to sell the freehold to another entity. This information is conveyed to the Land Registry in the form of a caution.

Because of the sensitivity surrounding the serving of the Enfranchisement Notice and the importance of the deadlines triggered by this document, the main leaseholder organiser should avoid being out of town for more than a few days at a time during the two months after the notice has been served. This is because it is essential for the enfranchisers to be able to respond quickly to any crucial issues that might arise, including a requirement to provide the landlord with access to the participants' flats or the original deeds.

 The leaseholder organiser should avoid being away during the two-month period following the serving of the Enfranchisement Notice on the landlord, in order to ensure a quick response to any time-critical correspondence from the landlord during this sensitive period.

Inspection of deeds and flats by landlord

Once the landlord has been served an Enfranchisement Notice, he has the right to inspect any participating flats in the building and to inspect the original deeds of the participating leaseholders, as we saw in chapter 4. Because the freeholder can provide as little as ten days' written notice for either of these inspections, the enfranchisers should complete the process of gathering all the original deeds and arranging possible access to the participants' flats before they serve the Enfranchisement Notice.

Leaseholders must comply with any request by the landlord to inspect, since failure to comply is a 'deemed withdrawal' and this would force the flat owners to wait one year before they are allowed to serve another Enfranchisement Notice on the landlord.

If the landlord wishes to inspect participating flats or deeds, this must be done before he serves his Counter Notice on the enfranchisers. Any inspection of flats is normally carried out by the landlord's surveyor, who is viewing the flats for the purpose of valuation. It can be awkward for the main enfranchisement organiser to put on hold all travel plans during the two months between the serving of the Enfranchisement Notice and the receipt of the Counter Notice, in order to wait for a possible request by the landlord to inspect the flats or deeds. In some cases, the landlord's surveyor, if asked by the enfranchisers, will advise whether or not an inspection of the flats will be required.

 The landlord's surveyor may, if asked by the enfranchisers, advise whether or not the landlord wishes to inspect the participating flats after having been served an Enfranchisement Notice.

Handling the landlord's Counter Notice

The second milestone in the official enfranchisement process is reached when the landlord serves the Counter Notice on the nominee purchaser. The Counter Notice must state whether the landlord acknowledges that the participating leaseholders qualify to enfranchise the building. If the landlord claims that they do not qualify, it might be because they lack the required 50 per cent of all the flats taking part or because the building itself does not qualify for enfranchisement.

If the landlord acknowledges that the participating leaseholders qualify to enfranchise the building, then he must state whether he agrees with the offer price contained in the Enfranchisement Notice. If the landlord disagrees with the offer price, he must state his 'counter offer' price. The landlord might state in the Counter Notice that he agrees with one part of the offer price, such as the offer price for the 'appurtenant property', such as driveways, pathways, garages and gardens, while disagreeing with the offer price for the freehold of the main building.

If the landlord owns flats in the building, he must state in the Counter Notice whether he requires a leaseback on these. As we saw in chapter 3, the landlord has a right to keep any flats in the building that he owns. He does this by exercising his right to a leaseback.

Enfranchisers should remember that the landlord is not required by law to serve a Counter Notice. If he agrees with the offer price presented in the Enfranchisement Notice, the landlord can simply proceed in selling the freehold to the nominee purchaser at the stated price. Even if the landlord is not a willing seller, the enfranchisers still have the right to buy the freehold at the stated offer price if the landlord fails to serve a Counter Notice. However, leaseholders should avoid a situation in which the landlord objects vigorously to the offer price but misses the deadline date for the Counter Notice. This is because some landlords in this situation will use the route of the County Court to protect against being forced to sell the building at the offer price. They do this by filing a claim in the County Court in which they ask the court to declare the Enfranchisement Notice invalid on some ground. Even if the landlord is unsuccessful in getting the County Court to declare the Enfranchisement Notice invalid, this tactic often delays the freehold purchase process by months and increases legal costs for the enfranchisers. Later in the chapter we examine what happens when a landlord files a claim in the County Court.

Flat owners often need to separate substance from bluster when they receive the Counter Notice, as some landlords apply pressure at this stage to persuade enfranchisers to drop their claim. I have seen intimidating letters sent by landlords' solicitors, accompanying the Counter Notice, demanding that the Enfranchisement Notice be withdrawn, threatening County Court action and offering to seek arbitration if the notice is withdrawn.

Leaseholders need to ensure that they are being well-advised by their project manager or solicitor if they get this kind of carrot-and-stick letter.

Once the leaseholders have received the Counter Notice, they need to prepare to do two things. They should get ready, through their chartered surveyor, to begin negotiations with the landlord and they should also prepare to apply to the LVT for a hearing to decide on the freehold price.

 After the enfranchisers are served the Counter Notice by the landlord, they should prepare both to negotiate with the landlord **and** to apply to the LVT.

Negotiations

Enfranchisement law has been designed to allow the leaseholders and the landlord sufficient time to reach a negotiated agreement on the price of the freehold. Indeed, a large majority of enfranchisement initiatives are concluded in a negotiated deal, while only a small minority end up going all the way through to an LVT hearing. We examine this subject in chapter 8.

By forcing leaseholders to wait two months from the date of the Counter Notice before they can apply to the LVT, the legislation aims to encourage leaseholders to use this time to start negotiations with the landlord. Since the enfranchisers have a maximum of six months from the date of the Counter Notice until they must file any application to the LVT, this is the period during which any negotiated agreement must be reached.

When leaseholders and the landlord negotiate in an enfranchisement, it is normally their chartered surveyors that do the negotiating. The issues over which they debate can include any of the valuation points we saw in chapter 3, including the estimated market value of the flats, the amount of marriage value, appropriate yield rate and whether there is development value and/or hope value to be paid. Enfranchisers may wish to instruct their surveyor to negotiate with the landlord's surveyor for a maximum period of time such as four hours, to try to reach agreement on as many valuation points as possible.

If the two parties do not reach a negotiated settlement, the next step is for the leaseholders to proceed to an LVT hearing. Even if negotiations at this stage fail to conclude in agreement, they can be a useful method for both sides to assess the strength of the other side's arguments and degree of determination. In some instances, when the landlord's counter offer price is considered by the enfranchisers to be unrealistically high, the residents might decide to forgo negotiations.

 Enfranchisement law is designed to allow a period of negotiation between the leaseholder and landlord once the Counter Notice has been served.

Applying to the Leasehold Valuation Tribunal

When the nominee purchaser is ready to apply to the LVT for a hearing that will decide on the price of the freehold, there is no form prescribed by law that must be used. However, the application must contain certain information. This information is identified in a government document called Leasehold Valuation Tribunal (Procedure) (England) Regulations 2003, in Regulation 3 and Paragraph 1 of Schedule 2 and also Paragraph 3 of Schedule 2. A sample application to the LVT is provided in Appendix 12.

It is normally the project manager or solicitor acting for the enfranchisers who sends the application to the LVT. The application must be sent to the nearest tribunal. Contact information for the five regional LVTs in England and the tribunal in Wales is provided in the section on 'Useful contacts' at the back of the book.

There is sometimes a significant backlog of enfranchisement applications at the LVT. Leaseholders can often get a hearing date about three months after sending their application, although the timeframe depends on the number of cases pending. Once the tribunal has received an application for a hearing, it will normally write to both parties and ask for dates to be avoided before scheduling the hearing. This is because it can be difficult to find hearing dates that the solicitors, surveyors and, if relevant, barristers acting for the enfranchisers and the landlord can all attend.

If the case concerns a large, complex enfranchisement, the LVT may hold a pre-hearing review, which is a kind of mini-hearing. Whether or not there is a pre-hearing review, the tribunal will require that both parties send certain documents prior to the hearing, referred to by lawyers as 'bundles', with an identical set of documents sent to the other party.

We have seen that it is important for leaseholders to apply to the LVT even if they are carrying out negotiations with the landlord that are expected to result in a negotiated settlement. This is because the existence of a scheduled LVT hearing increases the enfranchisers' leverage when seeking to reach agreement with the landlord. The fact that each party has to pay its own legal and surveyor fees at an LVT hearing creates a disincentive for landlords to go all the way through to a hearing. It is not unusual for a large corporate landlord to express interest in reaching a negotiated settlement with enfranchisers a few weeks before a scheduled tribunal hearing begins. The leaseholders and their advisers need to be ready for this.

Enfranchisers must remember not to miss the four-month window during which they can apply to the LVT, which starts two months after the date of the Counter Notice and ends six months after the date of the Counter Notice. If the landlord has demanded a higher price for the freehold in his Counter Notice than was offered in the Enfranchisement Notice, and if the leaseholders subsequently fail to apply to the LVT during the required four-month period, then this is a 'deemed withdrawal', as the leaseholders are considered to have dropped their enfranchisement claim. As with any deemed withdrawal, leaseholders must wait one year before they can serve another Enfranchisement Notice on the landlord.

 If the enfranchisers fail to apply to the LVT during the four-month period starting two months and ending six months after the Counter Notice, this is considered a deemed withdrawal of their Enfranchisement Notice and they must wait one year before they can serve a new Enfranchisement Notice.

County Court claims

Some enfranchisement projects are thrown into confusion if the leaseholders are served with a County Court claim before their case is heard by the LVT. We have seen that the landlord can file a claim in court if he believes the Enfranchisement Notice that he received is invalid.

Similarly, enfranchisers can file a claim in the County Court if they believe that the Counter Notice sent by the landlord is invalid, but I strongly recommend against such action by leaseholders because of the delays and additional legal costs that are likely to result.

If the landlord wishes to file a claim in the County Court, he can do so any time before the LVT hearing takes place. Some large corporate landlords, in an apparent attempt to create maximum delay, disruption and frustration for the enfranchisers, wait until a few days before the scheduled tribunal hearing before filing their claim in the County Court. They then ask the LVT to adjourn the hearing until after the court case has been decided. I have seen such action by large landlords cause delays of more than one year in large enfranchisements.

If the leaseholders' nominee purchaser receives this type of County Court claim, the enfranchisers should not panic. If the Enfranchisement Notice was properly prepared, then the leaseholders should recognise the County Court claim as hard-ball tactics by the landlord. Leaseholders need to be ready for this, especially when the landlord is known to fight hard against enfranchisement initiatives. As explained earlier, some landlords use the County Court route as a means to avoid having to sell their freehold at the enfranchisers' offer price if the landlord has missed the Counter Notice deadline. Other landlords use the County Court as an arena in which to place leaseholders at maximum disadvantage, since increased legal costs, delay and distraction all increase the probability that the enfranchisement project will collapse.

Once a hearing is held in the County Court, if the landlord is successful in persuading the court to declare the Enfranchisement Notice invalid, then the leaseholders are back to square one. It is as if they never served an Enfranchisement Notice. If they wish to pursue their freehold purchase project, they must prepare and serve a new Enfranchisement Notice.

If the landlord is unsuccessful in the County Court and the court finds that the Enfranchisement Notice **was** valid, then the leaseholders have the right to request that the LVT schedule a hearing.

 A scheduled LVT hearing will be adjourned if the landlord files a County Court claim against the enfranchisers, pending the outcome of the court case.

A sale of a participant flat after the Enfranchisement Notice is served

Organisers of an enfranchisement need to remain focused once the Enfranchisement Notice has been served on the landlord and as they await the Counter Notice, because of the statutory deadlines we have discussed. It can be frustrating for the organisers to discover at this busy time that one or more participants are moving from the building. While organisers of a freehold purchase might like to freeze time and prevent any participant from selling a flat until the enfranchisement has been concluded, this is obviously not possible.

We have seen that the validity of the Enfranchisement Notice that has been served on the landlord will not be jeopardised if one or more participants move away. The requirement for a minimum 50 per cent of all flats to take part in order for leaseholders to qualify to enfranchise is a requirement that must be fulfilled only at the time that the Enfranchisement Notice is served. However, organisers will want to take all reasonable precautions to prevent the number of participants from diminishing, as this would leave a smaller number of leaseholders each paying a larger proportion of the freehold cost than originally envisaged.

If a project participant announces that he is selling his flat, the organisers will need to arrange for his original deeds to be sent to his solicitor. This should be done by DX, a system for sending documents that is used by solicitors' firms. The organisers should send written instruction to the solicitor who is holding the original deeds to send the relevant deeds for the flat by DX to the seller's solicitor and for the buyer's solicitor to send the deeds back to the enfranchisers' solicitor after the sale has been completed.

One of the most time-consuming requirements in this process is briefing the prospective buyer of the flat and the buyer's solicitor about the enfranchisement project. If the enfranchisers have hired an outside project manager, the project manager might do the briefing. If there is no outside project manager, organisers can save themselves time by declining to give multiple briefings and by insisting on speaking directly with the buyer of the participating flat or his solicitor. I have seen many enfranchisement organisers spend long hours giving briefings to anyone involved in the sales chain, including the seller, the seller's solicitor, the estate agent, the buyer and the buyer's solicitor, none of whom fully appreciates the personal cost to the organiser of carrying out this unpaid labour-intensive work. While the organisers have an interest in being helpful and informative to participants and future participants, they should refuse to engage in endless briefings about the freehold purchase at this time.

Organisers will save themselves time by having ready the documents that the seller's solicitor will need to show to the prospective buyer. These include a copy of the Memorandum and Articles of Association ('MemArts') of the nominee purchaser company, the Participation Agreement, the Enfranchisement Notice and the share certificate of the nominee purchaser. It is also useful to have a brief confidential information sheet ready on the freehold purchase project, including the dates of the Enfranchisement Notice, the Counter Notice and the LVT application. The organisers should not agree to send the original share certificate, as the loss of this important document can create many hours of unnecessary work for the enfranchisers.

As we saw in chapter 2, the organisers should get any participant that is moving from the building to sign a J30 Stock Transfer Form, as shown in Appendix 17. The buyer should also sign the brief form shown in Appendix 16 that confirms that he will abide by the terms of the Participation Agreement. In chapter 6 we look at how to transfer shares from a founding participant of the enfranchisement to the buyer of his flat. Finally, organisers need to remind the seller, buyer and their solicitors that the enfranchisement is a strictly confidential process. The organisers should not be drawn into a discussion on how much the leaseholders eventually expect to pay for the freehold, as this information could find its way to the landlord and weaken the enfranchisers' negotiating position.

 Organisers should avoid taking on unnecessary extra work in the event that a participant flat is sold after the Enfranchisement Notice has been served by having ready an information pack for the buyer of the flat and his solicitor.

Project management and liaising with advisers

Flat owners are often surprised at how quickly things start moving once they serve their Enfranchisement Notice on the landlord, with business-critical deadlines every other month. Focused project management is crucial for the success of an enfranchisement, particularly in a large building. Whether leaseholders have outsourced this task by hiring a professional project manager or whether they do this work themselves, they must identify the organiser in the building that has ownership of the project on a day-to-day operational level. This individual should be the single point of contact for the project both internally and externally.

Ineffective project management has resulted in some disasters in enfranchising buildings, including unnecessarily large advisers' fees, leakage of confidential information to the landlord and, in some cases, a collapse of the project. It is understandable for each enfranchisement participant to want to be kept up to date and to find out how the freehold purchase project is going. But organisers must avoid a situation in which any participant other than the agreed single point of contact in the building is liaising with the external project manager, solicitor and/or chartered surveyor.

The diagram below illustrates the chaotic and inefficient flow of information that can result when there is weak internal and external project management of an enfranchisement. In this situation, many participants of the project are contacting the solicitor and the surveyor, often asking the same questions without communicating with one another. Some solicitors and surveyors will charge the nominee purchaser company, as the client, for every one of these contacts. In the scenario depicted in the diagram below, this would result in some large bills. To make matters worse, there is no external project manager, and the solicitor and surveyor are not communicating with one another – an unfortunate situation that occurs in many enfranchisements. The flow of information in this scenario is extremely inefficient, as the solicitor and surveyor are providing similar information repeatedly to individual participants. This kind of inefficiency places enfranchisers at an increasingly great disadvantage vis-à-vis the large corporate landlord and heightens the project's risk of failure.

Communication flow in a collective enfranchisement with weak internal and external project management

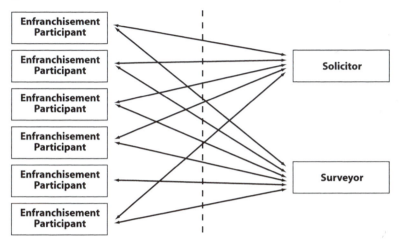

By the time leaseholders in a building are ready to serve their Enfranchisement Notice on the landlord, it is essential to have in place focused internal project management with an identified single point of contact amongst the leaseholders and, if possible, an experienced external project manager. The diagram below shows the efficient flow of communication that results in an enfranchisement that has strong internal and external project management. In this situation, the internal and external project managers work closely together and keep one another informed. They also each liaise with the relevant advisers, participants and other stakeholders in a co-ordinated manner that avoids duplication of effort.

Communication flow in a collective enfranchisement with strong internal and external project management

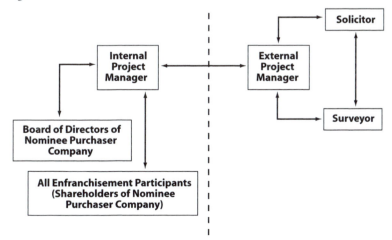

The internal project manager will be communicating with two bodies within the building, the board of directors of the nominee purchaser company and the shareholders as a group. Often the internal project manager will be a member of the board of directors.

When the enfranchisers have tight project management in place, there is a greater chance that major milestones will be met and costs will be controlled. But strong project management requires the ability to say 'no'. The internal project manager must make clear that participants need to direct to him any questions or input, and must not contact the external project manager, solicitor or surveyor, except in an emergency. It should be agreed from the beginning of the project that the external project manager, solicitor and surveyor will only deal with the single-point-of-contact leaseholder within the building.

In the well-organised enfranchisement shown in the diagram above, the external project manager ensures a smooth flow of information not only with the single point of contact inside the building, but also with the solicitor and surveyor, who will also be encouraged to communicate with each other as needed.

 Even if the enfranchisers succeed in instructing a professional project manager, they need to identify the project manager's single point of contact amongst the leaseholders.

Keeping participants updated

It is not easy for the internal project manager of a large enfranchisement to work effectively with the external project manager while also keeping all participants fully informed. Enfranchisement law is complex and there are many issues that can crop up and create confusion in a freehold purchase project beyond the information that can be reasonably covered in, say, a two-hour residents' meeting. A key task is for the board of directors of the nominee purchaser to establish a communications plan for the enfranchisement and for the internal project manager to stick to this plan.

When busy flat owners feel that they are being kept up to date on important developments, they are more likely to remain enthusiastic about and committed to the project, and to leave the organisers to get on with the work at hand. But when the leaseholders feel that they are being left in the dark, they are more likely to bombard organisers with questions and complaints.

It is best practice in freehold purchase projects for an update note to be emailed to all participants at each major milestone. By sending an update note, for instance, when the Enfranchisement Notice has been served, the Counter Notice has been received and the application has been made to the LVT, participants will be getting fresh news every other month, an appropriate frequency at this stage of the project. The freehold purchase organisers will need to keep a centralised, updated list of all the participants' contact information, including email addresses. None of this confidential information should be released to anyone, including to residents in the building, without permission from the relevant individual. Update notes that are emailed to participants should not reveal the email addresses of other participants, as this represents a breach of confidentiality.

One of the greatest communications challenges is to keep updated those leaseholders that live overseas and that rent out their flat in the enfranchising building or that use it as a pied-à-terre when they are in the UK. Many enfranchisement organisers have told me with exasperation over the years about being rung up early on a Sunday morning or late at night by an absentee leaseholder that had arrived in town and was demanding an instant, individualised briefing on the status of the freehold purchase project. The solution here is to reply with a polite, but firm 'no' to such requests and to explain that an update will be sent at the appropriate time to all participants.

We have seen the importance of moral authority when leaseholders set out to organise and implement a large enfranchisement project. Creating consensus and persuading one's fellow leaseholders to join forces to buy the building freehold involves persuading, rather than forcing, people. This moral persuasion must come through effectively when the internal project manager communicates with participants, if he is to help keep the level of morale and commitment high. But the internal project manager must also be firm in requiring co-operation from participants, including saying 'no' to unreasonable requests for individual briefings.

While the organisers need to strike a delicate balance with participants by being inclusive, yet focused and efficient, the solution is more clear-cut when requests for information come from non-participants. In this instance, the enfranchisement organisers should reply with an emphatic 'no'. They should state briefly that all leaseholders were invited to join the project, the sign-up deadline has passed and no information is to be made available until this confidential project has been concluded. We examine this important issue in more detail in chapter 7.

 Organisers should create a communication plan for the enfranchisement, which includes sending an update note to all participants at each project milestone and which avoids providing individual one-on-one briefings to visiting absentee leaseholders.

Leaseholders have reason to feel encouraged once they serve their Enfranchisement Notice on the landlord. By the time they reach this stage, they will have got a large part of the work done. Once they serve the notice, which equates to our long-distance runner taking off at the start of the race, leaseholders will have increased dramatically the chances of success of their freehold purchase project. This is because they will have moved beyond the prolonged discussion and debate, as we saw in chapter 1, that prevents many enfranchisement projects from ever getting off the ground.

As leaseholders reach each new milestone in the process, with the receipt of the landlord's Counter Notice and application to the LVT, the internal project management should make it clear to the participants that progress is being made. But the project manager must also take care to manage expectations, as there is no guarantee of success in an enfranchisement until the freehold has been purchased, and there are numerous pitfalls along the way.

I have seen some leaseholders in large, troubled buildings ready to declare victory once they had served their Enfranchisement Notice, so great was their relief that they had finally reached the starting point of the race. But flat owners need to take a longer view of enfranchisement and remember that a good start does not ensure a good finish. In the next chapters we look at the awkward issues that can create obstacles for enfranchisers and we identify ways in which to manage these risks.

CHAPTER 6

Maintaining participant numbers

Many leaseholders feel that they have guaranteed the success of their enfranchisement once they have obtained participation from the minimum 50 per cent of all the flats or once they have served the Enfranchisement Notice on the landlord. While it is important to take satisfaction at each milestone, leaseholders need to remember that many freehold purchase initiatives collapse months after they start. It is essential for the organisers to stay focused on keeping the project moving forward, from the earliest planning stage until the freehold has been bought.

It can be difficult for organisers to hold together a large enfranchisement because of the diverse priorities of the households involved. Organisers need to be prepared for the fact that even the most strongly-committed participant at the start of the project can announce months later that he is moving from the building and dropping out of the project. Leaseholders in a block of flats represent a dynamic, evolving community. Changing circumstances such as a new job, marriage, the birth of a child or divorce can prompt a participant quickly to alter plans and sell his flat.

Many leaseholders discover at later stages in the project that the landlord represents the least of their worries in the enfranchisement. They find that the leaseholders themselves are placing the project at risk because of a lack of understanding of or compliance with rules of the enfranchisement. The solution is for organisers to rely not only on the moral authority we have seen is so important in such a project. They must also put in place an infrastructure to protect the cohesiveness of the enfranchisement until the end. This chapter examines this infrastructure.

How to juggle ten screaming cats for one year

Organisers can find it frustrating to spend time and effort ensuring that all statutory requirements are met in an enfranchisement, only to get bogged down in the individual problems of the participants. In extreme cases, organisers can feel as though they are being expected to juggle ten screaming cats for a year. The directors of the nominee purchaser company, including the single-point-of-contact organiser, need to keep the participants informed while also providing firm leadership if they want to avoid the kind of dissent and lack of co-operation that can cause such a project to unravel.

It is just as important at this stage for the organisers to know what to do as it is to know what **not** to do. A key goal is to maintain the focus and momentum of the project. While many participants will be clear about upcoming milestones, there are often one or two participants in a large block of flats that insist on revisiting old issues, such as encouraging leaseholders to withhold their service charges in protest against the landlord. It is important for enfranchisers to avoid being drawn into these old debates, which can waste valuable time and effort, and can create an impression of weak project management of the freehold purchase.

Some participants will want to have detailed discussions about action the nominee purchaser will take after the freehold purchase has been completed, including how the building will be managed. Again, it is crucial for the organisers to focus their limited resources on the most urgent and important tasks, which normally involve ensuring that the next project milestones are reached. While the board of directors of the nominee purchaser company should listen carefully to all shareholders and acknowledge their input, participants should be told that future management of the building will be addressed in detail after the enfranchisement has been concluded.

Enormous distraction can be caused in an enfranchisement project by non-participants. I have seen many instances in which a small number of leaseholders in a building who decided not to join the freehold purchase project went on to create havoc for the project organisers and other participants, including placing the project at risk. One way in which non-participants can do this is to disseminate confidential information about the enfranchisement to the landlord or other non-participants. Organisers of the freehold purchase need to take a firm line in this situation. They should not be drawn into discussions with non-participants about the enfranchisement, which is a confidential venture of the participants. They should also make it clear that non-participants should not take any action, including dissemination of information, that could place the project in jeopardy. Ways to address residents who are hostile to an enfranchisement project are examined in chapter 7.

Leaseholders who are working hard to move a large enfranchisement from one stage to the next can help avoid upset by preparing themselves for the likely event that one or more participants will move from the building before the freehold has been purchased. Indeed, organisers need to take specific steps to prepare for the worst, i.e. that at least one participant will fail to inform organisers that he is moving or will refuse to pay the required share of the freehold cost at the end. Carrying out this risk management at an early stage has saved many enfranchisements from crumbling.

 Enfranchisement organisers in a large block of flats need to prepare early in the project for the likely event that one or more participants later on will seek to drop out of the project, sell their flat without informing the nominee purchaser or refuse to pay their share of the freehold cost.

Gathering and locking in commitment

Too many organisers of enfranchisements rely on the goodwill and sense of fair play of participants when they hope that all the participants will meet their obligations within the project. This is a mistake. Although a freehold purchase initiative is, by its nature, a joint undertaking with a communitarian element, the organisers need to create an infrastructure that locks in the commitment of participants. If the organisers simply assume that each participant will pay his share of the freehold cost at the end because this is the right thing to do, there is unlikely to be full compliance.

Whether each participant completes a Sign-Up Form and pays a deposit to the internal organisers at the start of the project or signs a contract and pays a deposit to an outside project manager, this written undertaking represents a crucial initial commitment. This commitment takes firmer shape when each leaseholder in the project signs the legally-binding Participation Agreement and the Enfranchisement Notice. Finally, by becoming a shareholder of the nominee purchaser company, the participant is bound by the Memorandum and Articles of Association, or 'MemArts', of the company. These documents help reinforce the message that the enfranchisement is not an informal agreement amongst friends or neighbours. It is a joint commercial venture that promises benefits to the participants, and that carries legal and financial obligations.

It is best practice for a nominee purchaser company to include a clause in the MemArts that says that if a shareholder ceases to own a flat in the building, then his shares in the company will be transferred automatically to the new leaseholder of the flat. It is important to have this in the MemArts to avoid the creation of a secondary market in shares in the nominee purchaser by people or companies outside the building.

The update note that the organisers send from time to time, normally at each project milestone, provides an ideal communication channel in which to inform shareholders of the nominee purchaser company of the latest developments and what to expect next, while also reminding them of their obligations as participants. While there will be questions and issues raised by participants once the project is under way, the update notes give organisers the opportunity to limit the number of time-consuming bilateral discussions they need to have with participants. Project organisers need to remember that the 80–20 rule applies at this stage in the project, since they will be spending 20 per cent of their time and effort communicating with the 80 per cent of the participants who are the most co-operative, while spending 80 per cent of their time and effort communicating with the 20 per cent of participants who are most difficult.

 Organisers of a collective enfranchisement should use best-practice documentation to create infrastructure that locks in the commitment of participants, including the Participation Agreement, and the Memorandum and Articles of Association of the nominee purchaser company.

Enforcing the Participation Agreement

While enfranchisement organisers need to use several documents to build a solid infrastructure for the freehold purchase initiative, it is the Participation Agreement that proves times and again to be the lynchpin that ensures cohesion and stability for the project. In chapter 2, we examined what goes into the Participation Agreement. Because of its importance, it is worth revisiting the Participation Agreement to examine its role in ensuring full compliance by participants with the rules of an enfranchisement.

We have seen that there is no legal requirement for leaseholders to use a Participation Agreement. However, it represents such an essential tool in maximising the chances of success for a freehold purchase project that enfranchisers should consider it a must-have document. By signing the Participation Agreement, each participant makes a legally-binding commitment to pay his share of the freehold cost at the end of the process and, if the participant sells his flat before the enfranchisement has been concluded, to sell to a buyer who will automatically take his place in the project.

While the Participation Agreement does not guarantee compliance by participants, it does provide the board of the nominee purchaser company with a compelling rejoinder when a participant says, 'I didn't realise that I had to pay my share of the freehold cost' or 'I didn't know that, if I sold my flat, I had to sell to a buyer who would take my place in the enfranchisement'. The sample Participation Agreement shown in Appendix 9 also helps enfranchisement organisers stay up to date on which participating flats are for sale in the building by obliging any participant who moves from the building to inform the nominee purchaser in writing within a maximum of ten days of the sale.

 As an enfranchisement moves from one stage to the next, organisers should use the Participation Agreement to ensure cohesion of the project, by legally obliging each participant to pay his share of the freehold cost at the end and if a participant moves from the building before the enfranchisement ends, to sell to a buyer who takes his place in the project.

Mitigating the risk of participants dropping out when they sell their flat

Many enfranchisers have described the participant who is so busy trying to sell his flat that he apparently forgets about obligations under the Participation Agreement. In such an instance, the organisers should send a written communication saying that the participant must advise his solicitor and prospective buyer about the Participation Agreement.

It can be exasperating for organisers to have to repeat again and again the obligations that enfranchisers have under the Participation Agreement, but the organisers must be patient and steel themselves for this. They should use the update notes to remind participants to send in any information on participating and non-participating flats for sale. By being aware of the sale of participating flats, organisers can step in quickly to get the seller to sign the J30 Stock Transfer Form, which we examined in chapter 2. They can also capture crucial information on the market values of flats in the building that will be needed by the chartered surveyor who is carrying out or has already completed the valuation of the freehold. The seller should be asked to advise the price at which the flat was sold.

 As soon as organisers within the nominee purchaser company learn of the planned sale of a participating flat, they should remind the seller in writing of his obligation under the Participation Agreement to sell to a buyer who automatically takes the seller's place in the enfranchisement and to advise the nominee purchaser once the sale has taken place.

Answering queries from prospective buyers and estate agents

In many residential buildings I have researched over the years, the main enfranchisement organiser is an efficient, busy person with a demanding day job. By the time this person has put in months of hard work to get the freehold purchase project up and running, and then has dedicated more months to oversee the official process after the serving of the

Enfranchisement Notice, patience can wear thin when confronted with unnecessary time-consuming tasks. I have seen the main organiser in a state of exasperation, for instance, after receiving phone calls at the office from a participant who is selling his flat, then from the participant's solicitor, the estate agent handling the sale, the prospective buyer **and** the buyer's solicitor. The solution in this case is for the enfranchisement organiser to compress the information chain and to agree to talk only with the decision maker, the buyer, and to refuse to provide numerous bilateral briefings.

We have seen that the organiser can save time and effort by having ready the main documents that comprise the infrastructure of the project. The organiser should be ready to email to the participant seller and/or his solicitor this information pack, with a copy of the Participation Agreemeent, the Enfranchisement Notice, the MemArts of the nominee purchaser company and a copy of the share certificate of the relevant flat.

While a participant who is in a hurry to sell his flat might view the obligations of the Participation Agreement as a hindrance, organisers should remind the participant and any prospective buyer that participating flats in the building carry a premium over non-participating flats because the former will be granted 999-year leases once the freehold has been purchased, while the latter will not.

 The single-point-of-contact organiser within the nominee purchaser company should save time by compressing the information chain when a participating flat is being sold and should aim to give one phone briefing only to the buyer as decision maker, rather than also to the estate agent, the seller's solicitor and the buyer's solicitor.

Managing newcomers when participants sell

Some enfranchisers get upset when many flats in the building are sold during or after the freehold purchase, but organisers need to prepare for this and should welcome the benefits that can result from bringing new blood into the building. The fact is, there are often a few participants in large blocks of flats who fail to grasp until the last minute the fact that they really **will** have to pay their share of the freehold cost, and so they decide to sell to avoid making this cash outlay. This can be exasperating for organisers because they have to communicate with prospective buyers of these flats and ensure that the number of participants does not diminish.

But this kind of churn in a large residential building that has been plagued for years by mismanagement can turn out to be a blessing. In many troubled buildings, frustrated leaseholders refuse to pay their service charges in protest against poor management. This leads a building into a downward spiral, since the landlord is not receiving service charges and is, thus, unlikely to provide an appropriate level of maintenance and repairs. The situation in the building becomes increasingly worse and residents grow ever more frustrated. I have seen many buildings in which a large enfranchisement project prompts the departure of leaseholders that had refused for years to pay their service charges. Newcomers arrive with fresh ideas, a sense of responsibility for paying their service charges and a lack of emotional baggage about past problems in the block.

Enfranchisement organisers should welcome newcomers who have bought participating flats in the building. But the board of directors of the nominee purchaser company needs to exercise caution regarding the enthusiasm of newcomers. Demographic changes have produced a cash-rich generation of young professionals who prefer to own a flat in an urban centre rather than a house in the suburbs, and these leaseholders are sometimes keen to be appointed to boards of nominee purchaser companies when they arrive in an enfranchising building. The directors and other shareholders need to ensure that anyone appointed to the board is a person of integrity and maturity, who fully grasps the responsibilities of the company director. I have seen instances in which a young investment banker buys a flat in an enfranchising block of flats, offers to serve on the board, and, within the same breath, demands an exemption to restrictions placed by the lease on all flat owners in the building in areas such as alterations, owning pets or installing satellite dishes. Enfranchisers can leap out of the frying pan and into the fire if they mistake enthusiasm of a would-be director with competence and appoint the wrong person to help run the nominee purchaser company.

Organisers should put in place efficient ways to bring newcomers to the project up to date, and to make them feel valued and included, without carrying out time-consuming individual briefings. In this long-distance race, the organisers need to pace themselves and guard against project fatigue, a subject we will examine in chapter 10. Newcomers to the building should be encouraged to attend the Annual General Meeting (AGM) of the nominee purchaser company. It is also a good idea for a director of the nominee purchaser who is not the single point of contact for the enfranchisement to meet with and brief each newcomer on the project, to help spread the work amongst directors.

 Organisers within the nominee purchaser company should welcome new shareholders who buy participating flats in the building and should provide them with helpful information on the enfranchisement project, but they should avoid providing time-consuming individual briefings.

Transferring shares to buyers of participating flats

One of the most time-consuming tasks for enfranchisement organisers when a participating flat is sold is to transfer the share certificate of the nominee purchaser company from the name of the seller to the name of the buyer. We have seen how important it is for the organisers to get the seller to hand over a signed, undated J30 Stock Transfer Form as soon as there are plans to sell the participating flat. The organisers need to keep the J30 form on file until they are ready to transfer the share certificate.

The enfranchisement organisers should never agree to have the share certificate for a participating flat transferred to a new owner until they have received an updated leasehold title from HM Land Registry that confirms the name of the new leaseholder. This is because the Land Registry title provides proof of ownership. It is also because the name that appears on the share certificate must be the same name as that on the leasehold title. I have seen numerous instances in which leaseholders have incorrectly identified the owner or owners of their flat. Sometimes a husband and wife are believed to own a flat, but the leasehold title confirms that the property is in the name of only one spouse. Or a man might describe himself as the leaseholder, while the leasehold title at the Land Registry reveals that he, his wife, his son and his daughter jointly own the property. In other cases, a leaseholder may say that he owns a flat, but it turns out that he owns it through a company. In this case, the company is the leaseholder and the share certificate must be transferred to the name of the company.

As we have seen, an updated leasehold title of any flat can be obtained online for £2 at www.landregisteronline.gov.uk. It can take several weeks after a flat has been sold for the leasehold title at Land Registry to be updated. Once the enfranchisement organisers have in hand the completed J30 Form and the updated leasehold title from the Land Registry, they need to hand over the J30 Form and the original share certificate to the company secretary of the nominee purchaser, so the name of the new shareholder can be registered at Companies House and the new share certificate can be issued. In chapter 10 we look at the importance for the nominee purchaser to outsource the work of the company secretary, to ensure that all required documents get filed with Companies House, while limiting the amount of legwork being done by of the directors of the nominee purchaser company.

The organisers should not agree for the seller to send the signed J30 Form to anyone other than the main organiser. There are many instances in which the seller's solicitor will want to hand over the signed J30 Form to the solicitor of the buyer on completion of the sale and the J30 Form is never received by the enfranchisement organisers. I have seen organisers spend months trying to get the share certificate of a participating flat updated.

 The nominee purchaser should only transfer a share certificate for a participating flat to the name of the buyer once a completed J30 Stock Transfer Form has been received and an updated Land Registry leasehold title document has confirmed the name of the buyer.

Keeping share certificates up to date

There may be instances in which the directors of the nominee purchaser company are not able to obtain a signed J30 Form from the seller of a participating flat. This can happen if a participant dies and the directors are unable to locate the executor of the late participant's estate. In other cases, a participant based overseas might simply refuse to respond to written requests from the directors to sign and send back the J30 Form.

If the directors are unable to secure from the seller a signed J30 Form, they will need to follow a different procedure to transfer the share certificate to the name of the new leaseholder. They will need to pass a resolution of the board that nominates one of the directors the attorney of the former leaseholder of the participating flat and that authorises the director to sign the J30 Form and transfer the share certificate to the name of the new leaseholder. In order to use this procedure, however, it is essential for certain clauses to be included in the MemArts of the nominee purchaser company. The MemArts must stipulate that no person can be a shareholder of the company without being a leaseholder of a flat in the building. The MemArts must also state that a shareholder who sells or otherwise transfers leasehold ownership of his flat must transfer to the new owner his shares. Finally, the MemArts must authorise the board to nominate a director as attorney for any shareholder who sells his flat, but fails to transfer the relevant share certificate to the name of the new owner.

One of the easiest ways for the board of directors of the nominee purchaser company to avoid unnecessary extra work, when addressing the sale of participating flats is to get all shareholders to agree that the board will keep custody of the original share certificates. In this way, directors avoid having to spend time tracking down the original share certificates each time a participating flat is sold.

 The board of directors of the nominee purchaser company should secure agreement from the shareholders for the board to hold all the original share certificates, to avoid any delays or extra work in transferring a share certificate from the name of a seller of a participating flat to the buyer.

Mitigating the risk of non-payment by participants

Every enfranchisement organiser dreads the possibility that, at the end of the process, one or more participants will refuse to pay their share of the freehold cost. Such a failure to pay can result in the collapse of a freehold purchase initiative on which organisers have volunteered years of hard work. Organisers must take all reasonable measures to ensure that participants pay their share when the time comes.

One way to protect against non-payment is to provide regular reminders of the estimated cost of the freehold. We saw in chapters 1 and 3 the importance of providing an informal cost estimate at an early planning stage and ways in which to arrive at this estimate. The organisers will want to send an updated cost estimate to participants once a chartered surveyor has carried out a formal valuation of the freehold, and they should include in the estimate legal and surveyor costs, stamp duty and conveyancing. Organisers should send this estimate around the time that the Enfranchisement Notice is being served, and they should advise that participants are likely to have to pay their share some six to eight months later.

At each project milestone, the organisers should provide to participants any relevant update to the cost estimate. After the valuation has been done and the Enfranchisement Notice served, the board of the nominee purchaser company should advise participants of the specific amount they are expected to have to pay. The letter should make clear that this is only an estimate, based on information available so far, and that the final figure will only be known nearer the conclusion of the freehold acquisition. When questions are repeatedly raised about the expected cost, for instance, in the event of the sale of a participating flat, the board of directors can refer back to this letter.

If a negotiated agreement on the price of the freehold is reached with the landlord after the Counter Notice has been received, this information should be conveyed in an urgent update note to participants. Every time a written communication is sent to participants that estimates either the grand total cost or individual costs for the freehold, it should be stated clearly that these figures represent only estimates and that they do not guarantee the final figures.

In the final months before the conclusion of the freehold purchase, some participants will want to arrange mortgage loans to pay their share of the freehold. The organisers should, if possible, send a frequently asked questions (FAQ) document to all participants to help in discussions with mortgage lenders. The FAQ should identify the number of flats in the building, the number of participating and non-participating flats, the number of years left on leases of participating and non-participating flats, and the fact that participating flats will get 999-year leases upon conclusion of the enfranchisement.

While most mortgage lenders are familiar with the growing trend by leaseholders of flats to buy the freehold of their building, the FAQ should provide a brief explanation of the way in which the freehold purchase and subsequent granting of 999-year leases is expected to increase the value of participating flats. If there are fewer than 80 years left on the leases of the participating flats, the FAQ should explain that the main cost element to each participant is the marriage value, which, roughly speaking, represents the expected increase in the value of the participating flats after they have been granted 999-year leases. The FAQ should explain that the participants have to pay half of the marriage value as part of the freehold cost.

The FAQ document should advise participants to ask their mortgage lender for a 'home improvement loan' rather than a loan for the purchase of a freehold, since many mortgage lenders understand the latter to refer to the freehold purchase of a house rather than a flat, and they require that the loan be sent to the borrower's solicitor instead of directly to the borrower.

In a large block of flats, even if the organisers provide cost estimates and other useful information, there is likely to be at least one participant who is considered likely to refuse or otherwise fail to pay his share of the freehold cost. The board of directors of the nominee purchaser company needs to identify such high-risk participants early on in the project and to prepare a plan of action in the event of non-payment. One best-practice option, if a participant fails to pay his share of the freehold by the specified deadline, is to sell to someone else the freehold interest of the non-payer's flat. This can be sold in the form of a 999-year head lease, as was described in chapter 3, to a shareholder of the nominee purchaser company or an outside investor.

Organisers must provide an appropriate amount of time for participants to raise the finance to pay for their share of the freehold. While brief reminders are helpful in the six months before the expected conclusion of the enfranchisement process, individualised letters should be sent to each participant no less than eight weeks before the end of the project. These letters should specify the exact amount to be paid, provide the bank details to which a BACS payment should be made and identify the deadline date by which the payment must be made. The payment to be made should include the share of freehold cost, legal and surveyor fees, stamp duty and conveyancing fee.

If a participant fails to pay by the specified deadline, an immediate written warning should be sent that says that the freehold interest of the flat will be sold by the nominee purchaser to a third party in the form of a 999-year lease and the non-payer will lose his status as a shareholder and his right to a 999-year lease extension. The nominee purchaser may also advise in writing that it plans to take legal action against the non-payer for violation of the legally-binding Participation Agreement. I have seen directors of a nominee purchaser company dragged into distressing phone conversations by difficult shareholders who insist that they did not know they would have to pay the amount of money in question and demanding that they be given a discount. These verbal communications should be kept to a minimum, as they are time-consuming and stressful for the directors, and they do not produce a required paper trail of information conveyed. Clear, simple written communication is preferable, and any letter or email should be copied to the non-payer's solicitor to eliminate doubt about expected next actions by the nominee purchaser. Many participants who threaten not to pay their share of the freehold cost engage in brinkmanship, only to pay once they receive a clear written warning that they will lose their right to the 999-year lease extension.

 Organisers should make clear that the board of directors of the nominee purchaser company will take firm action, including, if appropriate, legal action, against any shareholder who fails to pay his share of the freehold cost at the end of the project, as non-payment represents a violation of the legally-binding Participation Agreement.

Paying service charge arrears and addressing other housekeeping issues

The months following the service of the Enfranchisement Notice represent an ideal time for participating leaseholders to get their building in shape for the acquisition. An important bit of housekeeping is to clear up service charge arrears. This is because the nominee purchaser, in many cases, must pay to the landlord any unpaid service charges for the building as part of the freehold purchase. Although the 1993 Act and the 2002 Act do not require this, it is common practice for landlords to put this requirement in the contract of sale of the freehold.

If all or most of the leaseholders in the building are participants in the enfranchisement, it is normally easier for organisers to ensure that all service charge payments are up to date. Problems can occur, however, when a significant number of leaseholders in the building have opted not to join the freehold purchase project, especially when non-participants include leaseholders who have refused to pay their service charges. This problem can be compounded by a failure on the part of the landlord to collect service charges.

Before the enfranchisement process has been concluded, the nominee purchaser should secure from the selling freeholder an assignment of the right, after the freehold purchase, to collect any unpaid service charges. In many cases, the requirement to pay unpaid service charges as part of the freehold purchase thus represents for the nominee purchaser more of a short-term cash flow problem than it does a long-term financing issue. Nonetheless, it can create havoc for enfranchisers to discover shortly before they are preparing to exchange contracts on the purchase of the freehold that the nominee purchaser, for instance, has to pay hundreds of thousands of pounds in service charge arrears. The board of the nominee purchaser must be clear about whether the contract of sale of the freehold says that the nominee purchaser must pay service charge arrears.

Organisers should manage the financing risk posed by service charge arrears by sending reminders to participants in update notes throughout the freehold purchase project that all service charge payments must be up to date by the expected conclusion of the enfranchisement.

 Organisers should send a written reminder to enfranchisement participants several times throughout the duration of the project of the requirement for all service charge payments to be made promptly, as the nominee purchaser is likely to have to pay service charge arrears as part of the freehold purchase.

Once leaseholders have served an Enfranchisement Notice on their landlord, they must maintain project momentum and take careful steps to minimise some of the well-known risks during this phase. In this chapter we have examined ways in which to avoid some of the most troublesome issues, including the possibility that participants drop out or refuse to pay their share of the freehold cost at the end.

We have seen that a departure by a participant from the freehold purchase project after the Enfranchisement Notice has been served will not threaten the validity of the notice, since it is only on the day that the notice is served that the required minimum of 50 per cent of all flats must be participating. However, a shrinkage in numbers of participants can still cause an enfranchisement to collapse by causing an unacceptable increase in cost for the remaining project members.

We have reviewed the importance for organisers to put in place a proper infrastructure to protect against these problems, including having all the participants sign a Participation Agreement before the Enfranchisement Notice is served. While issues of mutual interests can help inspire leaseholders initially to join forces to buy their freehold, the organisers must take an increasingly businesslike approach once the Enfranchisement Notice has been served in order to ensure full compliance by participants.

Leaseholders involved in organising an enfranchisement take on a serious commitment when they agree to serve as directors of a nominee purchaser, since they are legally bound to comply with the Companies Act. It is appropriate, therefore, that the directors demand a high level of commitment from shareholders and that they make it clear that exceptions will not be made for any shareholder wishing to drop out of the project or to be given a discount on the cost of the share of the freehold. Referring back to the Participation Agreement makes it easier for the board of directors to remind each shareholder of the responsibility to pay his share of the freehold cost at the end of the project and, if moving from the building before the enfranchisement has been concluded, to sell to a buyer who will take the seller's place in the freehold purchase project.

CHAPTER 7

Managing the opposition

There are compelling reasons for enfranchisers to seek participation by all qualifying leaseholders in a freehold purchase project. One obvious motivator is financial, as it is more attractive to share the costs of the acquisition amongst as large a number of participants as possible. But there are also important social and political reasons for seeking 100 per cent participation in an enfranchisement, as flat owners are more likely to maintain harmonious relations in a building if they have all taken part.

Organisers of a freehold purchase need to remember, however, that 100 per cent participation is unusual in a large block of flats. Indeed, once the nominee purchaser has concluded the enfranchisement, it can take several years to bring all the non-participants on board. We will address this post-enfranchisement issue in chapter 10.

One of the most stressful aspects of organising an enfranchisement in a large building, as described to me by leaseholders over the years, is the occasional fierce resistance presented by one or more non-participants. In some cases, hostility within a building to a planned freehold purchase can become nasty, with non-participants engaging in acts of harassment against project organisers. Fortunately, such conduct does not occur in every block of flats, but it is important for organisers to be aware of and to plan for the possibility, since some enfranchisement initiatives have been destroyed by a dedicated minority of leaseholders.

Importance of inviting all leaseholders from the start

Some leaseholders, in organising an enfranchisement, decide to invite only a selected number of people in the building to join, to try to reduce the eventual price of the freehold. The organisers do this in order for the nominee purchaser to avoid paying marriage value on as many non-participating flats as possible. We have seen in chapter 3 that this is a dangerous strategy and is to be avoided.

It is best practice for organisers to invite **all** of the qualifying leaseholders in the building to join the enfranchisement, rather than to invite a selected subset. We have seen that a landlord can seek to have an Enfranchisement Notice invalidated if he can prove the nominee purchaser has had conversations behind closed doors with non-participants in which non-participants were promised a share of the freehold and/or lease extensions at a specific price following the freehold purchase. We revisit this scenario of the Section 18 Notice later in the chapter. Leaseholders should avoid trying to be clever and should send the same invitation on the same date to all qualifying leaseholders.

There is another compelling reason for organisers to play it straight by inviting all flat owners from the start to join the enfranchisement. If there are non-participants in a building, the landlord might demand that the nominee purchaser pay 'hope value' for these flats as part of the freehold price. As we saw in chapter 3, hope value is payment demanded by the landlord for what he describes as the hope that the nominee purchaser will sell lease extensions to non-participants after the freehold has been purchased. Enfranchisers can strengthen their argument that there is no hope value to be paid by producing evidence that every qualifying leaseholder was invited to join the freehold purchase project and that non-participants have shown themselves unlikely to want a lease extension.

In some buildings, there can be a compelling reason not to invite every qualifying leaseholder to participate in an enfranchisement. This includes instances in which the freeholder owns one or more leasehold flats in the building through a family member or associate. While these long lease flats might qualify by law to take part in an enfranchisement, it can hurt the project's chances of success to reveal to the freeholder early on the intention to pursue the purchase of the freehold. If the flats that are indirectly owned by the landlord have very long leases – in many cases these flats have more than 100 years on the lease – then there will be no marriage value payable. Thus, the financial participation by these flats would bear little, if any, benefit to the enfranchisement project.

 Organisers can reduce certain project risks later in an enfranchisement by sending the same written invitation on the same date at the start of the project to all qualifying leaseholders.

The legislative requirement on inviting all the leaseholders to participate

The Commonhold and Leasehold Reform Act 2002 broadened the rights of leaseholders to collectively enfranchise their building, but it also introduced some unpleasant surprises for flat owners. One such surprise was the requirement for leaseholders who are enfranchising their building to provide a written invitation to all non-participants, including a cost estimate of the freehold, after the nominee purchaser company has been set up. This clause on 'Invitation to Participate', which is contained in Part 2, Chapter 1, Section 123 of the 2002 Act, gives a non-participant the right to join the enfranchisement at any stage, no matter how late, before the freehold purchase has been completed.

Fortunately, legislators have apparently realised that this clause is unfair to enfranchisers and is so impractical as to be virtually impossible to enforce. The clause is unfair because it obliges enfranchisers to produce a cost estimate for non-participants that is not required for participants and that can jeopardise a freehold purchase project by disseminating confidential information to non-participants who have no obligation to join nor to treat the information confidentially. The clause is impractical because a decision by a non-participant to join would, in many cases, change the value of the freehold by increasing the amount of marriage value payable. This is because there is no marriage value to be paid for a non-participating flat, while there is marriage value to be paid on any participating flat with less than 80 years left on the lease. Therefore, when the non-participant joins the project, the enfranchisers would need to rehire the chartered surveyor to recalculate the value of the freehold and they would need to rehire the solicitor to redraft the Enfranchisement Notice containing the offer price. Section 123 of the 2002 Act effectively gives non-participants the power to scupper an enfranchisement by repeatedly interrupting the project and introducing new costs for participants in the form of advisers' fees.

The good news is that Section 123 on 'Invitation to Participate' has never become law and appears unlikely to do so. The 2002 Act, as 'primary legislation', creates a foundation on which 'secondary legislation' is required in order to make the various sections and clauses enforceable. No secondary legislation has been created for Section 123, following an uproar amongst leaseholders who recognised the enormous problems that it would introduce for enfranchisers. Another important part of the 2002 Act that has not yet become law and that is not expected to do so is the section dealing with 'right to enfranchise' companies, or RTE companies. Sections 121 and 122 of Part 2, Chapter 1 of the 2002 Act say that leaseholders must set up their nominee purchaser company as an RTE company, with prescribed Memorandum and Articles of Association. Leaseholders have understandably welcomed the fact that no secondary legislation has been created to implement this section of the law, as it would have placed unnecessary constraints on enfranchisers, who are normally better off simply setting up a company limited by shares.

While the 2002 Act represented a poorly-executed legislative attempt to force enfranchisement organisers to invite all qualifying leaseholders in the building to join the project, extending such an invitation at the start of the project does remain best practice.

 The legal requirement that was anticipated in the 2002 Act for enfranchisers to invite all qualifying leaseholders, including latecomers, to participate in the freehold purchase has not become law, but an early invitation to all remains best practice.

Unlikelihood of 100 per cent participation in large enfranchisements

It is surprising to see that some residents' associations spend years delaying an enfranchisement project because they are determined to get every leaseholder in the building to join in. As we have seen, this goal of achieving 100 per cent participation in a large block of flats is unrealistic. Not only can such a goal waste an enormous amount of time, but it can create an unnecessary amount of labour-intensive work. This is because, according to ever-relevant 80–20 rule, the organisers normally spend 20 per cent of the time and effort getting 80 per cent of participants on board and then spend the remaining 80 per cent of their time and effort trying to get the remaining 20 per cent of participants to join.

As we saw in chapter 1, different leaseholders in a building have different budgets and priorities. I have come across many residential buildings in which a minority of leaseholders, often senior citizens, have decided not to join a collective enfranchisement, but have lent moral support to the initiative. Organisers should welcome this moral support and move on, rather than harangue flat owners that don't want to take part. Those involved in the early organising stage need to keep reminding leaseholders that only a minimum of 50 per cent of all flats in the building need to participate in order for the building to qualify for enfranchisement. Under no circumstances should organisers allow a small number of non-participants to hold the project hostage.

 Organisers of an enfranchisement in a large building should not delay the project in an effort to secure 100 per cent participation, as unanimity is rare.

Dealing early in the project with possible later requests by non-participants to join

One way to secure a maximum level of participation in a planned enfranchisement is to address early on misunderstandings that often arise later. For instance, as we saw in chapter 1, organisers need to make clear that project participants will get 999-year leases at the end of the freehold purchase process while non-participants will not. They also need to emphasise that the deadline for joining the project is a real deadline and that those wishing to join after the deadline date will not be allowed to do so.

A common problem in a large building with several non-participants is the application for lease extensions. We have seen that, once an Enfranchisement Notice is served, the landlord is not allowed to grant any lease extensions until the freehold purchase process has been concluded. But there are still cases in which a non-participant, after the Enfranchisement Notice has been served, sends an individual notice to the landlord applying for a 90-year lease extension. The landlord must, by law, inform the leaseholder that no lease extension can be provided while the enfranchisement is under way and he must inform the nominee purchaser of the lease extension application. At best, this event is distracting for the enfranchisement organisers. At worst, it strengthens the landlord's claim for hope value.

 Organisers should minimise the damage that can be caused to an enfranchisement project by non-participants by making clear early on that latecomers will not be granted 999-year leases.

Essential nature of confidentiality after the sign-up deadline has passed

Enfranchisement organisers should maintain a firm position on the confidentiality of the project once the deadline for joining has passed. While it is normal for there to be participants **and** non-participants in a large building, and while all residents should be treated with respect, non-participants have no right to be briefed on the freehold purchase project that they have opted not to join. We have seen that the tone of the undertaking by residents should change from a loose, informal discussion to a carefully-planned joint commercial venture once the deadline for joining the project has passed. Organisers must remind participants in writing that they are not to discuss any aspect of the enfranchisement or its existence with any non-participant.

In many large buildings, non-participants contact the organising team or other participants after the joining deadline has passed, to request information. In such a case, an organiser should reply that the matter is confidential and cannot be discussed with any non-participant until the process has ended.

Participants of an enfranchisement should be reminded in writing several times in the months following the start of the project not to discuss this confidential undertaking with any non-participant.

Decreasing the risk of information leaks to the landlord by non-participants

Some flat owners find it uncomfortable to refuse to talk with a neighbour about a freehold purchase project, even if the neighbour has opted not to join the initiative. This can produce awkward moments amongst residents in the lift or main lobby of the building, when a question posed by a non-participant is met by embarrassed silence. However, participants must understand the business-critical nature of keeping all aspects of the enfranchisement, including its existence, strictly confidential and preventing any leakage of confidential information to the landlord.

Many landlords behave properly during an enfranchisement by respecting the legal right of leaseholders to buy their freehold and they comply with their responsibilities. A powerful minority of large corporate landlords, however, have been known to behave in a manner that creates such serious problems for enfranchisements that many such projects collapse. It comes as sobering news to many leaseholders that some landlords strike deals with non-participants by forgiving their service charge arrears in exchange for information on an enfranchisement project.

While no resident wants to expect the worst of his neighbour, enfranchisement participants must make every effort to prevent the dissemination, even if inadvertent, of information that could hurt the project's chances for success. Leaseholders need to remember that a porter, even a friendly porter who is popular amongst residents, is an employee of the landlord or the managing agent company hired by the landlord to run the building. Under no circumstances should any discussion take place with the porter or other staff in the building about an enfranchisement project.

We have seen that residents that take steps to enfranchise a large block of flats often pursue this route because their building is plagued by poor management and that this poor management can prompt some leaseholders to withhold their service charges. Unfortunately, the strategy of withholding service charges frequently backfires, by creating an ever-larger debt for the individual leaseholder, a debt that the landlord has a legal right under the lease to collect. Enfranchisers must be aware of the vulnerability of leaseholders in a building of striking a deal with the landlord if these leaseholders have large service charge debts.

We have examined the many ways in which enfranchisers suffer from a David-and-Goliath inequality vis-à-vis the landlord. They are placed at an even greater disadvantage if the landlord is provided with information about the timeframe of the enfranchisement, the number and identity of the participants, the lawyer, surveyor or project manager being used by the leaseholders, the discount rate envisaged or even the fact that the enfranchisement is being planned at all.

 Participants should be warned about the possibility of information on the enfranchisement being leaked by non-participants to the landlord.

Section 18 invalidation of an Enfranchisement Notice

Organisers should tell participants that there is a business-critical reason why the project should not be discussed with non-participants until the freehold has been purchased. The reason is that any such discussion can, in theory, be used by the landlord to have the entire enfranchisement initiative thrown out. We saw in chapter 3 that this is because of what lawyers refer to as a 'Section 18 Notice'.

Section 18 of Part 1, Chapter 1 of the Leasehold Reform, Housing and Urban Development Act 1993 places strict obligations on enfranchisers not to enter into any agreements regarding the freehold purchase without informing the landlord. This section of the law, which comes under the section heading of 'Duty of nominee purchaser to disclose existence of agreements affected specified premises', also bans the nominee purchaser from issuing shares in the company to anyone other than the identified participants of the enfranchisement.

The logic behind Section 18 is clear. If the enfranchisers were allowed to make deals behind closed doors with non-participants, they could get a minimum number of leaseholders formally to join the freehold purchase project in order to minimise the amount of marriage value payable, while agreeing secretly to grant non-participants 999-year lease extensions and shares of freehold after the enfranchisement at the opening price. This process would deny the landlord a fair price for the freehold.

Section 18 says that, in the event of a failure by the nominee purchaser to advise the landlord of an agreement reached with a non-participant, the nominee purchaser will be liable to pay to the landlord the increase in freehold price that would have resulted from the agreement. In a worst-case scenario, we have seen that a landlord can seek to have the Enfranchisement Notice declared invalid. Organisers of an enfranchisement need to make all the participants aware of Section 18 and the absolute necessity that no discussions take place with any non-participants about the freehold purchase project.

 Organisers need to protect against any possible Section 18 Notice by the landlord by ensuring that there are no behind-closed-door discussions between the nominee purchaser and non-participants about letting non-participants join later at the beginning price.

Addressing efforts by non-participants to sabotage an enfranchisement

Leaseholders can make every best effort to organise an enfranchisement in a large building in a manner that is fair and democratic, but they can still find that some non-participants object strongly to the project. Instances of downright hostility by non-participants often come down to the issue of service charge arrears. I have seen several instances in troubled buildings in which a small number of non-participants who owe tens of thousands of pounds of service charges, dating back many years, set out with great determination to foil the freehold purchase initiative.

The motivation of such non-participants is powerful and should not be ignored. We have seen that if the enfranchisement succeeds, the nominee purchaser is likely to have to pay to the landlord any service charge arrears at the time of the freehold acquisition. This means that the participants can end up paying off significant service charge debts that have been accumulated by non-participants. The requirement for the nominee purchaser to pay these service charge arrears can create short-time financing pain, but most resident management companies have an excellent record for collecting service charges once they have bought the freehold.

Resident management companies should always take a no-nonsense approach in ensuring that all leaseholders pay their service charges fully and promptly. A failure to do so means that some leaseholders are subsidising their neighbours, since the resident management company will likely have to borrow money from the bank to fill any financing gap and leaseholders will be charged for the bank interest. It is not acceptable for any leaseholder to be forced to subsidise another leaseholder. Some non-participants of large enfranchisements understand, therefore, that they are likely to be forced to pay their large service charge arrears to the new landlord, which is owned by a majority of leaseholders in the building, once the freehold purchase has been completed. If the service charge debt is large enough, a leaseholder may have to sell his flat in order to repay it.

This situation explains, unfortunately, why some non-participants adopt a do-or-die approach towards trying to prevent an enfranchisement. Again, we see a situation where the leaseholder's worst enemy in a freehold purchase can end up being his fellow leaseholder.

Many freehold purchases involve harmonious relations amongst flat owners. But I have come across enough efforts by non-participants to sabotage enfranchisements to provide a warning and some practical tips. An attempt by one's neighbour to ruin a collective initiative to buy the building freehold can come as a shock to organisers. But enfranchisers should take a firm stance in addressing this possibility.

One means of trying to sabotage an enfranchisement, as we have seen, is for non-participants to talk about the freehold purchase with the landlord or the managing agent that has been instructed by the landlord. I have witnessed some extraordinary instances in which non-participants have called a so-called residents' meeting with the managing agent, supposedly to discuss future repairs and maintenance in the building, only to reveal to the managing agent confidential information about the planned enfranchisement. In other cases, non-participants might post confidential information about the freehold purchase project on a bulletin board by the lift, where the porter, managing agent, landlord and anyone else entering the building can see it.

Not only do these efforts to sabotage an enfranchisement deliver confidential information to the landlord, but they also create enormous distraction for the project organisers. This is because the organisers are forced to take swift action to put a stop to such destructive activity by non-participants. Because of the huge organisational imbalance that exists between the under-resourced residents' association and the heavily-resourced landlord, this kind of distraction and extra work for organisers can result in an enfranchisement losing momentum, failing to reach project milestones, losing support of its participants and ultimately collapsing.

 If some leaseholders are hostile to the freehold purchase project, organisers need to prepare to take swift action in the event of any efforts to sabotage the enfranchisement.

Being firm with non-participants who pose a threat to the project

There are various ways in which organisers can deal with non-participants who are trying to sabotage an enfranchisement, but it is crucial that firm action be taken immediately. Participants must understand that such saboteurs pose a real threat to the success of the project. In the same way that all leaseholders in a building should be invited from the start to join in an enfranchisement, no individual should be allowed to jeopardise the success of this important joint undertaking.

If one or more non-participants do something that endangers the freehold purchase project, organisers should tell them to stop immediately. This should be communicated in writing. Verbal communication should be avoided, because it fails to leave a necessary paper trail and can increase stress for the organisers without clear benefit. While organisers should hope to nip in the bud any mischievous attempts by non-participants to foil the enfranchisement, they need to keep in mind that this issue could end up in legal action, so they need to keep a careful record of all relevant communication.

While enfranchising a large building brings its own complexities, organisers can mobilise a powerful force by getting shareholders of the nominee purchaser company to send emails or other written communication to the non-participants in question asking them to stop the action that is creating risks for the project. It depends on the personalities involved whether organisers are able to bring non-participant troublemakers quickly and easily into line. This is, unfortunately, a moment in the project when the gloves come off and the organisers need to get tough with any would-be saboteurs.

 TOP TIP Organisers should tell non-participants in writing to cease any action that threatens the enfranchisement and should get other participants to send the same message.

Don't get personal, even if others do

Flat owners in a large enfranchisement need to be prepared for things to get nasty if there are non-participants who are deeply hostile to the freehold purchase project. Organisers must strike a careful balance between being firm with opponents in the building, while at the same time maintaining a proper, respectful tone. A freehold purchase is about money and people's homes, and people can get extremely emotional. In the many blocks of flats I have researched, I have seen some instances in which non-participants have launched vicious verbal and written attacks on organisers. Enfranchisers should steel themselves for this possible scenario.

In some buildings, I have seen hostile non-participants heckle enfranchisement organisers at residents' meetings. In others, would-be saboteurs have sent anonymous hate mail to organisers or posted offensive letters on the bulletin board by the lift for all to see. I have seen a small dedicated group of opponents to an enfranchisement in a large building engage in shameless slander and libel of the main organiser. These events can be deeply distressing, particularly given the fact that many enfranchisement organisers are busy people who do this work on an unpaid volunteer basis. But it is essential for those who are initiating and overseeing a freehold purchase to rise above this kind of petty nastiness.

Eleanor Roosevelt, wife of former US President Franklin Delano Roosevelt, had useful advice in the early 1900s for young people when facing mud-slinging attacks. 'Never take things personally – even if they are meant personally,' she said. Organisers of a large enfranchisement, in playing an important leadership role, must prepare themselves for the possibility that they might earn some enemies in the building for a while.

The board of directors of the nominee purchaser must, from the start, set the tone for the future freeholder of the building. By refusing to engage in or respond to personal attacks by hostile non-participants, the board provides a clear distinction between the old regime and the new, more professionally run resident management company. While it can be difficult to look down the road a few years when organisers are busy enfranchising a large building, they need to adopt the tone that will be applied later on, once the freehold purchase has been completed. This will help maximise the chance that bad blood created by would-be saboteurs can dissipate and harmony can return to the building after the enfranchisement has been concluded.

 Directors of the nominee purchaser company should maintain a professional tone towards all interlocutors, including hostile non-participants, and should not be drawn into making or responding to personal attacks.

Many leaseholders are caught off guard by efforts from within the building to delay, derail or destroy an enfranchisement project. Some flat owners have described these events to me as the worst aspect of having taken on the job of organising the freehold purchase initiative. The sense of dismay is often compounded by the sheer shock of seeing one's neighbour actively seek to ruin an initiative being pursued by a majority of people in the building and/or to engage in personal attacks on fellow leaseholders.

Enfranchisers often expect the greatest threat to their freehold purchase initiative to be presented by the landlord. They are then horrified to discover that the greatest obstacle exists in their midst, in the form of the hostile non-participant. Indeed, a landlord can sometimes sit back and wait for an enfranchisement effort to self-destruct if opponents within the building are sufficiently determined. Or the landlord can help foment opposition and conflict by offering special deals to non-participants, while being difficult with participating leaseholders.

This is inevitably an unpleasant interlude, but enfranchisement organisers must keep their cool and maintain their focus. The more they pursue a business-like approach to the freehold purchase project, the greater is the likelihood that would-be saboteurs will stand down. The directors of the nominee purchaser company need to remember that they are responsible for protecting the interests of shareholders and they must act accordingly. Above all, even if opponents to an enfranchisement engage in petty mud-slinging, the organisers must rise above these personal attacks and keep their eye on the finish line of this long-distance race.

CHAPTER 8

Negotiate or not?

Flat owners are often surprised to learn that a large majority of collective enfranchisement initiatives are concluded in a negotiated purchase of the freehold by participating leaseholders. Of those residents' groups that serve an Enfranchisement Notice on their landlord, only a small percentage go all the way through to a Leasehold Valuation Tribunal (LVT) hearing. This chapter examines why negotiated settlements are so prevalent in enfranchisements and how you can maximise your chances for successful negotiations.

Timing is everything in an enfranchisement. While attempts by leaseholders to get their landlord to agree to a negotiated sale of a building freehold might fail to produce results over a period of years, the same landlord may well agree to a negotiated deal once the leaseholders have served an Enfranchisement Notice. We examine in this chapter the differing degrees of negotiating leverage that enfranchisers enjoy at various stages in the process and how to identify the right moment at which to pursue a negotiated settlement.

Enfranchisers are too often lulled into complacency once they do reach a negotiated agreement with the freeholder and they forget that they have an identified period of time within which they must exchange contracts on the sale. This chapter provides practical tips on how to avoid missing crucial deadlines and what to do if the landlord agrees on a sale price for the freehold, but then fails to exchange contracts.

Why most enfranchisements conclude in negotiated acquisition

Many leaseholders believe that they face two mutually-exclusive options when buying their freehold, that is, to reach a negotiated agreement with the landlord or else force the landlord to sell by collective enfranchisement. These options, however, are not mutually exclusive. They **both** come into play in most enfranchisements. The government does not provide statistics on the subject, but my research over the years involving hundreds of residential buildings suggests that as few as one in every 200 Enfranchisement Notices ends up in an LVT hearing, with the remainder being concluded in a negotiated sale.

Money explains why so many statutory freehold purchases are resolved by negotiated settlement. As we saw in chapter 1, leaseholders must pay the landlord's reasonable legal and surveyor fees during an enfranchisement, but this only applies to fees incurred when the landlord handles the Enfranchisement Notice, and prepares and serves the Counter Notice. If the freehold purchase initiative goes to a tribunal hearing, then each side must pay its own costs in preparing for and attending the hearing. An LVT hearing for an enfranchisement that is complex will ordinarily last two days, and the enfranchisers and the landlord will typically be represented by a barrister, solicitor and surveyor.

To avoid incurring these LVT costs, most landlords seek a negotiated agreement with the enfranchisers on the freehold price. As we see later in the chapter, a negotiated settlement can be reached by both parties at different stages in the process. The timing of the statutory deadlines in an enfranchisement is meant to encourage leaseholders and landlords to conclude freehold purchases by negotiated agreement.

 A large majority of collective enfranchisements conclude in negotiated settlement, as most landlords are keen to avoid paying for a barrister, solicitor and surveyor at an LVT hearing.

Capital gains rollover relief

A landlord who is disposing of a freehold has a Capital Gains Tax incentive to sell as a result of a collective enfranchisement rather than by pure negotiated agreement. This important financial motivator, unfortunately, escapes the notice of many leaseholders. On 17 September 1993 the Inland Revenue announced that landlords that were forced to sell a building freehold or a lease extension under the Leasehold Reform Act 1967 or the Leasehold Reform, Housing and Urban Development Act 1993 could claim tax rollover relief on the capital gains made from the sale. The Inland Revenue said that this was similar to the rollover tax relief that landlords could claim under Section 247 of the Taxation of Chargeable Gains Act 1992 regarding a compulsory disposal of land by a landlord to an authority.

While many freeholders wish to avoid incurring LVT costs at the end of an enfranchisement, it is important for leaseholders to remember that landlords only get to claim tax rollover relief on the capital gains made from the freehold sale if they have been served an Enfranchisement Notice. This Inland Revenue rule creates a disincentive for many landlords to agree to sell a freehold unless they are being forced to do so as a result of a formal enfranchisement process.

 Landlords have a greater tax incentive to sell their freehold only **after** being served an Enfranchisement Notice by leaseholders, rather than by pure negotiation, since the enfranchisement process enables landlords to claim capital gains rollover relief on the sale.

Two-stage negotiations

A freeholder can reach a negotiated settlement with the leaseholders at any time during the formal enfranchisement process, but there are two stages at which most successful negotiations occur. The first is the period after the landlord has served the Counter Notice on leaseholders. The second is the period immediately before a scheduled LVT hearing.

By the time the leaseholders have served their Enfranchisement Notice and the landlord has then sent his Counter Notice, both parties know what price has been offered for the freehold by the buyer and what price is being requested by the seller. Lawmakers purposely banned leaseholders from making an application for a hearing at the LVT any earlier than two months from the time of the Counter Notice to give both parties sufficient time to carry out negotiations.

In large buildings, negotiations often occur in two phases, with the surveyors that represent both parties seeking to reach agreement on the freehold price during the weeks following the Counter Notice and then, failing a settlement, resuming negotiations in the weeks prior to the tribunal hearing. Enfranchisers need to remember that a failure to reach a negotiated settlement immediately after the Counter Notice does not rule out the possibility of striking a negotiated deal later on, before the LVT hearing.

It is worth noting that a large number of landlords reach a negotiated agreement with the enfranchisers even earlier in the process, thus eliminating altogether the Counter Notice stage. This happens in many small residential buildings and in buildings that are owned by small landlords, including individuals. For the small landlord, who lacks the scale, organisational resource and experience of the large corporate freeholder, the receipt of an Enfranchisement Notice serves as a sufficient incentive for the landlord to agree to a negotiated price. If a landlord agrees to the offer price presented in the Enfranchisement Notice and does not serve any Counter Notice, the leaseholders can proceed to purchase the freehold. But leaseholders should not formally withdraw their Enfranchisement Notice until they have concluded the purchase, in order to provide protection in case the negotiated deal falls through.

 Leaseholders should be prepared to negotiate with the landlord after receiving the Counter Notice and again before the LVT hearing.

Increased negotiating strength before an LVT hearing

We have considered many areas in which the enfranchiser, like the long-distance runner, must pace himself and employ tenacity and single-minded drive to reach the finish line. Preparation and readiness for negotiations represents one such area. Many freehold purchase organisers are exhausted by the time they approach a scheduled LVT hearing, as this is normally at least eight months after the serving of the Enfranchisement Notice and can be years after the project was initially conceived. But the organisers must be ready for what is often an eleventh-hour negotiation.

Indeed, the negotiating position of leaseholders increases as a tribunal hearing approaches and it is important for enfranchisers to make best use of the timing. Flat owners also need to understand that many large corporate landlords which have hundreds of buildings in their portfolio only begin to pay serious attention to an enfranchisement when it enters the final phase, that is, in the run-up to an LVT hearing. Leaseholders can decide for a variety of reasons to drop an enfranchisement initiative. But by the time the enfranchisers and the landlord are, say, two weeks away from a tribunal hearing, the landlord knows that he is very likely to have to sell the building and it is now often a question of cutting losses and agreeing on a mutually-acceptable price.

A large number of enfranchisements are concluded in a negotiated settlement within the two-week period prior to the scheduled LVT hearing. Of these, many agreements are reached within the LVT building, minutes before the hearing begins. Leaseholders need to be ready for this and must stay on their toes. It is the responsibility of the board of directors of the nominee purchaser to reach any negotiated settlement, while taking advice from a professional project manager, surveyor or lawyer. The nominee purchaser should not delegate crucial decision-making power regarding such deals to an adviser.

 Leaseholders enjoy increasing negotiation leverage the nearer they get to a scheduled LVT hearing.

Must-have and want-to-have negotiating points

Negotiations on a freehold purchase are normally carried out by the chartered surveyor representing the leaseholders and the landlord. In reviewing the debating points covered, one can see that some 'horse trading' takes place in large enfranchisement negotiations, with each surveyor trying to secure an improved deal for his client. While enfranchisement organisers in a large block of flats should entrust the negotiations to their surveyor, they need to agree with him beforehand on the must-have and want-to-have elements of the freehold acquisition.

It is unusual for each surveyor simply to present his overall valuation figure and to press for this figure. Typically, each side will be putting forward a proposed discount rate for the capitalised ground rent and for the reversion. While some surveyors argue that one discount rate should apply to both of these cost elements, others say that one discount rate should apply to the ground rent, while a different rate should apply to the reversion. In many large hotly-contested enfranchisements, the landlord's surveyor argues that there is development value in the building, while the leaseholders' surveyor argues there is not. If a significant number of leaseholders in the building have decided not to join the freehold purchase initiative, the freeholder's surveyor might argue for hope value, while the enfranchisers will resist having to pay this.

Leaseholders need to ensure that their project manager, surveyor and solicitor have done their homework and that the offer price for the freehold contained in the Enfranchisement Notice can be substantiated. If the landlord is demanding an unreasonable amount for development value by claiming he plans to build an additional storey with flats to be sold, even though planning permission for this has been denied, leaseholders need to have documentation backing up their argument that no such development value exists. But enfranchisers might wish to agree a trade-off on one or more valuation points. If, for instance, enfranchisers deny that there is hope value in a building, they might still instruct their surveyor to be ready to concede on this point if the landlord's surveyor agrees to a discount rate that is acceptable to the leaseholders.

When an enfranchisement gets all the way to an LVT hearing, the tribunal panel considers, amongst other things, the degree to which each party has made a reasonable effort to arrive at a negotiated settlement. Although the law provides a statutory formula for the main cost elements of a freehold valuation, there is enormous scope for differing valuations, especially when a landlord claims that there is development value and/or hope value. The LVT panel considers each side's argument and the strength with which the valuation is substantiated by market evidence. A surveyor who backs up his freehold valuation with relevant examples of property sales can hope to be accorded more credibility than one who provides no such 'market comparables'.

 Enfranchisement organisers should instruct their chartered surveyor to do the negotiating, but should agree beforehand with the surveyor on must-have and want-to-have negotiating elements.

Negotiations before starting an enfranchisement

Deadlines set down in enfranchisement law provide crucial protection for leaseholders against the possibility that a freehold purchase process will drag on for years and years. If flat owners decide to negotiate with the landlord on the freehold purchase without first starting the statutory process, they enjoy no such protection. However, there are cases in which the landlord is ready to sell the freehold at a price considered reasonable by the leaseholders.

If would-be enfranchisers have reason to believe that the landlord is a willing seller, this information should be confirmed as quickly as possible without allowing it to create long delays for the freehold purchase project. The leaseholders should send a letter to the landlord with an offer price for the freehold and they should require that the landlord provide them with a contract of sale within a specified period of time, such as one month. If the landlord provides the contract of sale within the specified period of time, the leaseholders can decide to forgo the statutory route of enfranchisement.

Flat owners need to remember, however, that even if the landlord is a willing seller, such as a senior citizen who wishes quickly to dispose of a certain property, he can inadvertently cause a delay of months or even years in a freehold purchase project by moving at a slower pace than would occur if the leaseholders served an Enfranchisement Notice. For this reason, the project organisers need to have compelling evidence that a purely-negotiated freehold acquisition can be concluded in a timely manner before they decide to rule out the statutory route.

If the landlord offers to reach a negotiated sale shortly before the leaseholders serve an Enfranchisement Notice, the leaseholders should require that the landlord produce a contract of sale at the leaseholders' offer price within one month, and, failing this, they should continue with their collective enfranchisement plan.

Negotiations as a delaying tactic

I have come across many buildings in which the leaseholders' efforts to buy the freehold have been unnecessarily delayed for years because the residents incorrectly determined whether the landlord was truly a willing seller. Flat owners need to remember that it is easy for a large corporate landlord to say that he is prepared to sell the freehold and that many freeholders use this as a delaying tactic to dissuade leaseholders from starting an enfranchisement. By the time the leaseholders realise that they have been strung along, the value of the freehold may have increased significantly.

It can cause great discouragement in a large building for residents to realise that they have wasted years trying to reach a negotiated deal with the freeholder. When the head of the residents' association or a key member of the association committee moves from the building or steps down, flat owners can feel that things are standing still or even moving backwards in their building. Organisers of an enfranchisement should use this experience as a valuable, if painful, lesson and as increased evidence of the need for a focused, structured process for buying the freehold.

There are often one or two flat owners in a large block of flats who insist that organisers of the freehold purchase project investigate the possibility of a negotiated acquisition before organising an enfranchisement. Ironically, individuals who urge organisers to carry out this kind of extra work are often residents who are unwilling to volunteer their own time for the freehold purchase project. Enfranchisement organisers need to be firm in communicating to the participants that they are not willing to commit unlimited numbers of hours to the project and they should place a limit on the amount of time spent seeking a purely-negotiated agreement with the freeholder.

By requiring that the landlord produce a contract of sale within a specific period of time such as one month, the leaseholders identify quickly whether to pursue a purely-negotiated purchase of the freehold. They produce clarity of issues and positions, and are able to move forward with the project. By keeping in mind the disincentives for many landlords to strike a purely-negotiated deal, including the absence of capital gains rollover relief, enfranchisers are able to follow a more efficient, focused strategy. As we have seen, leaseholders place themselves in a much stronger position to reach a negotiated deal after they have served their Enfranchisement Notice on the landlord.

 Leaseholders need to beware of the landlord who suggests a purely-negotiated sale of the freehold as a delaying tactic in order to dissuade flat owners from pursuing a collective enfranchisement.

A negotiated deal that goes to a Vesting Order in the County Court

Enfranchisers often feel a great sense of relief when they reach a negotiated agreement with the landlord on the freehold price, whether this occurs shortly after the serving of the Enfranchisement Notice or just before an LVT hearing. The impression is that of the long-distance runner who has finally crossed the finish line. However, leaseholders need to remember that the process is not yet over and that their enfranchisement can still collapse.

When leaseholders arrive at a negotiated settlement with the freeholder, the nominee purchaser has a maximum of four months from the time that the terms of the deal are agreed to exchange a contract of sale with the freeholder. A failure to do so is seen as a deemed withdrawal, meaning that the leaseholders are considered to have withdrawn their Enfranchisement Notice and dropped their claim. It comes as a shock to many flat owners to learn that their long-fought enfranchisement effort can come to naught, even though they have put in months of hard work, have got all the way to a scheduled LVT hearing and have then managed to strike a deal with the landlord in the days before the hearing.

Fortunately, the law provides two types of protection for leaseholders against their enfranchisement collapsing if there is no exchange of contracts within the required four-month period of time. The bad news is that both types of protection require the enfranchisers to do additional work and to incur additional costs.

The first area of protection is the County Court. If the nominee purchaser and the landlord have agreed to the price and to all other terms of the freehold purchase, including the wording of the contract of sale, but no exchange of contract has occurred within the four-month period, then the nominee purchaser, in order to protect its position, must file a claim in the County Court asking the court to agree to a Vesting Order. This Vesting Order says that the nominee purchaser can pay the agreed freehold price to the court and that the landlord must then collect the money from the court.

A dangerous mistake made by some enfranchisers is to fail to record immediately in writing the details of a negotiated agreement reached with the landlord. I have seen horrific instances in which highly-experienced lawyers and surveyors were representing an enfranchising group when a negotiated deal was struck with the landlord, but no one recorded in writing the agreed price of the freehold, date of agreement and other details, such as the amount of legal and surveyor fees that the enfranchisers would pay to the landlord. Then, to the exasperation and disbelief of the enfranchisers days later, the landlord claimed to have agreed to figures that were higher than those being quoted.

There is a simple remedy for this type of confusion. The enfranchisers should have a brief letter – three sentences will normally suffice – sent to the landlord within a day or two of the negotiated agreement, which recaps the date and place of the agreement, the agreed price of the freehold, any agreed amount of legal and surveyor fees to be paid to the landlord by the enfranchisers and the names of the people who were witness to the agreement. If the project manager or solicitor representing the leaseholders refuses to send this letter as soon as the negotiated agreement has been reached, then the enfranchisement organisers should send it.

 If the leaseholders agree a contract of sale with the landlord, but fail to exchange contracts within four months of reaching a negotiated agreement, they must seek a Vesting Order from the

County Court that will enable them to pay the agreed price to the court.

A negotiated deal that goes back to the Leasehold Valuation Tribunal

The second area of protection for leaseholders who reach a negotiated agreement with the landlord, but fail to exchange the contract within the required four-month period is the LVT. If the nominee purchaser has not reached an agreement with the freeholder on all the terms of the sale, that is, the contract of sale, then the nominee purchaser must reactivate its earlier application for a hearing at the tribunal.

This application for a hearing can easily be reactivated if the advisers representing the enfranchisers have done their job properly by requesting, as soon as the negotiated agreement was reached, for the scheduled LVT hearing to be adjourned. Because the enfranchisers did not withdraw their application for the hearing, the application can simply be reinstated. Unfortunately, leaseholders are often obliged to wait several weeks before they can get another scheduled tribunal hearing, because of the backlog of cases at the LVT.

By reverting back to the tribunal, the enfranchisers are once again asking the LVT panel to decide on the freehold price at which the landlord must sell. The panel will examine arguments and evidence presented by both sides, as we will see in chapter 9, and panel members will consider the efforts made by both parties to reach a negotiated settlement. Two key messages, therefore, for leaseholders when they reach a negotiated agreement with the landlord on the freehold price is, firstly, to remember that these deals sometimes fall through and, secondly, to remain alert to the options that must urgently be pursued if a negotiated settlement does not result in an exchange of contracts within the four-month deadline period.

 If the leaseholders fail to agree a contract of sale within four months of a negotiated agreement with the landlord, they must reactivate their application for an LVT hearing.

Limiting the cost of negotiations

Leaseholders should control project costs by setting clear parameters for the chartered surveyor who is carrying out negotiations with the landlord on their behalf. Poorly-defined parameters can result in unnecessarily long and unproductive negotiations, and enfranchisers can get a nasty surprise when they receive the bill from the surveyor. Many surveyors charge by the hour for carrying out negotiations, so the enfranchisement organisers should agree on a maximum number of hours. A four- to five-hour timeframe is normally sufficient for a surveyor to determine whether he can reach a negotiated agreement with the landlord's surveyor.

Some enfranchisers consider it a waste of money, time and effort to have their surveyor carry out negotiations on their behalf with the landlord's surveyor if the landlord has demanded an absurdly high price for the freehold in his Counter Notice. But leaseholders should remember that the law creates little disincentive for landlords to demand a realistic price for a freehold. While leaseholders run a real risk of having their Enfranchisement Notice declared invalid in the County Court if the landlord can argue compellingly that the offer price is so low as to be unrealistic, it is difficult to find evidence of large corporate landlords being penalised for counter offer prices that are so high as to be unrealistic. Therefore, enfranchisers should not conclude that they will have to pay an outrageously high price for the freehold just because the landlord has demanded such a price in the Counter Notice. Leaseholders need to remember that this may simply represent a tough opening position for negotiation.

Finally, enfranchisers should make best use of the negotiations route, if only to assess the strength of the landlord's case. A surveyor experienced in enfranchisement will be able to report back to the leaseholders on whether the landlord's surveyor can substantiate a demand for a higher freehold price. He will also be able to provide valuable information on the apparent level of determination of the landlord to fight the enfranchisement all the way through to an LVT hearing.

 Enfranchisers should instruct their chartered surveyor to carry out a maximum number of hours of negotiations at any defined stage, such as four or five hours.

We have reviewed in this chapter the degree to which a large majority of enfranchisements are concluded in a negotiated purchase of the freehold before an LVT hearing is held. While leaseholders should make best use of the protection that enfranchisement law provides, in the form of statutory deadlines that prevent a freehold purchase process from dragging on endlessly, they should also be ready to strike a negotiated deal with the landlord at the right price. Such a conclusion will save the leaseholders the cost of a surveyor and one or more lawyers that they might otherwise incur at the LVT.

Enfranchisers should not be unduly discouraged if a first round of negotiations with the landlord, after receipt of the Counter Notice, fails to end in a settlement. They will often find that a subsequent negotiating effort, in the weeks before a scheduled tribunal hearing, will produce the desired agreement with the freeholder. Even landlords that demand a ridiculously high price for a freehold in the Counter Notice are often ready to negotiate sensibly once they see that an LVT hearing is imminent and that a negotiated agreement will save the landlord from incurring tribunal costs.

Organisers of a freehold purchase must have a solid understanding of the main valuation issues, but they also should delegate the negotiating to their chartered surveyor. The main organiser needs to keep an open line of communication with the surveyor and to agree with him on negotiating strategy, tactics and the parameters of a possible deal. While the surveyor is the owner of technical knowledge on valuing freeholds, it is only the nominee purchaser that can decide on the lowest reasonable offer price for the freehold and also the maximum price the nominee purchaser is willing to pay in a negotiated settlement.

It can appear a nightmare scenario for enfranchisers if they reach a negotiated agreement with the landlord, only to get to the end of the four-month period with no exchange of contract. But leaseholders must steel themselves for this possibility and take necessary urgent steps to ensure that the enfranchisement project does not collapse. Whether this involves applying to the County Court for a Vesting Order or reactivating the earlier application for an LVT hearing, project organisers need to take a deep breath and press on.

Many consumers say that enfranchisement law creates too many loopholes for landlords on the one hand, while presenting unfair costs and obstacles for the leaseholders on the other. It is true that homeowners would be well served by a change in the law that would remove these inequities. Until that happens, leaseholders wishing to buy their freehold under the existing legislation must prepare themselves for the many pitfalls and project risks that we have identified.

CHAPTER 9

Crossing the finish line

By the time the organisers of a large collective enfranchisement approach the end of the freehold purchase process, they are often exhausted. If they have opted to project manage the enfranchisement themselves rather than to outsource this work to a professional project manager, these volunteer workers are even more likely to view the finish line of the race with a sense of impatience and desperation. In the final stretch of this long-distance race, our runner must watch carefully to avoid obstacles that can trip him up before he reaches the finish line.

This chapter examines the three final ways in which an enfranchisement is concluded. Whether leaseholders reach the end of the process by negotiated agreement, a right-of-first-refusal acquisition or the Leasehold Valuation Tribunal (LVT), the freehold purchase is not over until the exchange of the contract of sale and completion, and many things can go wrong in the final weeks. One of the most awkward but predictable obstacles to the smooth conclusion of an enfranchisement is a failure by a participant to pay his share of the freehold cost. We provide practical tips in this chapter for this crucial area of risk management.

At the end of a large enfranchisement, a process that we have seen can take years, leaseholders must work hard to avoid creating their own hurdles. In this chapter we review how project organisers should take action to ensure that all service charges in the building are paid up by the time the freehold purchase project nears conclusion, to avoid leaving the nominee purchaser and shareholders that own it from having to pay any service charge arrears. We also look at best practice for granting 999-year leases to enfranchisement participants, a final step that is sometimes neglected until long after the freehold acquisition has been completed.

The negotiated freehold purchase agreement

We saw in chapter 8 that a large majority of enfranchisements are concluded in a negotiated agreement with the landlord and never proceed all the way to an LVT hearing. Once a settlement has been reached, the next step is for enfranchisers to reach agreement with the landlord on a contract of sale for the freehold. If the landlord is exercising his right to a leaseback on one or more flats that he owns in the building, the enfranchisers also need to agree with the landlord on the exact wording of the new 999-year lease for these flats.

When the contract of sale and any leaseback leases have been agreed, both parties can proceed to an exchange of contract and subsequent completion. A colour plan should be attached to the contract of sale that identifies the freehold property being acquired and any property over which the enfranchisers have secured a right of way. The exchange of contract and completion is normally carried out by the lawyers acting for both parties. It is not necessary for the enfranchisement participants to be present.

 The nominee purchaser must agree on the wording of any leaseback leases being granted to the landlord as part of the freehold purchase.

Completing a freehold purchase through the right-of-first-refusal process

When enfranchisers are served a Right of First Refusal Notice by the landlord and they accept to buy the freehold at the landlord's asking price, several stages are eliminated from the normal enfranchisement process. We saw in chapter 4 that a landlord wishing to sell the freehold to a third party must first serve a Right of First Refusal Notice or Section 5 Notice on qualifying residents in the building that identifies the landlord's asking price and the two-month deadline date by which leaseholders must reply if they wish to buy the building.

If leaseholders, before serving an Enfranchisement Notice on the landlord, decide to buy through the right of first refusal, they do not make any application to the LVT for a hearing to be held. In many right-of-first-refusal processes, there are no negotiations between the leaseholders and the landlord. This is because, as we have seen, the leaseholders have no legal right to demand that the landlord negotiate with them over the price of the freehold in a right-of-first-refusal purchase.

If more than 50 per cent of all qualifying residents, with each flat in the building counting as one resident, wish to buy the freehold at the landlord's asking price, they must notify the landlord in writing within two months of the Section 5 Notice by sending a Section 6 Notice. The next step is for the leaseholders to advise the landlord in writing within two months of the Section 6 Notice of the identity of the person or entity that will be buying the freehold, that is, the identity of the nominee purchaser.

Once the leaseholders have notified the landlord of the identity of the nominee purchaser, the landlord must send a contract of sale to the nominee purchaser within a maximum of one month. Within the following two months, the nominee purchaser must return to the landlord a signed contract and a deposit for a maximum of ten per cent of the freehold price. On receipt of the signed contract, the landlord must exchange contracts with the nominee purchaser within seven days or else withdraw from the sale. After the exchange of contract has taken place, completion follows in the manner set out in the contract.

As we saw in chapter 4, if the enfranchisers are served with a Section 5 Notice by the landlord, but they do not agree to buy the freehold at the landlord's asking price, they can carry on with their enfranchisement.

 TOP TIP Enfranchisers who are served and who accept a Right of First Refusal Notice from the landlord proceed directly to agreement on and exchange of a contract of sale, and they skip the normal enfranchisement stages of negotiating with the landlord on the freehold price and applying to the LVT.

The Leasehold Valuation Tribunal hearing and decision

For the minority of enfranchisements that go all the way to the LVT, the hearing at the tribunal can last as little as half a day for the simplest case or as much as three or more days for the most complex. For many large buildings, the procedure lasts two days. The LVT hearing, which is open to members of the public, is meant to be more informal and less intimidating than a formal court case. Enfranchisers can present their own arguments and are not obliged to hire a solicitor, barrister or surveyor. However, leaseholders in most large enfranchisements do instruct such advisers to represent them.

As we saw in chapter 1, each LVT hearing is presided over by a panel comprising two or three members. If the panel has two members, one member is a lawyer and the other is a valuer. A three-member panel comprises a lawyer, a valuer and a layperson specialising in enfranchisement. The tribunal, as part of the Residential Property Tribunal Service, adjudicates on a wide range of disputes between landlords and residents. Contact information on the five regional LVTs in England, which are located in London, Chichester, Cambridge, Birmingham and Manchester, and the Housing Directorate of the Welsh Assembly Government in Cardiff, is provided in the 'Useful contacts' section.

A few weeks prior to a scheduled hearing, the enfranchisers and the landlord will be instructed by the tribunal to send in valuation and related documentation supporting claims for a specific freehold price. During the hearing, each side presents its case. In large enfranchisements, this is typically done by a barrister and a chartered surveyor. After the hearing, the LVT panel will usually visit the property in question. A decision is reached by the panel after the hearing and is sent in writing to both parties, with most panels sending their decision within about six weeks of the hearing. Typically, an LVT decision will run to ten to 20 pages, will present each sides' arguments and will explain the tribunal's decision. Importantly, the decision identifies the price at which the landlord must sell the freehold.

If the nominee purchaser does not wish to buy the freehold at the price determined by the LVT, it can walk away from the deal. It is not allowed, however, to start a new enfranchisement initiative for one year.

The fact that a large majority of enfranchisements are concluded in negotiated agreement, including many in the run-up to a scheduled LVT hearing, has created awkward scheduling problems for the tribunal. In anticipation of many hearings being cancelled at the last minute as a result of settlements reached between enfranchisers and landlords, the tribunal has often purposely overbooked cases. In some instances, leaseholders arrive at the LVT building only to find that their two-day hearing that was scheduled to begin that morning has been bumped off the roster and will not be heard for weeks. This can cause frustration for weary enfranchisement organisers, who are keen to cross the finish line. But leaseholders need to be prepared for this possibility and, if appropriate, to use this as an opportunity to try to reach a negotiated agreement with the landlord in one of the available conference rooms at the tribunal building.

Many leaseholders have complained over the years about what they describe as abuse by large landlords of the LVT system in which landlords fail to send required case documentation by the pre-hearing deadline stated by the tribunal. Many enfranchisers have told me that the tribunal appears to lack crucial legal clout or is unwilling to use such clout to force both parties to send the required bundles of documents on time. It is not unusual for large corporate landlords to send bundles of documents to the LVT days before a scheduled hearing instead of by the stated deadline weeks earlier and for the tribunal panel to accept these documents. Leaseholders appear to have no immediate remedy for this exasperating situation.

 A three-member panel at the LVT normally presides over a hearing lasting two days in the enfranchisement of a large building, although the length of a hearing can vary from a half day to three or more days depending on the complexity of the case.

Appealing a Leasehold Valuation Tribunal decision

Once the LVT has sent its written decision to both parties, either side can appeal the decision to the higher-level Lands Tribunal. However, an appeal can only be made on a point of law and only if written permission to appeal has first been obtained from the LVT or the Lands Tribunal. Any request to appeal must be made to the LVT within 21 days of the LVT decision or by an extension date identified by the LVT. If the LVT refuses a request to appeal, a written request can be made to the Lands Tribunal, but this must be done within 21 days of the LVT refusal. The requirement to get permission to appeal was created with the passage of the Commonhold and Leasehold Reform Act 2002. Prior to the 2002 Act, leaseholders complained of a common practice by some large landlords to appeal regarding any LVT decision not to their liking. Contact information for the Lands Tribunal is provided in the 'Useful contacts' section.

An appeal of an LVT decision to the Lands Tribunal can delay a large enfranchisement by a year. This kind of delay often works in favour of the landlord, since most leaseholders are keen to complete the freehold purchase process as quickly as possible and because delays in the process can prompt participants to drop out. As a result, it is unsurprising that most appeals to the Lands Tribunal are made by landlords rather than enfranchisers. While only a small percentage of LVT decisions are appealed to the Lands Tribunal, leaseholders need to be aware of this risk and of the possibility that an appeal will drag out the process for an extended period of time. Enfranchisement organisers also need to assess whether their landlord is one of the few that is well-known for appealing to the Lands Tribunal. A small number of the biggest residential landlords make effective use of their corporate clout and deep pockets by appealing LVT decisions to the Lands Tribunal, thus increasing delays and costs for enfranchisers and leaving the enfranchisers more amenable to reaching a negotiated settlement.

 The nominee purchaser or landlord can appeal an LVT decision to the higher-level Lands Tribunal, but this can only be done once the relevant party has received written permission to appeal from the LVT or the Lands Tribunal.

Timeline for the exchange of contract and completion of the freehold purchase

When the enfranchisers' nominee purchaser has exchanged contracts with the landlord on the purchase of the freehold, the next step is to complete on the sale. There is no deadline set down in law by which the completion must take place. In some small residential buildings, enfranchisers will exchange and complete with the landlord on the same day, while in large buildings it is best practice to complete on the sale four to six weeks after the exchange of contract.

If the exchange of the contract and completion take place on different dates, a deposit is normally paid by the enfranchisers on exchange and the balance is paid on completion. It is essential for leaseholders to have the money ready and in the right location in time for payment of the deposit and the balance. Normally these funds are transferred from the enfranchisement bank account to the client bank account of the solicitor acting for the enfranchisers. When the deposit and final balance are paid, it is the solicitor acting for the enfranchisers who makes these payments to the solicitor acting for the landlord. When the leaseholders are transferring a large amount of money from the enfranchisement bank account to their solicitor's account, they should talk with their bank manager to ensure that the transfer will go through quickly and smoothly. Many banks, for instance, do not allow account holders to make same-day internet transfers that total more than £50,000.

 There is no timeframe prescribed by law between the exchange of contract and completion in a freehold purchase, but a gap of four to six weeks represents best practice for most large buildings.

Paying service charge arrears as part of the freehold acquisition

It is important for enfranchisers to remember that their nominee purchaser company is likely to have to pay to the landlord, as part of the freehold purchase, any service charges owed by leaseholders in the building. The nominee purchaser, once it has completed the enfranchisement process, has the right to collect these debts from the relevant leaseholders in its capacity as the new freeholder. However, the nominee purchaser must be sure to get the outgoing freeholder to assign the right to collect these debts.

Ideally, the enfranchisers should try to get the leaseholders in the building to clear up any service charge arrears before the freehold purchase process has been concluded. We have seen that this task is easier to accomplish if the leaseholders in the building are participants in the freehold purchase process, since the participants will not want to have to pay any money on top of their share of the freehold cost to cover such service charge arrears.

In chapter 7 we examined troubled buildings in which a significant minority of leaseholders have not joined the enfranchisement and have, over the years, refused to pay their service charges in protest over poor building management. It is not unusual in blocks of flats in central London for leaseholders that have engaged in this kind of 'rent strike' to owe tens of thousands of pounds in service charges by the time their fellow leaseholders have completed a freehold acquisition. This kind of rent strike creates two serious obstacles for project organisers. Firstly, the organisers must raise extra funds from participants or an outside source to pay off these service charge arrears to the landlord at the time of completion of the sale. Secondly, the new resident management company, formerly the nominee purchaser, must chase after residents in the building to get them to pay their arrears. This can represent an unpleasant task for the new resident-owned freeholder and can create tension in the building.

We have seen that organisers should send written reminders throughout the course of the project that participants must keep their service charge payments up to date, to avoid lumbering the nominee purchaser with any of this debt at the end of the project. A second way to drive home the message and also gather crucial information is to carry out an audit of service charge payments amongst participants. It is not recommended for enfranchisers to contact non-participants about the status of service charge payments unless the freehold purchase is believed to be just weeks away, as this can encourage non-participants to ask questions about the status of the confidential freehold purchase project that they have opted not to join.

When leaseholders are approaching the final stages of the enfranchisement process, they need to obtain from the landlord a breakdown of any service charge arrears in the building. Some landlords are forthcoming in providing this information, while others are downright unhelpful. This can be a disheartening moment in the freehold purchase initiative if the organisers are informed of significant arrears, especially regarding money owed by non-participants. Unfortunately, there is little that can be done other than for enfranchisers to raise the necessary finance and pay off the debt, then to have their resident management company collect these arrears from the relevant leaseholders after the enfranchisement has been completed. Organisers should take the necessary action, in the weeks prior to an exchange of the contract of sale, to raise funds in the form of a bank bridging loan, a loan from the participants or another source in order to pay any required service charge arrears.

The conclusion of an enfranchisement often marks a change in culture in a residential building. Before the freehold purchase, disgruntled leaseholders may have expressed their unhappiness about poor building management by withholding their service charges. The practice of non-payment of service charges, however, is rarely tolerated after the leaseholders have bought their freehold. Indeed, resident management companies have an excellent track record for ensuring compliance when it comes to paying service charges, since non-payment equates to a resident forcing his neighbours to finance his presence in the building. In chapter 10 we look at other ways in which the enfranchised building can clean up its act and eradicate inappropriate practices of non-compliance.

> Organisers should take the necessary action, in the weeks prior to an exchange of the contract of sale, to raise funds in the form of a bank bridging loan, a loan from the participants or another source to pay off any required service charge arrears.

Paying the deposit for the freehold

The landlord has a right to require payment of a deposit upon exchange of the contract when leaseholders are collectively enfranchising. The deposit can be for a maximum of ten per cent of the price of the freehold. The enfranchisement organisers should send this deposit to the solicitor handling the freehold acquisition and should ensure that the solicitor has received the money about a week before the anticipated date of exchange, to avoid any possibility of reaching the exchange date without the required funds.

Some enfranchisers decide to collect the share of the freehold cost due from each project participant in two separate tranches, to cover the deposit and the subsequent balance due. However, this is not an advisable approach. The enfranchisers should instead ensure that each participant sends just **one** amount of money to the organising team, to cover both the deposit and the subsequent balance due. There is a very high transaction cost to the organisers of an enfranchisement in collecting money from participants. Because of this, the work involved in this process should be streamlined as much as possible. The transaction cost is paid for by the organisers with their time, rather than cash, so participants often fail to recognise that there is a problem. It is not unusual, for instance, for each participant to communicate with the main organiser three or four times, whether by email or phone, when sending a large payment for a share of the freehold cost. In a building with, say, 50 flats, this means the organiser is being swamped with as many as 200 separate communications while carrying out the task of collecting the money.

 A landlord selling a building freehold in an enfranchisement has the right to require payment by the nominee purchaser on the exchange of the contract of a deposit representing a maximum ten per cent of the freehold price.

Collecting money from enfranchisement participants

Gathering the funds from each participant at the end of an enfranchisement can represent one of the most difficult tasks of the project, especially if the initiative was conceived years earlier. I have heard many accounts from exasperated organisers about leaseholders who started as enthusiastic supporters of a freehold purchase project and who knew throughout the project of expected final costs, yet who expressed surprise when asked at the conclusion of the enfranchisement to pay their money.

This is where a carefully-devised communications strategy is crucial. Organisers of an enfranchisement must provide useful information to participants on cost estimates of the freehold and related items such as the leaseholders' legal and surveyor fees, and the landlord's legal and surveyor fees. But they also need to avoid overloading participants with **too much** information about cost estimates and they must take care not to overwhelm themselves by agreeing to update cost estimates at unreasonably frequent intervals.

We saw in chapter 6 that organisers can usually strike an appropriate balance by sending three cost estimates to enfranchisement participants over the duration of the project. The first is the informal estimate at which the organisers arrive when leaseholders in the building are trying to decide whether to pursue the purchase of the freehold. The second should be provided once the enfranchisement project has started and a formal valuation of the freehold has been carried out by a chartered surveyor. This should advise participants of the conservative estimate made by the chartered surveyor, that is, the amount that participants should be prepared to pay. The third cost estimate should be sent to participants no later than eight weeks before the scheduled exchange of contracts, once the precise cost of the freehold has been determined, whether by negotiated settlement with the landlord or by an LVT.

We have seen that the organisers should send individualised letters identifying the total amount to be paid by all participants and the individual amounts to be paid by the recipients of each letter, with a deadline date. The letters should provide bank details for making the payment by BACS bank transfer or by cheque. The clearer the information provided in this letter, the more likely that the organisers will avoid having to answer the same questions again and again at this busy stage in the project.

I have been asked by leaseholders in many buildings how the cost of the freehold should be allocated amongst participants. There are several cost allocation models, including using the cost breakdown per flat that is provided by the chartered surveyor. However, the model I recommend in most cases is to allocate a share of the freehold cost according to the percentage of service charges paid by all the leaseholders in the building. While each cost allocation model has its own merits and drawbacks, I have found the service charge percentage model to create the fewest problems. One advantage of this model is its simplicity and transparency. It is easy for a participant to understand why he is paying, for instance, two per cent of the cost of the freehold, if this leaseholder is already paying two per cent of the annual service charges in the building. If some residents in a block of flats are not participating in the enfranchisement, it is a simple calculation using an Excel spreadsheet to recalculate the percentages in order to strip out the non-participants and to make service charge percentages of participating flats add up to 100 per cent.

The possible scenario in which one or more participants threaten not to pay their share of the freehold cost at the end of the enfranchisement was examined in chapter 6. The organiser who is communicating with the participant that is threatening non-payment should state in writing that the participant should urgently consult his lawyer on this subject. I have seen instances in which an enfranchisement organiser gets bombarded by phone calls and letters both from the participant threatening non-payment and from the solicitor representing the participant. The organiser is under no obligation to hold two series of bilateral discussions in this instance. To save time and effort, and to avoid any misunderstanding, the organiser should communicate in writing with just one person, say, the participant, and copy each letter to the solicitor.

If a participant fails to pay his share of the freehold cost at the end of the process, the nominee purchaser will have to raise the extra funds from the other participants, a third party inside the building or someone outside the building. In some cases, the nominee purchaser may wish to get a bridging loan from a bank to cover the financing gap. If a significant number of leaseholders in the building have not joined the freehold purchase project and if several of these residents are expected, after the enfranchisement has been concluded, to want to buy lease extensions from the new freeholder, the nominee purchaser should inform the lending bank about these expected funds. Such expectation of lease extension sales will often increase a bank's willingness to lend to a resident-owned freeholder. In some cases, the nominee purchaser might need to raise the amount of annual ground rent payable by all the leaseholders, to cover bank interest charges.

 As soon as the price of the freehold has been determined, each enfranchisement participant should be sent an individual letter by the organising team that identifies the exact amount due for his share of the freehold cost, the deadline date for payment and full details required for payment by BACS bank transfer or cheque.

Selling the freehold interest of a non-payer flat

We have seen that if an enfranchisement participant fails to pay his share of the cost of the freehold, the nominee purchaser needs to take immediate steps to sell the freehold interest of the non-payer's flat. Enfranchisers must remember that, by acquiring the freehold, they are each buying a piece of property. Each participant is buying a share of the entire building and he is also buying the freehold interest for his flat. It is this freehold interest of the flat that enables the participant to get a 999-year lease at the end of the process. By failing to pay the money due, a non-paying participant loses the right to secure the freehold of his flat and thus loses the right to a 999-year lease. The board of directors of the nominee purchase will need to remove the non-payer from the list of shareholders.

The freehold interest of the non-payer flat can be sold to a third party in the form of a head lease for the flat. We saw in chapter 3 how a person, company or other entity can hold a head lease for the entire building, which is an intermediate ownership sitting below that of the freeholder and above that of the leaseholders. Similarly, the head leaseholder of a flat in an enfranchised building would be sold a 999-year head lease for the flat. In this way, if and when the leaseholder or a subsequent leaseholder of the flat wants to buy a lease extension, they would need to buy the lease extension from the head leaseholder.

It is important for enfranchisement organisers to make clear to any participant who threatens not to pay his share of the freehold that, by taking such action, the non-payer will forgo the right to get a share of the freehold and a 999-year lease. The right for leaseholders to collectively enfranchise their building is a one-off right. Once a building has been enfranchised, leaseholders do not have a legal right to enfranchise the building again. An individual leaseholder has the right to compel the landlord, including a resident-owned freeholder company, to sell to the leaseholder a 90-year lease extension, and to do so at a fair market price within a statutory timeframe. But he does not have the right to force the landlord to sell him a share of the freehold of the enfranchised building or a 999-year lease. After the enfranchisement has been concluded, the new resident-owned freeholder might decide to sell a share of the freehold and/or a 999-year lease to the non-participant, but there is no legal obligation to do so.

We have seen that, in the final months of the enfranchisement project, the organisers should carry out a risk management exercise regarding the possible non-payment by one or more participants. They should identify those leaseholders considered most likely to fail to pay their share of the freehold cost. The organisers should also, if possible, identify a potential buyer inside or outside the building for the freehold interest of the non-payer flat. While it is important to have this contingency plan in place, this subject should be handled discretely by the organising team in order not to cause alarm amongst participants. If the nominee purchaser decides to take legal action against a non-payer flat, this should be pursued as a separate action after the enfranchisement has been completed. This kind of litigation should not be allowed to create delay or distraction until the freehold purchase process has finished.

While project organisers need to put in place a contingency plan to sell the freehold interest of any non-payer flat, they should make every reasonable effort to avoid having to sell head leases of individual flats in the building. A central goal of enfranchisement is to streamline the ownership structure in a building by eliminating the ownership layer represented by the outside freeholder. It can be counter productive to introduce at this time a new layer of complexity by creating head leases of individual flats. In any event, many organising teams are able to ensure full payment by all participants of money due at the end of the enfranchisement by communicating clearly in advance the consequences for any would-be non-payer.

 In the final stage of the enfranchisement, the organisers should identify possible buyers inside or outside the building of a 999-year head lease of any non-paying participant flat.

Granting 999-year leases after the freehold purchase

Once the enfranchisers have completed the freehold purchase, they will need to grant themselves new 999-year leases. These leases will show the name of the new freeholder, the nominee purchaser company, which now becomes the resident management company, and the leaseholder of the flat. Some flat owners believe mistakenly that by buying the freehold of the building, they will eliminate the need for leases. This is not correct. The flat owners continue to be leaseholders after the enfranchisement has been concluded, but their leases now have 999 years and they are also shareholders, or joint owners, of the company that owns the freehold of the building.

Organisers of an enfranchisement can arrange with their solicitor to prepare the new leases of participants immediately upon completion of the freehold purchase or they can choose to wait until after the project has ended and the dust has settled. The granting of 999-year leases after an enfranchisement represents an ideal time to get rid of any defects or inconsistencies in the existing leases, and to draft new leases that are in modern form. Many leases for the century-old red-brick mansion blocks located across central London, for instance, have old-fashioned clauses that refer to coal storage or the maintenance of gas lamps. Leaseholders can delete these outdated clauses and can insert clauses regarding the installation of television satellite dishes that are missing from the old leases.

Another important improvement to be made to many leases after an enfranchisement is the insertion of a clause that allows for the freeholder to create and maintain a sinking fund or reserve fund on behalf of the leaseholders. One reason that so many London mansion blocks are poorly-managed is that the leases do not allow for a sinking fund. This means that the service charges must be collected each year for any maintenance, repairs or major works to be carried out in the following year. If a large project, such as roof repairs, is undertaken, then the leaseholders receive one or more staggeringly large service charge invoices. The creation of a sinking fund makes it possible to spread over a period of several years the collection of money from the leaseholders for these big repair projects.

We saw in chapter 4 that the organisers of a freehold purchase, before serving the Enfranchisement Notice on the landlord, should collect all of the existing leases of the participants. This makes it easy, once the enfranchisement has been concluded, for the solicitor acting on behalf of the participants to replace the old leases with the new 999-year leases without delay. If the enfranchisers decide not to prepare the new leases immediately upon completion of the freehold purchase sale, they should take care not to let the process drag on for too long. In some buildings, the organisers of a freehold purchase are so exhausted by the time the process has been completed that they neglect for a year or more to have the 999-year leases created.

Every leaseholder in an enfranchised building gets a new freeholder, whether or not each leaseholder has participated in the freehold purchase project or not. But it is not necessary to replace the leases of the non-participants immediately after the enfranchisement. The Land Registry leasehold title for all flats in the building will need to be updated in order to identify the new freeholder, but non-participants can be left with their existing leases. If and when a non-participant wishes to buy a lease extension, the resident-owned freeholder can grant the new lease at that time.

We have seen that a landlord owning a flat in an enfranchising building can keep this flat by exercising his right to a 'leaseback'. In this case, the nominee purchaser must grant the landlord a 999-year lease for the flat with zero, or a 'peppercorn', ground rent. When the nominee purchaser drafts the leaseback lease, which happens when the contract of sale for the freehold is being agreed, care must be taken not to introduce any clause that does not exist in the other leases in the building, since the landlord has the right to a lease that is consistent with the other leases. However, according to enfranchisement legislation, the landlord has the right to demand that the leaseback lease contain no restrictions on the transfer or assignment of the flat.

 When the enfranchisers grant themselves new 999-year leases after the completion of the freehold purchase process, they should use the opportunity to eliminate defects in and to modernise the leases, including by inserting a clause that allows for creation and maintenance of a sinking fund or reserve fund.

Participants of a large collective enfranchisement are right to feel encouraged as they enter the final phase of the project, since finally the end is in sight. But the organisers are likely to be runners with tired legs, and they need to watch out for events that can cause them to stumble and fall before crossing the finish line. One pitfall to avoid, as we have seen, is the deemed withdrawal that results if the enfranchisers fail to exchange a contract of sale for the freehold with the landlord within four months of reaching a negotiated agreement.

Another obstacle that can trip up our weary athlete is an appeal by the landlord to the Lands Tribunal of a decision by the LVT. By foreseeing this possibility, enfranchisement organisers can prepare the participants and then, if necessary, retrain their sights on a longer race.

We have seen in this chapter how a freehold purchase project can be disrupted, even destroyed, if the nominee purchaser is forced to pay off large service arrears to the landlord as part of the enfranchisement. Organisers can help eliminate or diminish this problem by impressing on the participants early in the project the importance of keeping all service charge payments up to date. We have also reviewed ways in which to handle one of the most stressful events of a large enfranchisement, when one or more participants fails to pay his or their share of the freehold cost at the end of the process. By planning for this possibility, organisers can limit the disruption caused by threatened non-payment. In the event that a participant fails to pay the money due, enfranchisers can proceed swiftly with the contingency plan I have identified in order to ensure that the freehold purchase project does not grind to a halt.

Thoughtful planning is essential throughout the process to ensure a successful enfranchisement. But the project will benefit in particular if organisers are far-sighted and review carefully at the **start** of the process what is likely to be happening at the **end**. The more that organisers can identify the steps required at the conclusion of the project, the more time and effort they will save themselves early on. For many enfranchisers, the freehold purchase understandably becomes the do-or-die event, with all enfranchisement activity ceasing after the exchange of contract and the completion of the acquisition. While it is fine to take a break following such a gargantuan undertaking, we have seen that it is important for the participants to get on with the business of granting themselves 999-year leases rather than to delay completion of this essential task.

CHAPTER 10

Beating burnout

The long-anticipated event finally occurs. The nominee purchaser company that was set up by the enfranchisers early in the project exchanges a contract of sale with the landlord for the freehold. The two parties agree that the completion of the sale will take place in six weeks. This is often a time for rejoicing amongst participants in a large building where overseeing the freehold purchase process to a successful conclusion has probably taken years. But the small number of individuals – or, in many buildings, the one person – responsible for getting most of the work done are often too tired to celebrate. In fact, it is not unusual for organisers of an enfranchisement to feel so burnt out by the process that they cease all involvement after the freehold has been bought.

This is a situation to be avoided. The long-distance runner who crosses the finish line, only to collapse a few yards further along and to spend the next few weeks in hospital, cannot be considered to have run a worthwhile race. I have seen large enfranchisements take a terrible toll on organisers by swamping them with unpaid work that damages their family life, careers and even health. It is important for organisers to recognise these problems early on and take action to ensure that they are not being overwhelmed by the end of the project.

Many newly-enfranchised buildings end up leaderless and in chaos for a different reason, when organisers of the project sell their flats and move from the building. We have seen that leaseholders in many large blocks of flats represent a fluid, ever-changing constituency. From the time leaseholders start to organise an enfranchisement in a large building until they have completed the project, it is not unusual for several flats to change hands.

This chapter addresses ways in which organisers of an enfranchisement can avoid experiencing burnout after the freehold purchase is completed. In addition, we look at practical strategies for running the resident management company, which started out as the nominee purchaser and is now the freeholder company. These strategies are aimed at establishing efficient processes that ensure good corporate governance and compliance, while decreasing the workload for the directors who normally work on a volunteer unpaid basis.

If directors of the resident management company fail to take action to avoid being swamped with work after the enfranchisement has been concluded, the freehold purchase can represent for them a Pyrrhic victory. This is, unfortunately, the case in many buildings where the enfranchisement organisers and participants insist on reinventing the wheel instead of following best-practice models for running a resident management company.

Why organiser burnout scuppers many freehold purchase projects

Because of the volunteer nature of the work involved in organising and supervising an enfranchisement, many participants fail to appreciate how much time and effort is spent by organisers. Many organisers have complained to me that participants seem to assume that organisers are doing this volunteer work because they have spare time to fill. We have seen that organisers need to set limits on the work they will do during an enfranchisement, including time spent communicating with participants. We have also identified the need for organisers to demand an appropriate level of commitment to the project and co-operation from the participants. In the absence of these safeguards, organisers can find themselves so weary and fed up at the end that the natural decision is to quit.

Organisers and participants can avoid a situation in which the organisers jump ship after the freehold has been purchased if they recognise the changing structure with which they are working. What started out as an informal residents' group is now a resident management company. The directors of this company must comply with the Companies Act and they are obliged by law to act in the interests of the shareholders, who own the company and who appoint the directors.

Many directors of resident management companies find themselves inundated with work in the months after an enfranchisement has been completed because they fail to create labour-saving procedures for an efficient, sustainable company structure. Too many participants of enfranchisements believe that anything goes regarding the manner in which their residential building can be run after the freehold purchase. They are mistaken. Enfranchisement must not be allowed to result in a free-for-all in the building. One common error is for enfranchisement participants to believe that the leases of flats in the building are no longer relevant after the freehold has been bought. This is incorrect. All leaseholders in the building continue to be leaseholders and their rights are defined in their leases, which continue to serve as a contract between the flat owner and the freeholder.

 Many freehold purchase initiatives collapse because the organisers become overwhelmed by the work involved and they drop out.

Importance of outsourcing for the resident management company

One of the most important ways in which directors of the resident management company can avoid burnout and create efficient procedures is to outsource certain functions. Buildings that experience organisational problems after leaseholders have bought the freehold are frequently those in which directors of the resident management company have been trying to do too much. This can result in a failure by the directors to carry out the work to an acceptable standard and/or the departure of one or more directors who refuse to carry on.

The work of the company secretary in a large residential building is one of the functions that I recommend be outsourced. In chapter 4, we saw that it is best practice for the nominee purchaser, which is set up early in an enfranchisement and that becomes the resident management company after the freehold purchase, to be incorporated as a limited company. We have seen that a limited company in England and Wales must have a minimum of one director and a company secretary, and the two cannot be the same person.

There are many service provider companies that carry out the work of the company secretary on an outsourced basis. One such company is Jordans Limited, which is based in Bristol. Jordans not only provides company secretary services, but it also specialises in doing this for resident management companies and offers a package for company incorporation, a company secretary service and the rental of a registered office address. Contact details for Jordans Limited are provided in the 'Useful contacts' section at the end of the book. Later in the chapter we look at the main tasks of the company secretary within a resident management company.

Another function that I suggest be outsourced by the resident management company is the preparation of the annual accounts. A qualified accountant or accountancy firm should be hired to prepare a Profit and Loss Account, and Balance Sheet for the latest financial year of the company.

A third function that I strongly urge resident management companies to outsource is the management of the building. Some enfranchisers proudly announce, once they have bought their freehold, that they are saving leaseholders money by sacking the managing agent and managing the building themselves. While this might work in a building with two or three flats, there are three reasons why it is a bad idea in a larger building. Firstly, it represents a false economy to claim that the leaseholders are being saved money, since it is likely that one or two directors of the resident management company are doing the work of the managing agent on an unpaid basis. They are thus subsidising others in the building. Secondly, it is unadvisable for the resident management company to manage the building because this is not the core competence of residents. All leaseholders in the building stand to benefit from hiring a professional managing agent firm. Finally, chaos often results when a director of a resident management company who has been managing a building on a volunteer basis sells his flat and leaves the building. The board of directors must put in place a workable system that is sustainable over time, even if one or more directors leave.

One area that cannot be outsourced by the resident management company is the responsibility of the board of directors to the company's shareholders. Too many directors of resident management companies fail to recognise that it is the shareholders that own the company and that appoint the directors to run it. Similarly, the board cannot rely on others to ensure that the company is run in a matter that is based on honesty and integrity. These are business-critical issues that can only be guaranteed by the board.

 Organisers of a collective enfranchisement should outsource the work of a company secretary, accountant and managing agent in order to create efficient procedures and to keep the board's workload to a reasonable level.

Avoiding being struck off at Companies House

Every year a large number of resident management companies are 'struck off' by Companies House, the government body that registers all companies and maintains their public file. The act of being struck off is the equivalent for a company of being declared dead. This can happen if a company fails to file required documentation on time with Companies House. The fact that resident management companies are the one category of company most often struck off each year reveals the alarmingly low standard of corporate governance found in many of these organisations.

When a company is struck off, all assets of the company officially become 'bona vacantia', which is Latin for 'ownerless goods'. When a resident management company is struck off, the freehold and all other company assets automatically become property of the Crown and are dealt with by the Crown's nominee government body, the Treasury Solicitor. To resuscitate the company and reverse this process, one must get the company 'restored'. This can take months of liaising with several government bodies and can cost more than £1,000. It is essential for the board of directors of the resident management company to put in place a system for ensuring that the company is not struck off. One of the best ways to do so, as we saw earlier in the chapter, is to hire a professional service provider to carry out the company secretary work.

Directors of the resident management company must ensure full compliance with Companies House's filing requirements, to avoid seeing the company struck off.

Company secretary work of the resident management company

We have seen that the board of directors is responsible for ensuring that the company is run in a manner that is based on honesty and integrity, and that serves the interest of shareholders. But in the company's day-to-day operations, it is the responsibility of the company secretary to ensure that any documents that need to be filed at Companies House get filed correctly and on time.

It is important for each director to be familiar with the accounts and the Annual Return that are filed with Companies House by the company secretary. Companies House publishes a useful free pamphlet called '*Flat management companies*' which explains what must be filed. The board of directors and shareholders can obtain the pamphlet by phoning Companies House on the number provided in the 'Useful contacts' section.

If the company accounts are prepared by an accountancy firm, it will often be the firm instead of the company secretary that files the accounts with Companies House. The accounts should contain a Profit and Loss Account, and Balance Sheet for the past two years.

The Annual Return, which is known at Companies House as Form 363, lists the company's registered address, and the name and address of the directors, the company secretary and shareholders. The return also identifies the amount of share capital. Companies House charges a £30 filing fee if the Annual Return is filed by post and a £15 filing fee if it is done electronically.

Other forms must be filed with Companies House to maintain an updated public file of the company. These forms include:

- Form 10, to identify founding directors and the company secretary on incorporation;

- Form 288C, for the change of address of a director;

- Form 288A, for the appointment of a director or company secretary after incorporation; and

- Form 288B, for the termination of the appointment of a director or company secretary.

These forms, copies of which are provided in Appendices 23 to 26, can be downloaded at www.companieshouse.gov.uk or obtained by post by contacting Companies House.

Another responsibility of the company secretary is to ensure that all share certificates remain up to date. We have seen that it is best practice for resident management companies to have a clause in their Memorandum and Articles of Association ('MemArts') that bans any person or entity that is not a leaseholder of a flat in the building from being a shareholder. We have also examined why it is important for the MemArts to have a clause that requires any shareholder selling his flat to sign a share transfer form to enable the company to transfer the shares to the buyer.

It is easier said than done to keep share certificates up to date. Even if the resident management company hires a professional company secretary, the company director with an overview of the share certificates can still spend a lot of time chasing after the required forms. As we have seen, much time and effort can be saved by getting the seller of a shareholder flat to sign but not date a J30 Stock Transfer Form as soon as he decides to sell the flat. Once the flat has been sold and the leasehold title at the Land Registry has been updated to include the name of the new leaseholder, the resident management company can have its company secretary destroy the old share certificate and issue a new one.

While I recommend that any sizable resident management company outsource the work of the company secretary, the board should still appoint one director to act as shadow company secretary. This person should keep all the essential company documents, including Annual General Meeting (AGM) documentation, minutes of board meetings, the MemArts and, if appropriate, the original share certificates. In some cases, the board may wish for the company secretary to hold the original share certificates. If so, the shadow company secretary should keep an updated set of photocopies of the share certificates.

The responsibilities of the company secretary of the resident management company include filing with Companies House an annual set of accounts and an Annual Return, which contains names and addresses of the directors and shareholders, and transferring share certificates when shareholder flats are sold.

AGM of the resident management company

Many volunteer directors of resident management companies groan when the time arrives to prepare documentation for the AGM. This is because many hours of detailed work are required. The board of directors must take care to send out the proper documentation, to send it on time and to send it to all the shareholders. The MemArts will normally state the minimum number of days' notice that must be provided to all shareholders regarding the date, time and location of the AGM.

There is no prescribed format for AGM documentation, but it is best practice for a resident management company to send the following to the shareholders along with a notice of the upcoming AGM:

- A proxy form that a shareholder can use to vote if he will not attend the meeting.

- Minutes of the previous AGM.

- A list of ordinary resolutions on which shareholders will vote.

- A list of any special resolutions on which shareholders will vote and explanatory information.

- A Profit and Loss Account, and a Balance Sheet for the last two financial years.

- A directors' report on important events and developments in the past year.

Some resident management companies bemoan the fact that many of their leaseholders live outside the UK, but the existence of absentee leaseholders should pose no problem for the running of a good AGM. The board must remember that all shareholders are to be treated equally. Whether shareholders live in the building or on the other side of the world, they all bear the same responsibility to pay their service charges.

The documentation sent prior to the AGM should state that any shareholder using a proxy form to vote must send in the form well before the meeting, for instance, one week before. This helps to avoid a last-minute scramble by directors in counting shareholder votes before the AGM.

I have attended many AGMs of volunteer organisations during which one 'block vote' is held for the entire committee by a show of hands. This is not best practice. Instead, shareholders should be asked to vote – for, against or abstain – for each director. While it takes a few more minutes to carry out voting in this way, it is the proper way to conduct the process. It also sends an important message to the shareholders about good corporate governance and about the shareholders' rights in appointing the directors.

Although it requires significant preparation work by the directors, the AGM provides a valuable, unique forum for shareholders of the resident management company. The AGM represents the one time during the year that any shareholder is guaranteed the chance to express his views, including any criticism about the way the company is being run. While it is reasonable for volunteer directors to require that shareholders show an appropriate level of commitment to and co-operation with the board, the board must also remember that it is the shareholders, not the board, that own the company, and that appoint and remove directors.

 The resident management company must hold an AGM each year and must send a notice of the meeting and related documentation to all shareholders as set out in the MemArts.

Directors' insurance for the resident management company

Some leaseholders are hesitant to serve as directors of a resident management company because they are afraid of the legal liability involved, including the possibility of being sued by a shareholder. The best-practice solution is for directors' insurance to be provided for all directors and for the company to pay for this insurance. While these directors are making an important commitment to the shareholders by carrying out this volunteer work, the provision of directors' insurance is one way in which shareholders show they are prepared to provide the necessary conditions for the directors to work effectively.

There are many companies that provide directors' insurance. Boards of resident management companies should be able to obtain a directors' insurance package covering all directors for an annual fee of £600. St Giles Insurance & Finance Services Limited in Liverpool provides a directors' insurance package that covers the whole board for just over £600 per year. Contact details for St Giles are provided in the 'Useful contacts' section.

 It is best practice for the directors of a resident management company to have directors' insurance against possible litigation and for this insurance to be paid for by the company.

Addressing queries from shareholders

Enfranchisement organisers have been telling me for years that one of the most time-consuming tasks of the freehold purchase project is communicating with participants, including sending periodic update notes and answering queries. It is important that this requirement to communicate with participants must not be allowed to overwhelm the project organisers or they may walk away from the enfranchisement initiative.

At the earliest stage, a freehold purchase project in a large block of flats gets off the ground when there is strong consensus amongst the participants and this consensus is built with effective communication. Not only do the organisers need to communicate well with the participants to keep the project moving forward, but they often end up doing some of the work that should normally be done by a managing agent, including receiving resident input about management problems in the building.

But the organisers who carried out the information blitz when the enfranchisement project was initiated must adopt a more sustainable communications strategy after the freehold has been acquired. A failure to do so is likely to result in burnout by the organisers, who by now are often directors of the resident management company. The directors should keep shareholders informed of shareholder issues by sending an update note at appropriate intervals. But they should decline to serve as recipients for any and all resident feedback about the building. Queries or input about building management issues need to be referred to the managing agent who is being paid to run the building.

 The resident management company should keep shareholders informed of shareholder issues by sending a periodic update note, but should leave the managing agent to answer queries about the management of the building.

Addressing queries from non-shareholders

The board of directors of the resident management company faces a different challenge when addressing queries and other communications from leaseholders in the building who are not shareholders. It is important for the board to address this issue and to have a plan in place, since leaseholders who decline to join a freehold purchase project in the early stages, when the success of the project is not guaranteed, often want to join after the work has been done and the enfranchisement has been completed.

In this situation, it is important for directors to maintain a clear distinction between the rights and responsibilities of the leaseholders in the building and of the shareholders. All leaseholders in a block of flats continue to be leaseholders after a freehold has been acquired through an enfranchisement. While participants of the project are normally granted 999-year leases by the resident management company, the number of years left on non-participant leases remains unchanged.

It is the job of the managing agent company, as instructed by the resident management company, to ensure that the rights of leaseholders are protected through full and proper enforcement of the leases. For this reason, the board of directors of the resident management company should refer any queries or input from non-shareholders about building management issues to the managing agent.

The board of directors has a different responsibility to shareholders than it does to non-shareholders, because it is the shareholders that own the resident management company. The board must stay focused on its job, which is often a busy one after the freehold has been purchased. One of the main tasks is to grant 999-year leases to shareholders and, in so doing, to eliminate any defects in the lease.

As directors prioritise their communications work, they need to avoid being drawn into unproductive debates with non-shareholders who take a 'sour grapes' view after the freehold has been purchased. Board members should restrict regular discussions in the building to shareholder-related matters with the shareholders who took a financial and personal risk by joining the enfranchisement. Board members need to steer clear of bilateral debates with non-shareholders who chose not to take part.

 After the enfranchisement has been completed, the resident management company should refer any queries from non-shareholders about building management to the managing agent and should avoid getting into personal bilateral debates with non-shareholders about the freehold company.

Bringing in non-participants after the enfranchisement

It is a common occurrence for leaseholders that decline to join an enfranchisement initiative at the beginning to contact the resident management company after the freehold has been purchased and to express a desire to obtain a 999-year lease and a share of the freehold. This can be an exasperating moment for the directors of the company, especially if they were involved in organising the enfranchisement from the start and were told 'no thanks' when they invited these non-participants to join.

The board has two main options in responding to such a request. The first option is to say 'no'. As we saw, the right for leaseholders to collectively enfranchise their building is a one-off right. Once the building has been enfranchised, leaseholders do not have the legal right to enfranchise it again. Similarly, a leaseholder who declined an invitation to join an enfranchisement has no legal right, after the freehold has been purchased by participating residents, to demand to be sold a 999-year lease and/or a share of the freehold. The non-participant, like any other leaseholder, does have a right, however, to compel the resident management company to sell to him a **90-year** lease extension.

The second option is for the board of directors to sell to the non-participant a 999-year lease and/or a share of the freehold. Although the resident management company cannot be legally compelled to do so by the non-participant, the company might decide that such a sale is in the best interests of the shareholders.

In a block of flats that has just been enfranchised, the resident management company will often aim to complete all the work required for granting 999-year leases for the shareholders before entering into discussions about possible lease extensions for the non-shareholders. Once the 999-year leases for the shareholders have been granted, the resident management company may decide to offer lease extensions, whether for 90 or 999 years, to the non-shareholders and, in so doing, to identify an asking price and a deadline date by which a deposit is required to accept the offer. In this way, the resident management company can create an incentive for each non-shareholder to buy a lease extension within an identified period of time and can manage the process efficiently. If a non-shareholder does not wish to buy a lease extension at the asking price, he has the option to do nothing or alternatively to seek to buy a 90-year lease extension through the statutory route. If the non-shareholder pursues the statutory route, he will be liable to pay legal and surveyor fees incurred by the resident management company in handling the statutory notice.

There can be complications when inviting non-participants after an enfranchisement to become shareholders of the resident management company. The board of directors must protect the interest of the shareholders by avoiding any unfair dilution of the financial interest of the founding shareholders. The financial interest of the shareholders can be damaged, for instance, if the shares of the freehold are sold to the non-participants after the enfranchisement has been concluded and if these newly-arriving shareholders enjoy equal rights to company dividends as do founding shareholders. Many resident management companies, when they sell lease extensions to non-participants after an enfranchisement, pay out these funds in the form of dividends to shareholders or else use the funds to repay loans made by the shareholders for the freehold purchase.

Some accountancy firms recommend the establishment of two separate companies in a newly-enfranchised block of flats to address this issue, to achieve tax efficiency and provide organisational clarity. The first company is the resident management company that was previously set up by the enfranchisers as the nominee purchaser. This company, which owns the building freehold, is run as a 'non-mutual trading company'. Its only function is to receive ground rent and to sell lease extensions. The second company, which is set up after the freehold purchase, is a 'mutual trading company' whose function is to collect service charges. The non-mutual trading company is liable for Corporation Tax, while the mutual trading company is not. The mutual trading company only pays tax on bank interest. One disadvantage to setting up the second company, the mutual trading company, is that all leaseholders in the building must become members or shareholders in order to achieve mutual trading company status. The other disadvantage is that the creation of two companies introduces a new layer of complexity and usually more work for the volunteer company directors.

 A resident management company created as part of an enfranchisement can be compelled to sell a 90-year lease extension and to do so at a fair market price within a statutory timeframe, but there is no legal obligation to sell a 999-year lease or a share of the freehold.

Collecting service charge arrears after the enfranchisement

By the time the enfranchisers have completed a freehold purchase, they are likely to know the precise amount of any service charge arrears in the building. As we saw in chapter 9, some freehold purchase initiatives collapse in the final stage when the landlord reveals to the participants a large amount of service charge arrears and obliges the nominee purchaser to pay the arrears. Once the enfranchisers get beyond this obstacle and have completed the freehold acquisition, they should take immediate action to enforce full and prompt service charge payment.

It is the responsibility of the managing agent who is running the building to calculate the amount of service charges due by each leaseholder, to send the invoices and to collect the money. But many managing agents take their lead from the freeholder company, whether it is a corporate landlord or a resident management company, to determine the degree to which full payment compliance will be enforced.

The directors of a resident management company usually have a lot of work to do in the months following the freehold acquisition. But they must waste no time in spreading the message that non-payment of service charges will not be tolerated. If a leaseholder fails to pay his service charge invoice by the due date, the managing agent, a solicitor or other professional adviser should be instructed to take swift action by demanding in writing that payment be made and by applying to the Leasehold Valuation Tribunal (LVT) for a determination of the reasonableness of the service charges if payment is not received. Armed with an LVT determination, the resident management company can go to the County Court to request the commencement of forfeiture proceedings. It is possible, although not easy, for a freeholder to secure forfeiture of a flat in the event of non-payment of service charges. It should be noted that a flat cannot be forfeited unless there are more than £350 in unpaid service charges or if the charges have remained unpaid for three years or more. A resident management company can also contact the mortgage lender of a non-paying leaseholder and demand payment of the service charges. Whichever route is followed, the resident management company must send out a clear message to leaseholders that non-payment of service charges will not be allowed.

After years of hard work, the leaseholders who now own the freehold, in their capacity as shareholders of the resident management company, need to join forces to establish in the building a culture of compliance by the leaseholders and the freeholder with all clauses in the lease. Some resident management companies succeed in eradicating virtually overnight any problem of non-payment of service charges by distributing to all residents a list of names of leaseholders who owe service charges and the amounts owed. This 'name and shame' tactic often results in non-payers quickly clearing up their debt.

The resident management company that becomes the freeholder after an enfranchisement should use the change in ownership to eliminate any culture of non-payment of service charges in the building.

Leaseholders of flats should welcome the fact that, since the passage of the Commonhold and Leasehold Reform Act 2002, they have enjoyed expanded legal rights to enfranchise their building. But this does not mean that reaching the conclusion of an enfranchisement is easy. The process presents so many pitfalls for leaseholders and so many opportunities for landlords to create delays, distraction and increased costs for enfranchisers, that many project organisers cross the finish line in an exhausted state. We have examined in this chapter several ways in which to help weary enfranchisement organisers avoid burnout after the freehold has finally been bought.

Solicitors and chartered surveyors who advise leaseholders on enfranchisement often fail to appreciate the enormous amount of unpaid work that is required by these flat owners to reach the end of the process. A newly-enfranchised building can be thrown into chaos if one or more directors of the resident management company are overwhelmed by the workload and quit. Participants of the project, who are now shareholders of the resident management company, should work actively towards preventing any such disintegration of the board. But they also need to be ready for the possibility that one or more directors will move from the building.

We have reviewed in this chapter the urgent need for the board to establish procedures that ensure good corporate governance and compliance of the resident management company, while also creating labour-saving efficiencies. In large blocks of flats, this includes outsourcing the work of the company secretary, hiring an outside accountant or accountancy firm to prepare the annual accounts and instructing a managing agent to run the building. Above all, the resident management company must ensure the full enforcement of all leases and must not allow the freehold purchase to be interpreted by any resident as the introduction of a free-for-all in the building.

Resident management companies in newly-enfranchised buildings must be careful to file all the required documents with Companies House, to avoid the cost and inconvenience created if the company gets struck off. Directors should make clear their commitment to shareholders and should require that shareholders provide the tools needed to do the job, including directors' insurance paid for by the company. We have seen the importance for directors to show good corporate governance in the preparation and running of the AGM, a unique forum each year in which all shareholders can express their views.

This chapter has analysed ways in which directors of a resident management company can avoid being swamped by communication from shareholders and how they should handle queries and input from leaseholders who declined to join the enfranchisement at the beginning. We have provided best-practice models for directors to address whether or not to sell 999-year leases and/or a share of the freehold to the minority of non-shareholders in the building. Finally, we have urged the boards of resident management companies to establish a culture of compliance regarding payment of service charges as soon as the enfranchisers have completed the freehold acquisition.

It is unusual for organisers to get all the way to the end of a large enfranchisement without feeling bone tired, like the marathon runner reaching the end of the race. However, by following best practice, by refusing to reinvent the wheel and by outsourcing appropriate functions, it is possible for volunteer directors to run a resident management company in a manner that is efficient and labour-effective, while also exemplifying good corporate governance.

Conclusion

Over the course of ten chapters, we have followed the long-distance race that is the collective enfranchisement. We have seen that the runner needs more than strong legs to get through all the preparatory work before the race begins, to stay on track in the months that follow the serving of the Enfranchisement Notice and to cross the finish line, once the freehold has been purchased and 999-year leases have been granted to the participating flats. We have reviewed the ways that landmark legislation, the Leasehold Reform, Housing and Urban Development Act 1993 and the Commonhold and Leasehold Reform Act 2002, has created important new rights for leaseholders of flats to compel their landlord to sell to them their building freehold, but we have also analysed the numerous ways in which many enfranchisement initiatives fail.

Having the legal right to buy one's building freehold does not mean that all flat owners should pursue this option. In the best of circumstances, it is an ambitious project. In a large block of flats, the process of organising an enfranchisement and seeing the project through to completion can take years. The 1993 Act and the 2002 Act, while providing important new legal ammunition for those wishing to buy their freehold, also make the process extremely difficult for many leaseholders. In the view of many owners of flats, these laws remain heavily skewed in favour of the landlord by providing loopholes that enable the freeholder to foil the freehold purchase initiative.

If leaseholders are to succeed in buying their freehold, they must understand the unique difficulties presented by this unusual project. Over the years many flat owners have described to me the terrible personal cost they paid for organising and supervising a large enfranchisement. These costs were borne in terms of damage caused by the workload and related stress of the project on the family and professional lives of the organisers, and, in several instances, on their health.

Organisers of an enfranchisement need to take specific action to avoid paying these hidden costs. The practical advice provided in this book and highlighted in the '100 top tips' should assist leaseholders in steering clear of pitfalls that cause many freehold purchase projects to collapse. While the legislation favours the landlord, it is ironic that it is often the participants of enfranchisements, not the landlord, who are responsible for the failure of these projects. By reading this book, leaseholders can equip themselves with the knowledge they need to make it successfully to the end of what is often an all-engrossing process.

We have seen that many leaseholders suffer from a crippling disadvantage in an enfranchisement because of their organisational weakness vis-à-vis the large corporate landlord. The challenge is great for the residents' association, which is typically a flat hierarchical structure whose leaders have little if any formal authority for getting things done. In many large blocks of flats, residents' associations are geographically decentralised, with many members living in other countries and renting out their London flats. We have examined the large corporate landlord that, on the other hand, often has a vertical command-and-control hierarchical structure, with paid employees whose job it is to protect the value and continued ownership of the company's property assets.

The book has addressed the many ways in which enfranchisers must overcome this David-and-Goliath mismatch if they are successfully to conclude the project. One way is for the residents' association committee, at the start of the project, to secure members' agreement that a sharp focus be applied to the single goal of purchasing the freehold and that the committee not get bogged down in time-wasting disputes with the landlord over service charges.

Leaseholders who complete enfranchisements in the quickest, most painless manner are usually those that identify a clear deadline at the start for those wishing to join the project. A surprisingly large number of flat owners have told me that 'we are in the process of buying our freehold', when, in fact, they mean that they have spent the last several years talking about the project without ever getting it started. Chapter 1 has identified the key steps for getting an enfranchisement off the ground. Organisers also need to know when to walk away from a freehold purchase project, including when fewer than 50 per cent of flats in the building are willing to sign up, and they should be flexible in choosing a phased approach, by getting lease extensions and/or the right to manage.

Many enfranchisements unravel because the organisers take on too much of the work and then they burnout or move away from the building. We have examined the ways in which enfranchisers can build sustainable processes that can outlive the presence of the original organising team. One important example is outsourcing the project management of the freehold purchase. While, years ago, leaseholders were more prepared to project manage an enfranchisement on a volunteer, unpaid basis, today's increasingly cash-rich, time-starved flat owners are more likely to hire a professional project manager who will take ownership of this complex endeavour. By instructing a project manager, leaseholders increase the chance of success for their enfranchisement, since an experienced project manager will bring in a chartered surveyor and solicitor with essential knowledge of this specialist area of residential property.

For leaseholders that choose to carry out the project management work themselves, we have identified the importance of hiring a surveyor and a solicitor with an established track record in enfranchisement. Whether or not enfranchisers instruct an outside project manager, they need to be familiar with the main documents used during the process and the basic principles in valuing a freehold. Chapter 2 has guided the reader step by step through a process that too many professional advisers describe as impenetrable. One of the key documents we examined was the Participation Agreement, which can help prevent the number of participants of the enfranchisement from dwindling over time.

In chapter 3 we saw that a basic understanding of concepts such as marriage value, development value and hope value can help enfranchisers ensure that the surveyor instructed by their project manager or by themselves has provided a robust valuation of the freehold before they serve their Enfranchisement Notice on the landlord.

The chances for a freehold purchase to succeed are strongly enhanced if the organisers set up a resident management company that embodies good corporate governance. We reviewed in chapter 4 how to set up and run such a company. We also identified the importance of distinguishing this entity, whose directors must comply with the Companies Act, from the less complex residents' association. Enfranchisers need to ensure good quality control in other areas as well as they complete the preparatory phase. This includes presenting an offer price in the Enfranchisement Notice that is to be served on the landlord that is a realistic offer, which can be substantiated by valuation evidence. By ensuring this, leaseholders diminish the likelihood that the freeholder will drag them into the County Court on a claim that the offer price is so low as to be unrealistic.

Although leaseholders have often completed most of the required work of a freehold purchase project by the time they serve the Enfranchisement Notice, they must stay on top of the situation once the official process begins. Chapter 5 has mapped out numerous steps with which the organisers need to hold the project together. This includes ensuring that each milestone is reached. In handling the Counter Notice that is served by the landlord, in applying to the Leasehold Valuation Tribunal (LVT) and in commencing negotiations with the freeholder, enfranchisers need to stay focused on statutory deadlines. Many freehold purchase initiatives have ended in tears after enfranchisers missed a statutory deadline and, since this equated to a 'deemed withdrawal', they had to wait a year to start the process again.

Many enfranchisement initiatives have unravelled after a few months because the organisers failed at the beginning to formalise and lock in the commitment to the project by all the participants. Chapter 6 has provided a best-practice model for ensuring that the number of participants remains constant through to the end, when the freehold purchase is completed. While the enthusiasm and moral authority of organisers represent key components for getting a large enfranchisement off the ground, the organisers must use the Participation Agreement and other formalised structures in the ensuing months to maintain momentum and keep the project moving forward.

The 1993 Act and the 2002 Act are meant to empower leaseholders of flats; they provide no clue as to what to do when one's neighbours get nasty during a freehold purchase initiative. Enfranchisers must be ready for this possibility and must steel themselves for any unpleasantness. In chapter 7 we have addressed the unfortunate, but all too frequent, situation in which one or more residents in a building not only oppose a freehold purchase project, but take steps to try to sabotage the venture. Enfranchisers need to address this situation in a no-nonsense, businesslike manner, especially when it involves leaseholders who decline to participate because they do not wish to pay significant service charge arrears for their flat.

Since a large majority of enfranchisements are concluded in a negotiated agreement with the landlord and never make it all the way to an LVT, we have examined the ways to reach such a settlement. In chapter 8 we have seen that landlords enjoy a tax advantage regarding capital gains rollover relief if they sell a freehold after being served an Enfranchisement Notice. This tax advantage makes it far more likely for the landlord, even if he is a willing seller, to reach a negotiated settlement with leaseholders only **after** being served with an Enfranchisement Notice, rather than before.

Flexibility is essential if the leaseholders are to succeed in enfranchising a large block of flats. Organisers must be prepared to cross the finish line in one of three main ways, as we have seen in chapter 9. They should be ready to agree a negotiated settlement with the landlord, if the opportunity arises. Failing this, enfranchisers need to be prepared to take their case all the way to an LVT, which will decide on the price at which the landlord will sell. Finally, flat owners must not be caught off guard if, when they are preparing to enfranchise, the landlord sends them a legal notification offering to sell them the freehold through the right-of-first-refusal process.

One of the worst nightmares for an enfranchisement organiser is the refusal of one or more participants to pay their share of the cost of the freehold at the end of the process. At best, such a possibility creates enormous stress for organisers. At worst, such a failure to pay can ruin a freehold purchase project. In chapter 9 we have reviewed emergency measures to be put in place by enfranchisers in case a participant fails to pay money due, including selling to a third party a 999-year head lease of the non-payer's flat. We have also presented practical solutions for enfranchisers that discover, late in the game, that they will have to pay off substantial service charge arrears as part of the freehold acquisition.

Enfranchisement organisers have represented the determined marathon runners of our story. By the time they cross the finish line, their leg muscles are burning. So, they need to plan carefully, from the earliest stages of the project, to ensure that business-critical tasks get completed at the end. This includes granting 999-year leases to participants after the freehold has been acquired and, if appropriate, using this as an opportunity to eliminate defects in the lease.

Buying one's freehold is only a course worth attempting if the athlete can cross the finish line and still be standing. For an enfranchisement to succeed over the long term, organisers must put in place processes and procedures that follow best practice, while keeping to a minimum the amount of work being done by the volunteer, unpaid directors of the resident management company. In chapter 10 we have seen the crucial aspect of outsourcing for these companies. While leaseholders need to get involved in order to get a freehold purchase project off the ground, they should **not**, for instance, take on the task of managing their building after the enfranchisement has been completed. This work should be outsourced to a managing agent company that has the required experience and expertise, and that will be accountable in a professional and transparent manner to the resident management company.

We have seen that two other areas that should be outsourced by the resident management company are the role of the company secretary and the preparation of the annual accounts. The company is more likely to ensure good corporate governance by hiring a qualified accountant to prepare the Profit and Loss Account, and Balance Sheet each year, rather than by depending on volunteer work in this area by a resident in the building. The resident management company is also more likely to comply with the filing requirements of Companies House if it hires a specialist company to perform the work of the company secretary. This will, amongst other things, help the company avoid being struck off by Companies House, a fate suffered by a shockingly large number of resident management companies each year.

Residential buildings that have suffered from shoddy management and short leases are often those that choose to gain control of their destiny by enfranchising. This means that, by the time the freehold acquisition has been completed, there is often a pressing need to change the culture in the building. While many leaseholders have traditionally gone on 'rent strike' by refusing to pay their service charges to landlords that have badly managed their buildings, enfranchisers need to put a swift end to any such practice of non-payment. In chapter 10 we have analysed ways in which to eliminate a destructive culture of non-compliance after the freehold has been bought. We have also provided practical advice for the resident management company, after the enfranchisement has been completed, when deciding whether to sell a share of the freehold and/or a 999-year lease to non-participants, or simply to fulfil the legal obligation to sell 90-year lease extensions.

A recurring theme throughout this book has been the heavy onus placed on leaseholders to get things right when they are attempting to enfranchise their building and not to make mistakes that can cause this fragile endeavour to fail. The landlord, while being forced into a compulsory sale in an enfranchisement, nonetheless can make several mistakes and still secure a fair price for his building. It may seem unfair that existing legislation obliges leaseholders to leap over so many hurdles in order to exercise their right to obtain full and permanent ownership of their homes. However, by understanding the unique disadvantages suffered by enfranchisers vis-à-vis the large corporate landlord, leaseholders can adopt a suitable strategy and maximise their chance of success.

We hope that our long-distance runner will consider that the race was worthwhile long after it has been run. Many leaseholders are shocked to discover that their resident management company is a more incompetent landlord than was the previous freeholder. One common complaint is that some resident management companies fail to recognise that leases remain in force after the freehold purchase has been completed and that these leases represent the central binding contracts between the freeholder and leaseholders. If the leaseholders view a post-enfranchisement building as a free-for-all, where a simple majority vote can be used to override legally-binding responsibilities contained in the lease, then flat owners can end up with a chaotic, poorly-run building. When the enfranchisers recognise that ownership of the freehold brings with it important responsibilities, they are best placed to ensure that the new resident-owned landlord represents a qualitative improvement over the last.

This book has described a process of collective enfranchisement that remains unreasonably difficult for leaseholders of flats, while providing many legal loopholes with which freeholders can scupper these initiatives. Some observers may conclude that homeowners should avoid enfranchising, given the many challenges they face. This is not the conclusion that I have drawn based on my study of hundreds of blocks of flats across England. As long as leaseholders approach the freehold purchase process with a strategic long view, they are often able to cross the finish line with a smile. And for those enfranchisers that go on to address the ownership of their freehold and the management of their building in a thoughtful, professional manner, the race is certainly worth running.

Appendices

Appendix 1: Useful contacts

Association of Residential Managing Agents (ARMA)
178 Battersea Park Road
London SW11 4ND

Tel: 020 7978 2607
Fax: 020 7498 6153
Email: info@arma.org.uk
Website: www.arma.org.uk

Companies House
Crown Way
Maindy
Cardiff
Wales CF14 3UZ

Tel: 0870 333 3636
Fax: 029 2038 0517
Email: enquiries@companieshouse.gov.uk
Website: www.companieshouse.gov.uk

Department for Communities and Local Government
Leasehold Reform Division
Zone 2/H10
Eland House
Bressenden Place
London SW1E 5DU

Tel: 020 7944 4400
Fax: 020 7944 3408
Email: leasehold.reform@dclg.gov.uk
Website: www.dclg.gov.uk

Federation of Private Residents' Associations (FPRA)
59 Mile End Road
Colchester
Essex CO4 5BU

Tel: 0871 200 3324/01206 855 888
Fax: 01206 851 616

Email: info@fpra.org.uk
Website: www.fpra.org.uk

HM Land Registry
Lincoln's Inn Fields
London WC2A 3PH

Tel: 020 7917 8888
Fax: 020 7955 0110
Website: www.landreg.gov.uk *or* www.landregisteronline.gov.uk

Jordans Limited
21 St Thomas Street
Bristol BS1 6JS

Tel: 0117 923 0600
Fax: 0117 923 0063
Email: customerservices@jordans.co.uk
Website: www.jordans.co.uk

Lands Tribunal
Postal address:

Procession House
55 Ludgate Hill
London EC4M 7JW

Street address:

Procession House
110 New Bridge Street
London EC4V 6JL

Tel: 020 7029 9780
Fax: 020 7029 9781
Email: lands@dca.gsi.gov.uk
Website: www.landstribunal.gov.uk

Leasehold Advisory Service ('LEASE')
31 Worship Street
London EC2A 2DX

Tel: 020 7374 5380
Fax: 020 7374 5373

Email: info@lease-advice.org
Website: www.lease-advice.org

Leasehold Valuation Tribunal (regional offices)

Eastern Leasehold Valuation Tribunal and
Eastern Rent Assessment Panel
Great Eastern House
Tenison Road
Cambridge CB1 2TR

Tel: 0845 100 2616
Fax: 01223 505 116
Email: eastern.rap@odpm.gsi.gov.uk
Website: www.rpts.gov.uk

London Leasehold Valuation Tribunal and London Rent
Assessment Panel
10 Alfred Place
London WC1E 7LR

Tel: 020 7446 7700
Fax: 020 7637 1250
Email: london.rap@odpm.gsi.gov.uk
Website: www.rpts.gov.uk

Midland Leasehold Valuation Tribunal and
Midland Rent Assessment Panel
2nd Floor, East Wing
Ladywood House
45–46 Stephenson Street
Birmingham B2 4DH

Tel: 0845 100 2615
Fax: 0121 643 7605
Email: midland.rap@odpm.gsi.gov.uk
Website: www.rpts.gov.uk

Northern Leasehold Valuation Tribunal and
Northern Rent Assessment Panel
1st Floor, 25 York Street
Manchester M1 4JB

Tel: 0845 100 2614
Fax: 0161 237 3656
Email: northern.rap@odpm.gsi.gov.uk
Website: www.rpts.gov.uk

**Southern Leasehold Valuation Tribunal and
Southern Rent Assessment Panel**
1st Floor, 1 Market Avenue
Chichester PO19 1JU

Tel: 0845 100 2617
Fax: 01243 779 389
Email: southern.rap@odpm.gsi.gov.uk
Website: www.rpts.gov.uk

Residential Property Tribunal Service (see also Leasehold Valuation Tribunals)
10 Alfred Place
London WC1E 7LR

Tel: 020 7446 7700
Fax: 020 7637 1250
Email: london.rap@odpm.gsi.gov.uk
Website: www.rpts.gov.uk

Royal Institution of Chartered Surveyors
Surveyor Court
Westwood Way
Coventry CV4 8JE

Tel: 0870 333 1600
Fax: 020 7334 3811
Email: contactrics@rics.org
Website: www.rics.org

St Giles Insurance & Finance Services Limited
8 Rodney Street
Liverpool L1 2TE

Tel: 0151 709 1911
Fax: 0151 709 3987

Email: enquiries@stgilesgroup.co.uk
Website: www.stgilesgroup.co.uk

The Stationery Office
PO Box 29
Norwich
Norfolk NR3 1GN

Tel: 0870 600 5522
Fax: 0870 600 5533
Website: www.tso.co.uk

Welsh Assembly Government
Housing Directorate
Cathays Park
Cardiff
Wales CF10 3NQ

Tel: 029 2082 5111
Fax: 029 2082 6989
Website: http://new.wales.gov.uk

Case study 1

Embassy Court – Protracted legal battle with the landlord

About the building

Embassy Court is a landmark building of 73 apartments overlooking the south-east coast in Brighton. Completed in 1935, it was designed by Wells Coates, a leading figure in the British modernist movement in architecture. In its early day, Embassy Court was home to several stars, including Rex Harrison and the comedian Max Miller. It remained a prestigious seafront location through the 1960s. However, by the 1980s the large block had fallen into disrepair and it passed through the hands of several freeholders who failed to halt the deterioration. In the early 1990s leaseholders joined forces to battle against the freeholder in court. The leaseholders sought to force the landlord to fulfil his responsibility under the lease to maintain the building and they in turn were sued by the landlord for failure to pay their service charges.

What happened?

The legal fight that started in the 1990s dragged on for a decade and repeatedly made national headline news. In 1997 the courts ordered the freeholder, a company called Portvale Holdings Limited which was run by David Marcel, to carry out necessary repairs at Embassy Court at a cost of approximately £1.5 million. Portvale subsequently went into liquidation and the freehold passed to the Crown Estate Commissioners. In 1998 the Crown awarded the freehold to the small group of campaigning leaseholders who had struggled to save the building. The leaseholders transferred the freehold to Bluestorm Limited, the company they had set up to buy and manage the freehold.

But securing the freehold did not bring an end to the conflict with the former landlord. It was now Portvale that took legal action against the resident-owned Bluestorm. David Marcel, although no longer the freeholder of the building, owned several flats there and he refused to pay his service charges, claiming that Bluestorm was failing to carry out necessary repairs. In March 2003 the courts ordered Portvale to clear up the unpaid service charges owed for flats that it owned at Embassy Court.

Portvale appealed, but lost its case in February 2004 when the Court of Appeal found in favour of Bluestorm.

With the protracted litigation finally ended, the board of directors of Bluestorm has focused on returning Embassy Court to its past architectural glory. Major refurbishment works were completed in November 2005 at a cost of £4.6 million, funded entirely by the leaseholders. The refurbishment represented an important turning point for the block, following the leaseholders' decade-long struggle to save their homes.

Why is this case important?

Emma Jinks, the Chairman of Bluestorm Limited since 2003, describes a bright future for Embassy Court and its residents, but she says the years of crippling litigation have taken a heavy toll on its leaseholders. Financially, the legal battle that started in the 1990s cost the leaseholders nearly half a million pounds in legal fees. But the most devastating toll was human. 'The residents who organised this effort gave their lives to it,' said Jinks, who bought her Embassy Court flat at auction in 2002. 'All of them got poorly. It destroyed them,' she said. 'We have saved a building of National Heritage importance. It is a great building. But the human cost was huge.'

Case study 2

Saxon Hall – Asset-stripping by the freeholder

About the building

Saxon Hall is a modern block of flats in the trendy Notting Hill Gate neighbourhood of London. Typical of residential buildings in this urban area, many of the 19 flats in the block are owned by busy professional people from around the world. Over the years Saxon Hall was managed so badly that the leaseholders went to court three times to force the landlord to comply with the lease. On one occasion, the freehold was sold illegally without informing the leaseholders. Residents later tried, but failed, to buy the freehold from the new owner. The leaseholders finally took away the landlord's right to manage the building by getting a managing agent appointed by the Leasehold Valuation Tribunal (LVT) and eventually they secured an official right to manage Saxon Hall.

What happened?

Bob Hrabal bought his flat at Saxon Hall in 1984. He subsequently was elected Chairman of the Saxon Hall Tenants Association and spent the following years fighting to improve conditions in the block. Building maintenance was a continual problem and the leaseholders sued the landlord in court on two occasions for failing to manage the building as set out in the lease. The leaseholders won both court cases, but the freeholder continued to mismanage the structure.

In the mid-1990s the leaseholders discovered that the freehold had been sold and that the landlord had violated the Landlord and Tenant Act 1987 by failing to offer a right of first refusal to the leaseholders. The leaseholders received no notification of the sale and it took them six months to confirm that there was a new landlord.

The new freeholder, unbeknownst to residents, then embarked on a programme of asset-stripping the building. He sold long leases of freehold space, including a car park and roof space, without informing the residents. By the late 1990s the landlord offered to sell the freehold to the leaseholders for £200,000 and the residents agreed. They paid a deposit of £25,000 through a law firm they had hired, only to discover at the last minute that the landlord was selling them a cut-down version of the freehold, minus the car park, roof space and basement areas. 'Residents in the building had no idea that the landlord had asset stripped Saxon Hall,' said Bob Hrabal. 'Having done that, he was then trying to sell us something called the freehold, but which really just represented our leasehold flats.' The leaseholders walked away from the deal and then filed a complaint with the Law Society against the law firm, claiming that it had been negligent and mishandled the deal. The Law Society ordered the law firm to refund the leaseholders £20,000, while the landlord kept the £25,000 deposit.

The landlord next sought planning permission to convert basement space at Saxon Hall into four flats, with the intention of selling these. The basement space had been used for 25 years by residents. Part of it housed the boiler for the building. The local council refused planning permission, but the landlord brought in a construction team anyway and work was started to gut the lower ground area. The leaseholders made repeated complaints to the local council, but only succeeded in stopping the construction and preventing the landlord from disconnecting the communal boiler by securing a court injunction. By the end, each leaseholder had spent approximately £6,000 on legal fees and the unrecovered deposit money.

In 2003 the leaseholders succeeded in taking away the landlord's right to manage the building. They filed an application at the LVT and got the tribunal to appoint a special managing agent to run the building for two years. By 2005 the Saxon Hall Tenants Association decided to secure permanent management rights, so it hired an outside project manager to initiate a right to manage application. A right to manage company was set up by the leaseholders and in early 2006 the company, Saxon Hall RTM Co. Limited, secured the legal right to manage the building, including appointing a managing agent of choice. Soon afterwards, leaseholders agreed on an ambitious £240,000 plan to refurbish the interior and exterior of the building.

Why is this case important?

Bob Hrabal says the problems at Saxon Hall illustrate how difficult it is for leaseholders of apartments to protect the value of their homes against unscrupulous landlords. 'The abuses are amazing. There is massive scope for abuse,' he said. 'There are so many loopholes in the law that make it easy for the landlord to escape his responsibility and that make it difficult for leaseholders to enjoy the most basic rights to enjoy their homes.'

When leaseholders hire the wrong adviser, they can find themselves in an bigger mess. 'Leaseholders have enough difficulty with a bad landlord. When you combine that with a bad or incompetent lawyer, the result is disastrous,' Hrabal said.

He said it was shocking to see how much effort was expended by honest hard-working homeowners to prevent their building from being run down, mismanaged and asset-stripped by the freeholder. 'The time that people spend just to protect the value of their property is unbelievable,' Hrabal said. 'It is a huge amount of work which is unpaid. Luckily, at Saxon Hall we were able to succeed because we had a strong sense of community and we stuck together.'

Case study 3

Palmer House – Problems with the surveyor

About the building

Palmer House is a graceful low-lying block of flats set back from Fortess Road in London's Kentish Town. The leaseholders owning flats there represent a dynamic group with a strong sense of community and commitment to the building. Several of the leaseholders live at Palmer House, while others reside elsewhere in London or in nearby counties, and rent out their Palmer House flat. One leaseholder lives in Australia and sublets her unit. After years of substandard management of the building, the residents decided to try to buy the freehold, but they were foiled in their efforts when the chartered surveyor firm they hired to advise them stepped in and snatched the freehold instead.

What happened?

Nicola Pharoah and her husband, James Clarke, moved to Palmer House shortly before the birth of their first child. Upon their arrival, they quickly learned from neighbours that all was not well in the building. The management had been considered inadequate for years. Because of this, the leaseholders were pleased to learn in 2001 that the landlord was seeking to sell the freehold. Each leaseholder was served a notice in which the landlord advised of his plans to sell the freehold at auction and which offered, as is required by law, the right of first refusal for the leaseholders in the building to buy at the price offered by the highest bidder at auction.

The leaseholders organised themselves to bid for the freehold. Their first step was to have a valuation done. They hired a chartered surveyor firm that was located nearby and paid the firm £800 to carry out a valuation of the freehold. The firm advised the leaseholders to make a bid of £40,000 at the auction. The residents busily collected the £40,000 that they hoped would represent the successful bid for their building. Unfortunately, they were outbid at the auction by just £2,000. Disappointment turned to shock later when they learned that the small company that outbid them at £42,000 and that subsequently became their new landlord had only been created weeks before the auction and that the chairman of the company was the father-in-law of the person who ran the chartered surveyor firm.

Things went from bad to worse at Palmer House as the new landlord doubled the annual service charges payable by leaseholders, but failed to manage the building properly, including getting basic cleaning done of the internal common parts. In fact, the quality of management deteriorated rapidly. At one stage, residents found that a 12-year-old boy had been sent to clean the internal stairwell at Palmer House. On another occasion, two men knocked on the door of an apartment owner to ask if she would provide products with which they could clean the inside of the building.

When the freeholder applied for planning permission to build an extra storey with four new flats on the roof, the leaseholders sent written objections to the local council, but planning permission was granted. During the construction, workmen's legs came through the ceiling of three top-storey flats, but the freeholder failed to make good the damage.

Lesley Fraser, a leaseholder at Palmer House, decided to withhold part of her service charges in protest over the inadequate management. In 2002 the new freeholder sued her in the County Court for approximately £2,000 in unpaid service charges. Her legal fight with the landlord over the following years was to cost her £5,000 in legal fees and her health. 'I ended up with stress-related illnesses which affected every part of my life,' Fraser said. 'I'm a law-abiding citizen who just wanted quiet enjoyment of my home.' Distressed by all the legal notices coming through her door, including threats by the landlord to forfeit her lease, Fraser finally felt forced to move away from Palmer House and to rent out her flat there to a subtenant. 'I just couldn't bear it any more,' she said.

The leaseholders made some progress eventually, when the LVT determined in 2005 that the landlord had indeed charged Fraser and the nine other leaseholders thousands of pounds in unreasonable service charges. 'But the landlord has failed to comply with the LVT decision and has continued to threaten me with court action,' Fraser said.

Why is this case important?

Pharoah said that the action taken at the auction by the chartered surveyor firm that had been hired to provide a valuation for the leaseholders had left apartment owners at Palmer House stunned. 'Here we are fighting against a landlord who has badly mismanaged our building and now we have a company that is supposed to be advising us but that, behind our backs, takes action against us,' she said. 'It was the most shocking violation of a professional code of conduct. How could a surveyor enter into that kind of conflict of interest without disclosing the conflict to the client?'

Pharoah said that the leaseholders were encouraged when they won their case at the LVT in 2005, but it was a small victory given the years of stress. 'The hardest thing to bear is the powerlessness of knowing that people are using your home to take advantage of you,' she said.

Fraser said that her professional work as a counsellor, which includes dealing with trauma, failed to prepare her for the health-destroying stress of learning that her home might be taken away. 'I felt powerless and completely isolated. I did not know where to turn,' she said. 'You're up against a corporate structure. You feel utterly impotent.'

Case study 4

Cornwall Crescent – Avoiding County Court

About the building

The building at 9 Cornwall Crescent contains three flats, is situated in a row of Victorian four-storey buildings in West London and was formerly owned by the local council. When two of the three leaseholders in the building set out to buy the freehold through the process of collective enfranchisement, they had no idea they would end up spending nearly two years in the County Court and approximately £65,000 in legal fees – over 300 times the amount they were advised by a chartered surveyor to offer for the building – and that they would end up with no freehold.

What happened?

When Annabel Cary and her fellow leaseholder set out to enfranchise their building, they had good reason to believe that they would be able to buy the freehold for a reasonable price. Their leases had 114 years, so there was no marriage value to pay to the landlord. Marriage value, which, roughly speaking, represents the expected appreciation in the value of the participating flats once the freehold has been bought and half of which must be paid by the enfranchisers to the freeholder, is only applicable if the leases have less than 80 years. The other elements of the freehold value at 9 Cornwall Crescent, including capitalised ground rent of only £10 per year, added up to small figures.

The two enfranchisers, based on advice by a chartered surveyor who is highly experienced in freehold purchases, served an Enfranchisement Notice on the landlord in 2002 that contained an offer price of £210 for the freehold. They were shocked when the landlord, the Mayor and Burgesses of the Royal Borough of Kensington and Chelsea, served a Counter Notice on them in January 2003 that demanded £130,000. The landlord's higher figure included £25,000 compensation for a small balcony off one flat and £100,000 in 'development value' for the roof, which the landlord said could be developed. Prior to the serving of the Enfranchisement Notice, Cary had obtained planning permission from the local council to build a loft conversion.

Cary and her fellow enfranchiser now faced three options – to try to reach a negotiated settlement with the landlord, to ask the LVT to decide on the freehold price or to file a claim in the County Court in which the court would be asked to declare the landlord's Counter Notice invalid on the grounds that the counter offer price was so high as to be unrealistic. If the court found the Counter Notice invalid, the enfranchisers would get to buy the freehold at their offer price of £210. The enfranchisers consulted their advisers and then filed the claim in the County Court. The case was called 9 Cornwall Crescent Limited versus the Mayor and Burgesses of the Royal Borough of Kensington and Chelsea.

In the court decision reached in January 2004, Judge Rich found in favour of the landlord by declaring that the Counter Notice was indeed valid. The enfranchisers challenged the ruling, but they lost subsequently in the Court of Appeal. Anthony Radevsky, the barrister who represented the landlord in the Court of Appeal hearing on 9 February 2005, argued that, while case law had established that the leaseholders had to include in their Enfranchisement Notice an offer price that was a realistic figure and that was not unrealistically low, the landlord was under no such obligation. Radevsky argued that the landlord did not have to include a counter offer figure in the Counter Notice that was realistic. Indeed, he argued in court that the landlord could include absolutely any figure in the Counter Notice, no matter how high. When asked by one of the three judges at the hearing whether this meant the landlord could have included a counter offer price of, say, £10 million in the Counter Notice, Radevsky said yes, the landlord could have done so without invalidating the Counter Notice.

Why is this case important?

By the time the enfranchisers lost their Court of Appeal case, they had spent nearly two years litigating to buy their freehold, had paid approximately £65,000 on legal fees and had little to show for it. Cary said it was an expensive way to learn that leaseholders should avoid the County Court when they are enfranchising their building. Professional advisers had explained that the enfranchisers had the legal right to challenge the validity of the Counter Notice in the County Court, but they had not provided strategy advice on whether this course of action would represent the fastest, cheapest and lowest-risk route to buying the freehold. Had Cary and her fellow leaseholder gone to the LVT after receiving the landlord's Counter Notice, they could have expected the tribunal to decide on a fair price for the freehold. By challenging the landlord in the County Court, the leaseholders placed themselves at a severe disadvantage, since the County Court has shown reluctance to enter into the minutiae of deciding freehold prices. 'If I knew then what I know now, I would have handled things very differently,' Cary said. 'I would have stayed far away from the County Court and I would have headed straight for the LVT.'

Case study 5

Ambling Court – Problems after the freehold purchase

About the building

Ambling Court is an elegant building of flats in West London that was constructed before the First World War. When it was built, the structure had five units, one on each of five storeys, with spacious storage under the roof. After the Second World War this storage space was converted into a sixth flat. Ambling Court was originally owned by a family trust which granted a 99-year head lease set to expire in 2006. Between 1968 and 1975, the head leaseholder granted long leases on all the flats in the building, with each lease running out in 2006. In 1980 the head leaseholder bought the freehold of the building from the family trust. (The name of the building and names of the individuals have been changed for the purpose of this case study.)

What happened?

The new freeholder set out to sell much longer leases at substantial prices to residents, but managed to sell only one lease. Over the following decade the freehold passed through several hands, with none of the landlords showing interest in carrying out necessary repairs on the building. Short leaseholders in the building made no move to buy long leases, which they considered too expensive, since they knew they had the legal right to stay on at Ambling Court as renting tenants when their leases expired.

The situation changed for leaseholders, however, when the law changed. Under the new legislation, renting tenants had to pay full market rents for their flats. The leaseholders at Ambling Court now had an incentive to try to secure long leases.

Richard Roe, a lawyer, bought a lease of a flat in the building in the late 1970s. By the early 1990s the freehold was sold to a property company that had little experience in managing rented properties. Roe galvanised his fellow leaseholders and together they served a notice requiring that the new freeholder carry out overdue repairs or sell the freehold to the leaseholders at a knock-down price. The freeholder did carry out repairs, but badly, and subsequently faced a lawsuit by the leaseholders. At this stage, the landlord agreed to sell the freehold to the residents. After the sale, the leaseholders became directors of the resident management company and they granted themselves 2,000-year leases.

But the directors soon fell out over how to run the company. Conflict erupted on the board regarding flat 6, which was located on the top floor. As a result of reduced mains pressure years earlier, water was not being carried to flat 6 with full pressure. Because of this, the resident of flat 6 had installed and maintained a pipe and pump to get water to the sixth floor. When the flat was later sold and the pump broke, the new leaseholder demanded that the resident management company replace and maintain it. She said the right to a supply of water through the pipes imposed the obligation on the freeholder to pump such water if the mains pressure fell.

Roe objected, saying this was not an obligation of the freeholder in the lease. But another director proposed that half the cost be borne by the leaseholder of flat 6 and half by the resident management company. The board voted five-to-one in favour, with Roe alone voting against. Pressure was placed on Roe by his fellow directors and the managing agent then running the building not to insist on compliance with the lease, but rather to go with a majority vote on contentious issues such as this.

The pump was installed and the resident management company paid half the expenses. Roe refused to pay any service charges towards the expense of the pump. He said that his lease imposed no liability on him to do so. The managing agent subsequently left and a new managing agent took over who now recovers from the new leaseholder of flat 6 all expenses connected with the pump and pipes for the top floor.

Why is this case important?

Richard Roe said the story of the pump showed how leaseholders could get rid of one landlord only to find themselves with a worse landlord – themselves. 'I was shocked to hear fellow directors of the resident management company say that the lease was irrelevant and that cost issues in the building should be decided by a simple majority vote,' he said. 'This is a dangerous way to run a residential building, as it provides no clearly-defined responsibilities on the part of the freeholder or the leaseholder.'

Roe said that the experience at Ambling Court highlighted the importance for residents to understand the advantages and the disadvantages of owning their building freehold. 'People need to realise that the resident management company has all the same responsibilities to the leaseholders as did the old freeholder,' he said. 'If the residents cannot cope with the responsibility that comes with ownership of the freehold, they might be better off leaving an outside landlord owning the building. It has to be said that, in general, the agents of an outside landlord can be expected to act in a disinterested way in making decisions affecting the financial interests of individual lessees.'

Case study 6

Acacia Mansions – Deception by a nominee purchaser

About the building

When the leases ran down to about 50 years at Acacia Mansions, a block of 16 flats in central London, the leaseholders began to experience difficulty in selling their flats. The chairman of the residents' association, Steve Jones, suggested to the association members that they buy the building freehold so that they could grant themselves 999-year leases. One member, Barry Smith, who lived in Suffolk, but owned and rented out a flat at Acacia Mansions, was one of several leaseholders keen to enfranchise. Jones hired a lawyer on behalf of the leaseholders, got the participants to sign an Enfranchisement Notice, served the notice on the landlord and then later told the leaseholders the freehold had been secured. So, the residents were stunned when they learned subsequently that Jones was the new landlord and that the leaseholders now had to buy their share of the freehold from him. (The name of the building and the names of the individuals have been changed for the purpose of this case study.)

What happened?

The landlord of Acacia Mansions, a man in his 80s, died in 2004 and his widow indicated that she was willing to sell the building. Steve Jones suggested to his fellow leaseholders that they follow the statutory route of collective enfranchisement, rather than negotiate to buy, in order to ensure a fair purchase price. Ten of Acacia Mansion's 16 leaseholders signed up for the freehold purchase project and Jones, on behalf of the members, instructed a lawyer to draw up the required Enfranchisement Notice. All the participants signed the notice and it was served on the landlord. In early 2005 the leaseholders were informed by Jones in a letter that 'we have got the freehold' and that the freehold had cost £120,000.

Then things went strangely quiet. Participants were puzzled as to why they had never been asked by Jones to pay their share of the freehold, despite their having offered to send to him money on several occasions. Jones had requested that the leaseholders pay their share of the legal fees incurred and they had done so. The participants now wrote to Jones and requested a meeting, but there was no immediate reply. Finally, several weeks later, participants received a letter with startling news. 'I am the new freeholder,' Jones wrote. 'If any of you want to buy a share of the freehold, you must buy it from me.'

It took the enfranchisement participants some time to figure out what had happened. By law, when leaseholders organise to enfranchise a building, they must appoint a 'nominee purchaser' as the person, company or other legal entity that is going to buy the freehold. It is the nominee purchaser, technically speaking, that serves the Enfranchisement Notice on the landlord and that buys the freehold. While it is best practice for the leaseholders to form a limited company as nominee purchaser and to become shareholders of the company, this had not happened at Acacia Mansions. Instead, the participants had agreed to Jones' suggestion that he be appointed as the nominee purchaser. So, he had technically become the new freeholder, but, in so doing, had misrepresented his intentions and had persuaded the leaseholders to sign an Enfranchisement Notice that they thought would deliver to each of them a share of the freehold.

The participants then discovered to their horror that Jones, as the new freeholder, had granted himself a long lease to the building's roof space and the basement area, something that had never been agreed as part of the freehold purchase project. 'We were tricked and deceived by a fellow leaseholder in the building,' Smith said. 'We have now ended up with a messy situation in which we either pay the price he is demanding for a share in the freehold or spend more money on a lawyer to sue this person for fraud.'

Why is this case important?

The leaseholders at Acacia Mansions could have avoided this distressing situation by following best practice when appointing a nominee purchaser. Had they set up a limited company, they would have all been shareholders and, as shareholders, they would have appointed a board of directors to run the company. This company would have had to comply with the Companies Act, which provides a strong legal and regulatory framework for corporate structures. By agreeing to appoint Steve Jones as the nominee purchaser, they had placed all their trust in this one individual, while failing to put in place appropriate checks and balances.

'Because he was the chairman of the residents' association, we trusted him,' said Barry Smith. 'We were partly responsible for the subsequent mess, because, in the early stages of the project, most of the participants did not pay close attention to the procedure. This created a huge scope for abuse.' But absentee leaseholders and senior citizens living in the building had seen no reason to distrust the head of their residents' association. 'We may have been naïve, but who would expect the chairman of the residents' association to defraud members in an enfranchisement?' Smith said.

Smith said that participants in the freehold purchase project should have been alerted to the fact that there was a problem when Jones hired one lawyer to handle the enfranchisement, then changed lawyers again and again. 'Things were not being done in a transparent manner. We should have recognised something was wrong when the lawyer handling the freehold purchase kept changing,' Smith said. 'We should have heard the warning bells.'

Case study 7

Westbourne Crescent – A landlord's offer to sell

About the building

The four residential buildings at 9–12 Westbourne Crescent, which comprise 21 flats, are located in a bustling part of Bayswater, a short walk from London's Hyde Park. One of the buildings, Crescent Court at 10 Westbourne Crescent, has 15 flats, while the adjoining structures are houses which were converted years ago into two-flat maisonettes. Most of the leaseholders know one another through the residents' association, which has operated actively for some time. The leaseholders say that they love the neighbourhood but for years were unhappy about the poor management of their property. When they complained to the corporate freeholder who owned the four buildings, they got little result. In 2005 the apartment owners decided to buy their freehold, but the process was nearly derailed by a surprise offer by the landlord to sell.

What happened?

Robert Neil Manning, the chairman of the 9–12 Westbourne Crescent Residents' Association, knew that the leaseholders stood to benefit from buying their freehold, because of his experience in dealing with many other blocks of flats in central London. As Managing Director of Granvilles Estate Agency, which is also a managing agent company, Manning had seen leaseholders of resident-owned blocks of flats introduce rapid and effective improvements in building management, while also granting themselves 999-year leases, after buying their freehold. But he also knew it could be difficult to get a large number of leaseholders to agree on such an ambitious project as collective enfranchisement.

In early 2005 the residents' association decided to pursue enfranchisement and to outsource the project management work. They instructed a specialist consultancy company that was located nearby to organise, supervise and see through their freehold purchase. Work began and within weeks Manning, the other members of his residents' association committee and the consultancy firm had succeeded in getting 19 of the 21 leaseholders to join the project, including paying a deposit. The next step was for the consultant to have a valuation of the freehold done by a chartered surveyor who specialised in enfranchisement.

In the summer of 2005, however, the leaseholders received an official notice from the landlord that caused panic and appeared to place at risk their enfranchisement project. The landlord served a Section 5 Notice on the leaseholders, advising that he planned to sell the freehold and offering the residents the right of first refusal to buy. The notice informed the leaseholders of a £185,000 sales price and it gave them, as is required by law, a maximum of two months to reply.

The residents had to move quickly. The consultant brought in the surveyor to carry out the valuation and the surveyor subsequently advised that the asking price was indeed reasonable, based on the statutory formula for calculating the value of a freehold in an enfranchisement. In September 2005 Manning convened a meeting of the residents' association and the leaseholders attending voted unanimously to buy the freehold at the asking price through the right-of-first-refusal process. Manning and the consultant worked together in the following weeks to complete the deal and, by early 2006, the new resident management company called 9–12 Westbourne Crescent Limited became the freeholder of the four buildings.

Why is this case important?

Leaseholders are often thrown into a panic when they receive a Section 5 Notice, whether or not they have been organising to buy their building freehold. But at 9–12 Westbourne Crescent, leaseholders had done their homework, had hired an outside project manager and were able to make the necessary decisions quickly when the Right of First Refusal Notices arrived. 'We had already gone through the process of analysing our options and debating about the best way forward,' said Manning. 'The residents' association had secured the consensus needed and so we were able to move swiftly when the landlord served the Section 5 Notices on us.'

Manning described the process of collecting the money due from each participant in the freehold purchase as surprisingly smooth, due largely to preparation with the consultant after the decision was taken to buy the freehold for £185,000. Manning instructed the consultant to send letters to the participants, who by now were all shareholders of the newly-created resident management company, which specified the amount to be paid by which deadline date and that provided all information for payments to be made by cheque or BACS transfer. 'Participants got all the information they needed, which meant that I had to spend very little time chasing after people and answering questions,' Manning said. 'It took just a few weeks to collect the money. We were pleasantly surprised at how quickly the project came to a successful conclusion.'

Appendix 3: Qualifying for enfranchisement

If leaseholders wish to buy their building freehold through the process of collective enfranchisement, the building and each would-be participant must qualify.

A building will be eligible for collective enfranchisement if:

1. it is a self-contained separate structure (this can include a building adjacent to and physically joined to another building, but that shares no common parts or common structural services with the adjacent building);

2. it has two or more flats;

3. at least two-thirds of all the flats in the building are held by leaseholders whose leases had more than 21 years when the leases were first granted;

4. not more than 25 per cent of the building floor space is for commercial use;

5. at least 50 per cent of all the flats in the building are participating, regardless of whether all the flats are leasehold or some are owned by the freeholder (if there are only two flats in a building, then both flats must participate);

6. the landlord is not a charitable housing trust or the Crown;

7. it is not a converted property of four or fewer flats, with the same person having owned the freehold since before the conversion and the freeholder or an adult member of the freeholder's family having lived in one of the flats continuously as his main home since the conversion.

There are a few other exemptions regarding building qualification. Any leaseholder in doubt should contact the Leasehold Advisory Service. Contact details are contained in the section on 'Useful contacts'.

A resident will qualify for collective enfranchisement if:

1. he has a 'long lease', that is, the lease term was for more than 21 years at the time it was granted; and

2. he does not own more than two qualifying flats in the building.

Appendix 4: The main stages of enfranchisement

There are five phases in the formal enfranchisement process, although a large majority of enfranchisement initiatives are concluded with a negotiated settlement and do not proceed all the way to a hearing at the Leasehold Valuation Tribunal (LVT). The five phases of the official process are described below.

Phase 1: The Enfranchisement Notice

The formal enfranchisement process begins when the Enfranchisement Notice is served on the landlord. This is normally served by the enfranchisers' project manager or solicitor. The clock now starts ticking regarding the deadlines established by enfranchisement legislation. The landlord has a maximum of two months by which he must reply by sending a Counter Notice to the nominee purchaser. The Enfranchisement Notice must state this deadline date. If the landlord misses the deadline, the nominee purchaser is allowed to buy the freehold at the offer price contained in the Enfranchisement Notice. It is unusual for large corporate landlords to miss the deadline.

Phase 2: The landlord's Counter Notice

Phase 2 begins with a Counter Notice being served by the landlord on the nominee purchaser. In the Counter Notice, the landlord must:

1. acknowledge that the participants qualify to enfranchise and agree with the offer price; or

2. acknowledge that the participants qualify to enfranchise, but state a counter offer price; or

3. challenge the right of the participants to enfranchise.

Many landlords choose option 2 by accepting the leaseholders' right to enfranchise, but disagreeing with the offer price. If the landlord chooses option 1, the nominee purchaser may purchase the freehold at the offer price contained in the Enfranchisement Notice. Under option 3, the landlord must state on which grounds the participants allegedly do not qualify to enfranchise. The nominee purchaser then has the right to challenge this, but it must do so within two months of the date of the Counter Notice.

Once the landlord has served the Counter Notice, if it contains a counter offer price, then the nominee purchaser and the landlord can begin negotiations and can agree the terms of the freehold sale. However, they must conclude a contract of sale within two months of the date on which the terms of the sale are agreed. If they do not agree on the terms of the sale, then either side can apply to the LVT to decide the price. It is usually the nominee purchaser, rather than the landlord, that applies to the LVT.

Phase 3: Application to the LVT

Phase 3 of the enfranchisement process begins when the nominee purchaser files an application with the nearest LVT. The nominee purchaser may make the application no sooner than two months and no later than six months after the Counter Notice. The nominee purchaser normally applies to the LVT through its project manager or solicitor.

Phase 4: The LVT hearing and decision

Phase 4 begins with the LVT hearing, which usually takes place about three months from the time of application. An LVT hearing for the enfranchisement of a small building often takes one day and for a large building two days. The LVT panel reaches its determination after the hearing and sends the written decision to both parties. The decision contains the purchase price at which the landlord is ordered to sell the freehold to the nominee purchaser. If the nominee purchaser wishes to proceed, it begins the process of buying the freehold.

Phase 5: Completion of the freehold purchase

Once the LVT has sent its written decision containing the price at which the landlord must sell the freehold, the landlord must prepare a contract of sale and must give this to the nominee purchaser within 21 days of the LVT decision or within 21 days of an agreement about this with the nominee purchaser. The landlord may require that a ten per cent deposit be paid at the time that the contract of sale is provided.

The table below presents the optimal timeframe if an enfranchising group of leaseholders moves from one phase of the project to the next at the earliest opportunity allowed by the legislation.

Event	Month in which event occurs
Enfranchisement Notice is served on the landlord by the nominee purchaser	Month 1
Counter Notice is served on the nominee purchaser by the landlord	Month 3
The nominee purchaser applies to the LVT	Month 5
The LVT hearing is held	Month 8
The LVT's decision is issued	Month 9

Appendix 5: OC1 Form

SPECIMEN

Application for official copies of register/plan or certificate in Form CI

Land Registry

OC1

Land Registry _____ Office

Use one form per title. If you need more room than is provided for in a panel, use continuation sheet CS and attach to this form.

1. **Administrative area** if known	
2. **Title number** if known	
3. **Property** Postal number or description	
Name of road	
Name of locality	
Town	
Postcode	
Ordnance Survey map reference (if known)	

4. **Payment of fee** *Place "X" in the appropriate box.*

☐ The Land Registry fee of £ [   ] accompanies this application.

☐ Debit the Credit Account mentioned in panel 5 with the appropriate fee payable under the current Land Registration Fee Order.

For official use only
Impression of fees

5. **The application has been lodged by:**
Land Registry Key No. (if appropriate)
Name
Address/DX No.

Reference
E-mail

Telephone No.	Fax No.

6. If the official copies are to be sent to anyone other than the applicant in panel 5, please supply the name and address of the person to whom they should be sent.

Reference

Appendix 5: OC1 Form (continued)

SPECIMEN

7. Where the title number is **not** quoted in panel 2, place "X" in the appropriate box(es).
   As regards this property, my application relates to:

   ☐ freehold estate   ☐ caution against first registration   ☐ franchise   ☐ manor

   ☐ leasehold estate   ☐ rentcharge   ☐ profit a prendre in gross

8. In case there is an application for registration pending against the title, place "X" in the appropriate box:

   ☐ I require an official copy back-dated to the day prior to the receipt of that application   **or**

   ☐ I require an official copy on completion of that application

9. **I apply for:** *Place "X" in the appropriate box(es) and indicate how many copies are required.*

   ☐ ___ official copy(ies) of the **register** of the above mentioned property

   ☐ ___ official copy(ies) of the **title plan or caution plan** of the above mentioned property

   ☐ ___ a certificate in Form CI, in which case **either:**

       ☐ an estate plan has been approved and the plot number is [ ]

       or

       ☐ no estate plan has been approved and a certificate is to be issued in respect of the land
       shown _____ on the attached plan and copy

10. **Signature of applicant** _____ **Date** _____

Appendix 6: Stamp duty on the cost of the freehold

When leaseholders buy the freehold of their building, whether through the process of collective enfranchisement or by negotiated agreement with the landlord, they must pay stamp duty to HM Revenue & Customs. The table below shows the rate of stamp duty that is payable, depending on the purchase price of the building.

Percentage of Purchase Price Payable to HM Revenue & Customs as Stamp Duty	Purchase Price of Residential Property
Zero	£0 to £125,000
1%	Over £125,000 to £250,000
3%	Over £250,000 to £500,000
4%	Over £500,000

Appendix 7: Invitation to participate in an enfranchisement

It is best practice for leaseholders that are collectively enfranchising their building to send a written invitation to all the qualifying leaseholders to participate, although there is no legal requirement to do so. A sample invitation is provided below.

INVITATION TO LEASEHOLDERS OF ACACIA MANSIONS TO PARTICIPATE IN THE COLLECTIVE ENFRANCHISEMENT OF ACACIA MANSIONS

This document contains an invitation to the leaseholders of Acacia Mansions, Long Road, London W11, United Kingdom to participate in the process of acquiring the freehold of Acacia Mansions through collective enfranchisement. It has been prepared by the Residents' Association of Acacia Mansions.

This document contains confidential information for Acacia Mansions leaseholders. It may not to be copied or distributed in whole or in part without the express written permission of the Residents' Association of Acacia Mansions.

Opening date of invitation to participate: *[dd-mm-yy]*
Closing date of invitation to participate: *[dd-mm-yy]*

An invitation to participate in collective enfranchisement

This document invites leaseholders of Acacia Mansions, a mansion block located on Long Road, London W11, to participate in the joint acquisition by the leaseholders of the freehold of the building through the process of collective enfranchisement. The duration of this invitation is six months, with an opening date of *[dd-mm-yy]* and a closing date of *[dd-mm-yy]*.

This document has been prepared by the Committee of the Residents' Association of Acacia Mansions, which adopted as policy at its Committee meeting in London on *[dd-mm-yy]* the goal of achieving collective enfranchisement for Acacia Mansions.

Collective enfranchisement refers to the right granted to the leaseholders by the Leasehold Reform, Housing and Urban Development Act 1993, as amended by the Commonhold and Leasehold Reform Act 2002, to compel their landlord (freeholder) to sell to them their building freehold, and to do so according to a statutory timeframe and at a fair market price as determined by a Leasehold Valuation Tribunal.

The number of participants required for enfranchisement

This document invites all 50 leaseholders of Acacia Mansions to join in the process of collective enfranchisement. In order for Acacia Mansions to collectively enfranchise, a minimum of 50 per cent of the flats, or 25 flats, must participate.

The timeframe of collective enfranchisement

The official process of collective enfranchisement is expected to take about one year. The organising team has set out the plan to enfranchise, including preparation work, in three phases.

Phase 1: Gathering the required number of participants

Phase 1 of the Acacia Mansions Collective Enfranchisement Project begins on [*dd-mm-yy*] and ends on [*dd-mm-yy*], and aims to secure a commitment to the enfranchisement project from a minimum of 25 leaseholders. This commitment must be made by:

1. paying £1,000 deposit into the Acacia Enfranchisement Fund; and

2. advising the Residents' Association of Acacia Mansions in writing of the desire to participate.

The £1,000 represents the first instalment of the total cost to each participant of taking part in buying the freehold. The remainder of the cost is to be paid near the end of Phase 2. The Collective Enfranchisement Project will progress to Phase 2 only if the formal commitment to the enfranchisement, as described above, is gained from a minimum of 25 Acacia Mansions leaseholders.

Phase 2: Preparation to enfranchise

If the required commitment to the enfranchisement is secured by [*dd-mm-yy*] from a minimum of 25 leaseholders, the project will progress to

Phase 2. Phase 2 is expected to last approximately four months and will involve hiring a project manager, or a solicitor and surveyor, having a valuation done of the freehold, carrying out leasehold searches on all the flats, setting up a resident management company, preparing a legally-binding Participation Agreement amongst the participants and preparing an Enfranchisement Notice.

Phase 3: The formal enfranchisement process

Phase 3 begins with the official commencement of the enfranchisement process, when the participating leaseholders serve notice on the landlord of their intention to enfranchise the building. Participants must pay towards the end of Phase 3 the remainder of the cost of buying the freehold. It is expected that the cost per participating flat of collectively enfranchising Acacia Mansions will range from £[amount] for the smallest flats to £[amount] for the largest flats, with an average cost of £[amount] per participating flat.

These figures are estimates only and do not represent a guarantee of the final cost of the freehold. The final cost per flat may be higher or lower, depending on the eventual price of the freehold, the level of professional fees and the number of participating flats.

Required action to participate in the collective enfranchisement

Any leaseholder wishing to participate in the enfranchisement of Acacia Mansions is required to carry out the following two steps before the closing date of [dd-mm-yy]:

1. Pay a £1,000 (one thousand pounds sterling) deposit into the Acacia Enfranchisement Fund, by cheque payable to 'Acacia Enfranchisement Fund' to: John Doe, Chairperson, Residents' Association of Acacia Mansions, 1 Acacia Mansions, Long Road, London W11, or bank transfer to Account Number [number], Sort Code [number], Account name: Acacia Enfranchisement Fund, HSBC Bank; and

2. Send a letter, fax or email stating 'I/we wish to participate in the collective enfranchisement of Acacia Mansions' to John Doe, 1 Acacia Mansions, Long Road, London W11.

Failure to gain the required number of participants

If, by the closing date of [*dd-mm-yy*], fewer than 25 Acacia Mansions leaseholders have joined in the enfranchisement project, then all deposits will be returned to the relevant leaseholders.

Withdrawal from participation in the collective enfranchisement

The payment of £1,000 to the Acacia Enfranchisement Fund and a written notice to the Residents' Association of Acacia Mansions of the intention to participate in enfranchising Acacia Mansions represent a firm commitment to the project. For this reason and due to the administrative costs of managing the project, the only circumstance under which deposits paid by leaseholders to the Acacia Enfranchisement Fund during the invitation period will be returned to leaseholders is a failure to gain the required minimum number of 25 participants. If the minimum number of 25 participants is achieved by the closing date of [*dd-mm-yy*], deposits made by the participants will be considered non-refundable.

Appendix 8: Sign-Up Form

There is no legal requirement for participants of a collective enfranchisement to sign an initial Sign-Up Form, but it represents best practice for the organising team to have such a form signed. A sample form is provided below.

SIGN-UP FORM
FOR COLLECTIVE ENFRANCHISEMENT
OF ACACIA MANSIONS

TO: The Committee of the Residents' Association of Acacia Mansions

I/We wish to participate in the purchase of the freehold of Acacia Mansions through the process of collective enfranchisement, if and when this project takes place.

_____

Name

_____

Flat number at Acacia Mansions

_____

Date

Appendix 9: Participation Agreement

Leaseholders are not legally required to use a Participation Agreement when they enfranchise their building, but use of such an agreement is strongly recommended. The following is a sample Participation Agreement.

PARTICIPATION AGREEMENT
ENFRANCHISEMENT OF ACACIA MANSIONS

This agreement is made on [*dd-mm-yy*] between Acacia Mansions Limited of [*registered address of nominee purchaser company*] (the 'nominee purchaser') and the participating qualifying tenants of Acacia Mansions, Long Road, London W11.

1. This agreement is made in accordance with the Leasehold Reform, Housing and Urban Development Act 1993, referred to here as 'the Act'.

2. It is the intention of the nominee purchaser to purchase the freehold of Acacia Mansions, Long Road, London W11 in a collective enfranchisement on behalf of the participating tenants of Acacia Mansions, a block of 50 flats, referred to here as 'the block'.

3. Each tenant confirms and guarantees that:

   (a) he is a qualifying tenant according to Section 5 of the Act of a flat in the block and will provide the nominee purchaser with Land Registry Office Copy Entries and a copy of the registered lease within seven days of a written request;

   (c) he does not know of any court order preventing the tenant from participating in the collective enfranchisement;

   (c) he will inform the nominee purchaser in writing within ten days of any change in (a) and (b) above;

   (d) he will not buy or otherwise acquire any other leasehold flat in the block without first advising the nominee purchaser in writing within seven days.

4. The nominee purchaser has prepared and will serve upon the freeholder and any other relevant persons the appropriate notices to enfranchise and will register the initial notice as a caution with

HM Land Registry and has complied or will comply with the procedure according to the Act.

5. The nominee purchaser has instructed [*name of project manager or solicitors' firm and surveyors' firm and address in England or Wales*] to advise on the preparation of the enfranchisement notices and other areas of compliance with the Act.

6. The nominee purchaser will inform the freeholder of any agreement reached with any non-participating tenant, in accordance with Section 18 of the Act.

7. A reasonable time after the completion of the freehold purchase, the nominee purchaser will grant and each participating tenant will accept and execute a counterpart of a lease of the respective flat and any related property and will surrender the existing lease, details of which are provided in the Schedule below.

8. Each tenant agrees that, if he sells or otherwise assigns his leasehold flat in the block before the completion of the freehold purchase, he will ensure that the purchaser or assignee of the lease will:

    (a) elect to participate in the collective enfranchisement of the block;

    (b) give the nominee purchaser notice of his intention to be bound by this Participation Agreement and to participate within 14 days of the assignment;

    (c) take up the tenant's share in the nominee purchaser.

9. (a) In this agreement 'each tenant's share of the freehold price' means the appropriate pro rata number of shares held in the nominee purchaser by each participating tenant or the agreed pro rata cost allocation.

    (b) The price to be paid for each new lease, after the freehold purchase, will not be more than each tenant's respective share of the freehold price and the lease will be in reasonable modern form for a term of 999 years.

    (c) Each tenant may be required to pay a deposit of ten per cent of the freehold price to the nominee purchaser or its agent, to be used for the deposit when the exchange of contract takes place for the freehold purchase.

(d) Upon completion each tenant will pay to the nominee purchaser:

    (i)   the balance of the tenant's pro rata share of the freehold price;

    (ii) all outstanding ground rent and service charges and other payments due under the old lease;

    (iii) the appropriate pro rata share of legal, surveyor and other costs incurred by the nominee purchaser in the enfranchisement;

    (iv) for the shares in the nominee purchaser (at par).

10. This agreement does not represent a Partnership Agreement.

Name of participating
qualifying tenant

Signature of participating
qualifying tenant

_____

_____

_____

_____

_____

_____

_____

_____

(Print name)

(Personal signature)

THE SCHEDULE

COLUMN 1	COLUMN 2	COLUMN 3	COLUMN 4	COLUMN 5
Name of Qualifying Tenant	**Flat Number**	**Date of Lease**	**Lessee as in Lease**	**Participation Status**
[Name]	*[Flat no.]*	*[Date on which lease commenced]*	*[Name of original lessee shown on lease]*	*[Participator/ non-participator]*
[Name]	*[Flat no.]*	*[Date on which lease commenced]*	*[Name of original lessee shown on lease]*	*[Participator/ non-participator]*
[Name]	*[Flat no.]*	*[Date on which lease commenced]*	*[Name of original lessee shown on lease]*	*[Participator/ non-participator]*
[Name]	*[Flat no.]*	*[Date on which lease commenced]*	*[Name of original lessee shown on lease]*	*[Participator/ non-participator]*
[Name]	*[Flat no.]*	*[Date on which lease commenced]*	*[Name of original lessee shown on lease]*	*[Participator/ non-participator]*

Appendix 10: Enfranchisement Notice

There is no prescribed form to be used when leaseholders serve notice notifying their landlord that they are enfranchising their building freehold, although certain information must be contained in the notice. The following is a sample Enfranchisement Notice.

INITIAL NOTICE BY QUALIFYING TENANTS
Under the Leasehold Reform, Housing and
Urban Development Act 1993

Part I, Chapter I, Section 13

Re: [*address of building*]

To: [*name of landlord*] of [*address of landlord*] [*Reversioner*]

This is an official Collective Enfranchisement Notice from the participating qualifying tenants of [*name and address of building*], a list of whom is provided in the attached Schedule (participating tenants).

1. The premises of which the freehold is proposed to be acquired under Section 1(1) of the Act are outlined in [*identify colour*] on the attached plan and known as: [*name and address of the building*].

2. The property of which the freehold is proposed to be acquired by virtue of Section 1(2)(a) of the Act is outlined in [*identify colour*] on the attached plan and known as: [*identify any garages, driveways, pathways, gardens and storage units*] at [*name of building*].

3. (a) The property over which it is proposed that the rights set out in 3(b) should be granted under Section 13(3)(a)(iii) of the Act is shown outlined in [*identify colour*] on the attached plan.

    (b) The rights referred to in the preceding paragraph are: [*identify, for instance, rights of way on foot and by vehicle rights of support and protection*].

4. The grounds upon which it is claimed that the specified premises are premises to which Part I, Chapter I of the Act applies are:

    (a) they consist of a self-contained building or part of a building;

(b) they contain two or more flats held by qualifying tenants;

(c) the total number of flats held by qualifying tenants is not less than two-thirds of the total number of flats contained in the premises; and

(d) the total number of participating flat lessees is 50 per cent of all the flats in the premises.

5. The leasehold interest proposed to be acquired under or by virtue of Section 2(1)(a) or (b) of the Act is: [*complete as relevant*].

6. The flats or other units contained in the specified premises in relation to which it is considered that requirements in Part II of Schedule 9 are applicable are as follows: [*complete as relevant*].

7. The proposed purchase price is:

£[*insert offer price for freehold*] for the freehold interest in the specified premises.

£[*insert offer price for other property, if relevant*] for the property within paragraph 2 of this notice.

For the leasehold interest(s) within paragraph 5 of this notice: £[*insert offer price, if relevant*].

8. The full names of all the qualifying tenants of flats in the specified premises, with the addresses of their flats and the particulars required by the Act, are as follows:

Full name of tenant: See Column 1 of the attached Schedule.

Address of tenant: The flat identified in Column 2 of the attached Schedule (unless otherwise stated in Column 1).

Address of tenant's flat: See Column 2 of the Schedule.

Details of lease:

Date: See Column 3 of the Schedule.

Parties: Lessor: [*name of landlord*] (unless otherwise stated in Column 4 of the Schedule) and Lessee: see Column 4 of the Schedule and any third party details of whom are set out in Column 4 of the Schedule.

Term: [*number of years in term of lease, from the beginning*] years.

Commencement of term: [*date on which lease originally commenced*].

Particulars of property (if different from address of flat): See Column 5 of the Schedule.

9. The full name of the person appointed to act as the nominee purchaser for the purpose of Section 15 of the Act is: [*name of nominee purchaser*].

10. The address to which notices should be sent to the nominee purchaser under Part I, Chapter II of the Act is: [*name and address of enfranchisers' solicitor in England or Wales*].

11. The date by which you must respond to this notice by giving a counter notice under Section 21 is: [*deadline date*].

12. Copies of this notice are being sent to the following relevant landlords:

_____

Dated

_____

Signed

_____

Participating qualifying tenants

Name of participating qualifying tenant	Signature of participating qualifying tenant
_____	_____
_____	_____
_____	_____
_____	_____
(Print name)	(Personal signature)

THE SCHEDULE

COLUMN 1	COLUMN 2	COLUMN 3	COLUMN 4	COLUMN 5	COLUMN 6
Name of Qualifying Tenant	Flat Number	Date of Lease	Lessee as in Lease	Any Additional Property in Lease	Status of Qualifying Tenant
[Name of leaseholder 1]	[Flat no.]	[Date on which lease commenced]	[Name of lessee in lease]	_____	[Participating/ non-participating]
[Name of leaseholder 2]	[Flat no.]	[Date on which lease commenced]	[Name of lessee in lease]	_____	[Participating/ non-participating]
[Name of leaseholder 3]	[Flat no.]	[Date on which lease commenced]	[Name of lessee in lease]	_____	[Participating/ non-participating]
[Name of leaseholder 4]	[Flat no.]	[Date on which lease commenced]	[Name of lessee in lease]	_____	[Participating/ non-participating]
[Name of leaseholder 5]	[Flat no.]	[Date on which lease commenced]	[Name of lessee in lease]	_____	[Participating/ non-participating]
[Name of leaseholder 6]	[Flat no.]	[Date on which lease commenced]	[Name of lessee in lease]	_____	[Participating/ non-participating]
[Name of leaseholder 7]	[Flat no.]	[Date on which lease commenced]	[Name of lessee in lease]	_____	[Participating/ non-participating]
[Name of leaseholder 8]	[Flat no.]	[Date on which lease commenced]	[Name of lessee in lease]	_____	[Participating/ non-participating]

There is no prescribed form to be used when a landlord serves a Counter Notice on his leaseholders, after receiving from the leaseholders an Enfranchisement Notice, but certain information must be contained in the notice. The following is a sample Counter Notice.

LEASEHOLD REFORM, HOUSING AND URBAN DEVELOPMENT ACT 1993 AS AMENDED BY THE COMMONHOLD AND LEASEHOLD REFORM ACT 2002
('The Act')
Section 21
Counter Notice
Admitting Claim

Re: [*address of building*]

Take notice that:

1. [*Name of landlord*] ('the Reversioner') admits that the participating tenants were on the relevant date entitled to exercise the right to collective enfranchisement in relation to the specific premises.

2. The following proposals contained in the Initial Notice are accepted by the Reversioner:

    (a) That the premises of which the freehold is proposed to be acquired by virtue of Section 1(1) of the Act are those shown edged red on the plan attached to the Initial Notice and known as [*address of building*].

    (b) That the purchase price for the property specified in paragraph 2 of the Initial Notice be £[*amount*].

3. The following proposals are not accepted:

    (a) That the property of which the freehold is proposed to be acquired by virtue of Section 1(2)(a) of the Act and shown edged green on the plan attached to the Initial Notice and known as garages 10 and 12, driveways, paths, amenity land, gardens and storage at [*address of building*].

(b) That the property over which it is proposed that the rights set out in 3(b) of the Initial Notice should be granted under Section 13(3)(a)(iii) of the Act are those shown coloured brown on the plan attached to the Initial Notice.

(c) That the purchase price for the freehold interest in the Specified Premises be £[amount].

4. In relation to the proposals which are not accepted, the Reversioner's counter proposals are as follows:

(a) That the property of which the freehold is proposed to be acquired by virtue of Section 1(2)(a) of the Act be limited to that shown shaded green on the plan attached to the Counter Notice and known as garage 10, driveways, pathways, amenity land, gardens and storage at [address of building].

(b) That the property over which it is proposed that the rights set out in 3(b) of the Initial Notice should be granted under Section 13(3)(a)(iii) of the Act are limited to those shown coloured brown on the plan attached to the Counter Notice.

(c) That the proposed purchase price for the freehold interest in the Specified Premises be £[amount].

5. The Reversioner desires to retain the following rights over the land shaded green on the plan attached to the Counter Notice ('the Appurtenant Land'):

(a) The right of way with or without vehicles at all times and for all purposes over and along the Appurtenant Land.

(b) The free and uninterrupted passage of water and oil, gas, electricity and other services from and to the land retained by the Reversioner ('the Retained Land') through such of the sewer's drains, pipes, channels, ducts, wires, cables, mains, watercourses, smoke vents, sanitary water, gas, soil and electrical apparatus and other conduits ('the Conduits') which now serve or shall within the period of 80 years from the date of the transfer of the Specified Premises and the Appurtenant Land to the nominee purchaser ('the Perpetuity Period') serve the Retained Land as are situate in, on, over, under or passing through the Appurtenant Land or Specified Premises and the free and uninterrupted use of all gas, electric, telephone and other services now serving or at any time hereafter within the Perpetuity Period serving the Retained Land.

(c) The right of subjacent and lateral support and shelter and protection for the Retained Land from the Appurtenant Land and the Specified Premises.

(d) The right of entry onto the Appurtenant Land and Specified Premises for the purpose of inspecting, maintaining, repairing and renewing the buildings now or within the Perpetuity Period on the Retained Land and the right to inspect, maintain, repair, renew, connect into, construct, alter and replace the Conduits so as to enable such services as the Reversioner requires to be provided to the Retained Land.

6. The following are the Reversioner's leaseback proposals:

   [*Leasebacks of Flats 4 and 5.*]

7. The Specified Premises are not within an area of a scheme approved as an Estate Management Scheme under Section 70 of the Leasehold Reform, Housing and Urban Development Act 1993.

8. The Reversioner's address for service is: [*address*].

_____

Dated

_____

Signed

Appendix 12: Application to the Leasehold Valuation Tribunal

There is no prescribed form to be used when leaseholders apply to the Leasehold Valuation Tribunal (LVT) to decide on a freehold price, after they serve an Enfranchisement Notice on their landlord in a collective enfranchisement and after they receive a Counter Notice from the landlord. However, certain information must be contained in the application. The following is a sample application to the LVT.

PARTICULARS TO BE INCLUDED IN APPLICATIONS TO THE LEASEHOLD VALUATION TRIBUNAL UNDER THE LEASEHOLD VALUATION TRIBUNALS (PROCEDURE) (ENGLAND) REGULATIONS 2003
Regulation 2(1) and (2) Schedule 2

1. Address of the property, the subject of the application: [*address of building*]

2. State of the purpose of the application and the relevant statutory provision: Section 24 of the Leasehold Reform, Housing and Urban Development Act 1993 – Collective Enfranchisement and determination of the Reversioner's costs under Section 91(2) of the Act:

3. (a) Name and address of the applicant: [*name and address of the nominee purchaser*]

   (b) The names and addresses of the tenants of the premises are set out in the Schedule to the applicant's Notice under Section 13.

4. Name and address of the applicant's representative (if any): [*name and address*]

5. Whether the applicant is the Reversioner or other freeholder or landlord, nominated person, nominee purchaser, tenant or, if none of these, the capacity in which the applicant makes the application: [*nominee purchaser*]

6. Name and address of respondent and whether he is the Reversioner or other freeholder, landlord, nominated person,

nominee purchaser or tenant or, if none of these, capacity of the respondent: [*name and address of landlord, c/o solicitors, if relevant*]

7. If the respondent is not the freehold, the name and address of the freeholder: [*name and address of freeholder*]

8. The name and address of any intermediate landlord which the applicant knows or which could reasonably claim: [*name and address*]

9. Name and address of any person having a mortgage or other charge over or interest in the property held by the freeholder or other landlord which the applicant knows or could reasonably obtain: [*none known*]

10. Copies of:

    (a) any lease (sample enclosed);

    (b) any notice served by any party;

    (c) any application to court or court order; and

    (d) any other documents which are relevant to the application and which the applicant has or could reasonably obtain.

11. Any terms which have already been determined or agreed between the parties including a copy of any draft conveyance or lease: [*none*]

12. Any terms which are in dispute: [*the price, costs, transfer and leaseback*]

13. If an amount or price is in dispute, the amount or price which the applicant considers to be appropriate: £[*amount*]

14. If the application is for the determination of the amount of compensation payable under Section 17 or 18 of the Leasehold Reform Act 1967, details of the circumstances under which the claim for compensation arises: [*N/A*]

15. If the application includes an application for determination of the amount of a subtenant's share of compensation under Section 21(2) of the Leasehold Reform Act 1967, the name and address of the subtenant and a copy of any agreement or subtenancy: [*N/A*]

16. If the application is made under Section 13 of the Landlord and Tenant Act 1987, the date on which the Landlord acquired the

property and the terms of acquisition including the sums paid: [*N/A*]

17. If the application is made under the Landlord and Tenant Act 1987 or under the 1993 Act, a map or plan showing the property and any appurtenant property which is relevant to the application: [*enclosed*]

18. If the application is for the apportionment of an amount under Section 91(2)(e) of the 1993 Act, the circumstances by which the need for apportionment arises and the apportionment which the applicant considers to be appropriate: [*N/A*]

19. If the application relates to the grant of leases back to a former freeholder under Schedule 9 to the 1993 Act, the name and address of any secure tenant, tenant under housing association tenancy, or subtenant to whose interests the tribunal is required to have particular regard: [*N/A*]

20. If the application is made under Section 21(2) of the Leasehold Reform Act 1967, the name and address of the subtenant and a copy of any agreement for the subtenancy: [*N/A*]

21. The applicant believes the facts stated in this application are true.

22. The date of the application [*dd-mm-yy*]

_____

Signed

(Name and address of signatory)

Appendix 13: Section 5 Notice

The following is a sample Section 5 Notice used by a landlord who wishes to sell the freehold of a building and is offering to his leaseholders the right of first refusal.

LANDLORD AND TENANT ACT 1987
Section 5
Landlord's Offer Notice: Private Contract

To   Qualifying tenant as defined by Section 3 of the Act

       Flat 1
       Mr and Mrs Doe (or the current lessee)
       Acacia Mansions
       Long Road
       London W11

From   The landlord as defined by Section 2 of the Act

       Freeholder Company Limited
       Short Street
       London W1

This Notice constitutes an offer by the Landlord to dispose of an interest in the property known as:

Acacia Mansions, Long Road, London W11

For a consideration of £[*amount*] on the terms set out in this Notice.

The estate or interest which the Landlord intends to dispose of is freehold.

The deposit required is £[*amount*].

The other principal terms of the contracts are: [*details*].

The Purchaser shall in addition to the purchase price pay to the Vendor the aggregate amount of all arrears of rent, service charge, insurance premium and other sums or payments due under the leases (if any) which are due or owing by the various tenants and are unpaid on completion.

This offer may be accepted by the requisite majority of qualifying tenants of the constituent flats at any time before [*dd-mm-yy*].

The further period within which a person or persons may be nominated to take the disposal is [*dd-mm-yy*].

_____

Dated

_____

Signed

Landlord's Agent

Landlord's Agent   Landlord Agent Company Limited
                              Middle Road
                              London W1

Appendix 14: Qualifying for right-of-first-refusal freehold purchase

If a landlord wishes to sell the freehold of a building and serves a Section 5 Notice, the leaseholders will be able to buy through the right of first refusal if the building and each would-be participant qualifies.

The right of first refusal can apply to all or part of a building. The right will apply to a property if:

1. it contains two or more flats held by 'qualifying tenants';
2. more than 50 per cent of the flats in the property are held by qualifying tenants;
3. not more than 50 per cent of the property's internal floor space is for commercial use, not counting common parts such as staircases, landings, lobbies and hallways;
4. more than 50 per cent of the qualifying tenants are participating in the purchase of the freehold;
5. the landlord is not a charitable housing trust or the Crown;
6. the building is not a house converted into flats in which the landlord occupies one of the flats as his only or main home and has done so for at least 12 months before the beginning of the freehold sale process.

There are other exemptions regarding buildings in which residents do not have a right of first refusal. Leaseholders in doubt should contact the Leasehold Advisory Service, contact details of which are provided in the section on 'Useful contacts'.

A resident will have a right of first refusal if:

1. he has a 'long lease', that is, the lease term was for more than 21 years at the time it was granted, or the resident is a 'regulated tenant';
2. he does not own or have a tenancy of more than two flats in the building;
3. he is not a 'protected shorthold tenant', an 'assured tenant', an agricultural-occupancy tenant, a business tenant, a resident subletting from a leaseholder or a resident with a tenancy that terminates upon the cessation of employment.

Appendix 15: Section 6 Notice

The following is a sample Section 6 Notice that leaseholders serve on their landlord if they wish to buy their building freehold through the right of first refusal and they have received a Section 5 Notice from the landlord.

LANDLORD AND TENANT ACT 1987
Section 6
Notice of Acceptance by Tenants

TO: Landlord Agent Company Limited
Middle Road
London W1

an Agent for the Landlord as defined by Section 2 of the Act

Freeholder Company Limited
Short Street
London W1

FROM: Project Manager Company Limited
Capital Road
London W2

representing a requisite majority of qualifying tenants at Acacia Mansions, Long Road, London W11, whose names and addresses are set out in the Schedule hereby attached

This Notice constitutes acceptance by a requisite majority of qualifying tenants of the offer by the Landlord to dispose of the freehold of the Property known as:

Acacia Mansions, Long Road, London W11

For the stated consideration of £[*amount*] on the terms set out in the Section 5 Landlord's Offer Notice dated [*dd-mm-yy*].

The identity of the nominee purchaser will be communicated in writing to you by the stated deadline of [*dd-mm-yy*].

_____

Signature of representative of participating qualifying tenants

Tenants' representative   Project Manager Company Limited
                                     Capital Road
                                     London W2

_____

Date

Appendix 16: Participation in an enfranchisement by a new buyer

It is best practice for enfranchisers to use a Participation Agreement and for the agreement to require that any participant selling his flat before the enfranchisement has been concluded to sell to a buyer who automatically takes the seller's place in the enfranchisement process. The following is a sample form to be signed by the buyer of a flat that is participating in an ongoing enfranchisement.

TO: Acacia Mansions Limited
Distant Road
London WC1

This is to confirm, as the new leaseholder of 2 Acacia Mansions, Long Road, London W11, that I/we elect to participate in the collective enfranchisement of Acacia Mansions and that I/we agree to be bound by the Participation Agreement dated [*dd-mm-yy*] between Acacia Mansions Limited and the participating qualifying tenants of Acacia Mansions, Long Road, London W11. I/We understand that the Acacia Mansions Limited share certificate for 2 Acacia Mansions will be transferred to my/our name(s) once the relevant Land Registry proprietor title document has been updated to reflect our purchase of 2 Acacia Mansions.

_____
Signed

_____
Print name(s)

_____
Date

Appendix 17: J30 Stock Transfer Form

SPECIMEN

STOCK
TRANSFER
FORM

J30

(Above this line for Registrars only)

Certificate lodged with the Registrar

Consideration Money £ . . . .

(For completion by the Registrar/Stock Exchange)

Full name of Undertaking.	
Full description of Security.	
Number or amount of Shares, Stock or other security and, in figures column only, number and denomination of units, if any.	Words	Figures
		(units of)
Name(s) of registered holder(s) should be given in full; the address should be given where there is only one holder.	In the name(s) of	Account Designation (if any)

If the transfer is not made by the registered holder(s) insert also the name(s) and capacity (e.g. Executor(s)) of the person(s) making the transfer.

I/We hereby transfer the above security out of the name(s) aforesaid to the person(s) named below *or to the several persons named in Parts 2 of Brokers Transfer Forms relating to the above security:*

Delete words in italics except for stock exchange transactions.
Signature(s) of

1. . . . .

2. . . . .

3. . . . .

4. . . . .

A body corporate should execute this transfer under its common seal or otherwise in accordance with applicable statutory requirements

Stamp of Selling Broker(s) or, for transactions which are not stock exchange transactions, of Agent(s), if any, acting for the Transferor(s).

Date . . . .

PLEASE SIGN HERE ⇨

Full name(s) and full postal address(es) (including County or, if applicable, Postal District number) of the person(s) to whom the security is transferred.

Please state title, if any, or whether Mr., Mrs. or Miss.

Please complete in typewriting or in Block Capitals

Account Designation (if any)

I/We request that such entries be made in the register as are necessary to give effect to this transfer.

| Stamp of Buying Broker(s) (if any) | Stamp or name and address of person lodging this form (if other than the Buying Broker(s)) |

Reference to the Registrar in this form means the registrar or registration agent of the undertaking, not the Registrar of Companies at Companies House

JFL0020 / Rev 5.2 10/99

Reproduced with the permission of Companies House

Appendix 17: J30 Stock Transfer Form (continued)

SPECIMEN

FORM of CERTIFICATE REQUIRED WHERE TRANSFER IS NOT LIABLE TO STAMP DUTY
Pursuant to the Stamp Duty (Exempt Instruments) Regulations 1987

(1) Delete as appropriate
(2) Insert "A", "B" or appropriate category

(1) I/We hereby certify that this instrument falls within category (2) _____ in the schedule to the Stamp Duty (Exempt Instruments) Regulations 1987, set out below.

*Signature(s)

*Description: "Transferor", "Solicitor", or state capacity of other person duly authorised to sign and giving the certificate from his known knowledge of the transaction.

Date _____

*NOTE - The above certificate should be signed by (i) the transferor(s) or (ii) a solicitor or other person (e.g. bank acting as trustee or executor) having a full knowledge of the facts. Such other person must state the capacity in which he signs, that he is authorised so to sign and gives the certificate from his own knowledge of the transactions.

SCHEDULE

A. The vesting of property subject to a trust in the trustees of the trust on the appointment of a new trustee, or in the continuing trustees on the retirement of a trustee.

B. The conveyance or transfer of property the subject of a specific devise or legacy to the beneficiary named in the will (or his nominee).

C. The conveyance or transfer of property which forms part of an intestate's estate to the person entitled on intestacy (or his nominee).

D. The appropriation of property within section 84(4) of the Finance Act 1985 (death: appropriation in satisfaction of a general legacy of money) or section 84(5) or (7) of that Act (death: appropriation in satisfaction of any interest of surviving spouse and in Scotland also of any interest of issue).

E. The conveyance or transfer of property which forms part of the residuary estate of a testator to a beneficiary (or his nominee) entitled solely by virtue of his entitlement under the will.

F. The conveyance or transfer of property out of a settlement in or towards satisfaction of a beneficiary's interest, not being an interest acquired for money or money's worth, being a conveyance or transfer constituting a distribution of property in accordance with the provisions of the settlement.

G. The conveyance or transfer of property on and in consideration only of marriage to a party to the marriage (or his nominee) or to trustees to be held on the terms of a settlement made in consideration only of the marriage.

H. The conveyance or transfer of property within section 83(1) of the Finance Act 1985 (transfers in connection with divorce etc.).

I. The conveyance or transfer by the liquidator of property which formed part of the assets of the company in liquidation to a shareholder of that company (or his nominee) in or towards satisfaction of the shareholder's rights on a winding-up.

J. The grant in fee simple of an easement in or over land for no consideration in money or money's worth.

K. The grant of a servitude for no consideration in money or money's worth.

L. The conveyance or transfer of property operating as a voluntary disposition *inter vivos* for no consideration in money or money's worth nor any consideration referred to in section 57 of the Stamp Act 1891 (conveyance in consideration of a debt etc.).

M. The conveyance or transfer of property by an instrument within section 84(1) of the Finance Act 1985 (death: varying disposition).

Instructional Notes

1. In order to obtain exemption from Stamp Duty on transactions described in the above schedule the Certificate must be completed and may then be lodged for registration or otherwise acted upon. Adjudication by the Stamp Office is not required.

2. This form does not apply to transactions falling within categories (a) and (b) in the form of certificate required where the transfer is not liable to ad valorem stamp duty set out below. In these cases the form of certificate printed below should be used. Transactions within either of those categories require submission of the form to the Stamp Office and remain liable to £5 duty.

FORM OF CERTIFICATE REQUIRED WHERE TRANSFER IS NOT LIABLE TO
AD VALOREM STAMP DUTY

Instruments of transfer are liable to a fixed duty of £5 when the transaction falls within one of the following categories:-

a Transfer by way of security for a loan or re-transfer to the original transferor on repayment of a loan.

b Transfer, not on sale and not arising under any contract of sale and where no beneficial interest in the property passes: (i) to a person who is a mere nominee of, and is nominated only by the transferor; (ii) from a mere nominee who has at all times, held the property on behalf of the transferee; (iii) from one nominee to another nominee of the same beneficial owner where the first nominee has at all times held the property on behalf of that beneficial owner. (NOTE - this category does not include a transfer made in any of the following circumstances: (i) by a holder of stock, etc., following the grant of an option to purchase the stock, to the person entitled to the option or his nominee; (ii) to a nominee in contemplation of a contract for the sale of the stock, etc., then about to be entered into; (iii) from the nominee of a vendor, who has instructed the nominee to deliver by some unstamped writing to hold stock, etc., in trust for a purchaser, to such a purchaser.)

(1) _____ hereby certify that the transaction in respect of which this transfer is made is one which falls within the category (2) _____ above
(3) _____

(1) "I" or "We".

(2) Insert "(a)" or "(b)"

*Signature(s)

*Description ("Transferor", "Solicitor", etc.)

(3) Here set out concisely the facts explaining the transaction. Adjudication may be required.

Date _____

*NOTE - The above certificate should be signed by (1) the transferor(s) or (2) a member of a stock exchange or a solicitor or an accredited representative of a bank acting for the transferor(s), in cases falling within (a) where the bank or its official nominee is a party to the transfer, a certificate, instead of setting out the facts, may be to the effect that "the transfer is exempted from Section 74 of the Finance (1909-10) Act 1910". A certificate in other cases should be signed by a solicitor or other person (e.g. a bank acting as trustee or executor) having a full knowledge of the facts.

This certificate relates to an instrument made on _____ between:-

JFL0028 / Rev 5.2 10/99

Reproduced with the permission of Companies House

Appendix 18: Present value table

The present value table shows the amount of money that would need to be invested today, for a specific number of years at an identified yield, to produce £1 at the end of the term, given interest that is compounded annually.

Present value of £1 to be paid in the future

Years	5.0%	5.5%	6.0%	6.5%
1	0.952381	0.947867	0.943396	0.938967
2	0.907029	0.898452	0.889996	0.881659
3	0.863838	0.851614	0.839619	0.827849
4	0.822702	0.807217	0.792094	0.777323
5	0.783526	0.765134	0.747258	0.729881
6	0.746215	0.725246	0.704961	0.685334
7	0.710681	0.687437	0.665057	0.643506
8	0.676839	0.651599	0.627412	0.604231
9	0.644609	0.617629	0.591898	0.567353
10	0.613913	0.585431	0.558395	0.532726
11	0.584679	0.554911	0.526788	0.500212
12	0.556837	0.525982	0.496969	0.469683
13	0.530321	0.498561	0.468839	0.441017
14	0.505068	0.472569	0.442301	0.414100
15	0.481017	0.447933	0.417265	0.388827
16	0.458112	0.424581	0.393646	0.365095
17	0.436297	0.402447	0.371364	0.342813
18	0.415521	0.381466	0.350344	0.321890
19	0.395734	0.361579	0.330513	0.302244
20	0.376889	0.342729	0.311805	0.283797
21	0.358942	0.324862	0.294155	0.266476
22	0.341850	0.307926	0.277505	0.250212
23	0.325571	0.291873	0.261797	0.234941
24	0.310068	0.276657	0.246979	0.220602
25	0.295303	0.262234	0.232999	0.207138

Present value of £1 to be paid in the future

Years	7.0%	7.5%	8.0%	8.5%
1	0.934579	0.930233	0.925926	0.921659
2	0.873439	0.865333	0.857339	0.849455
3	0.816298	0.804961	0.793832	0.782908
4	0.762895	0.748801	0.735030	0.721574
5	0.712986	0.696559	0.680583	0.665045
6	0.666342	0.647962	0.630170	0.612945
7	0.622750	0.602755	0.583490	0.564926
8	0.582009	0.560702	0.540269	0.520669
9	0.543934	0.521583	0.500249	0.479880
10	0.508349	0.485194	0.463193	0.442285
11	0.475093	0.451343	0.428883	0.407636
12	0.444012	0.419854	0.397114	0.375702
13	0.414964	0.390562	0.367698	0.346269
14	0.387817	0.363313	0.340461	0.319142
15	0.362446	0.337966	0.315242	0.294140
16	0.338735	0.314387	0.291890	0.271097
17	0.316574	0.292453	0.270269	0.249859
18	0.295864	0.272049	0.250249	0.230285
19	0.276508	0.253069	0.231712	0.212244
20	0.258419	0.235413	0.214548	0.195616
21	0.241513	0.218989	0.198656	0.180292
22	0.225713	0.203711	0.183941	0.166167
23	0.210947	0.189498	0.170315	0.153150
24	0.197147	0.176277	0.157699	0.141152
25	0.184249	0.163979	0.146018	0.130094

Present value of £1 to be paid in the future

Years	9.0%	9.5%	10.0%	10.5%
1	0.917431	0.913242	0.909091	0.904977
2	0.841680	0.834011	0.826446	0.818984
3	0.772183	0.761654	0.751315	0.741162
4	0.708425	0.695574	0.683013	0.670735
5	0.649931	0.635228	0.620921	0.607000
6	0.596267	0.580117	0.564474	0.549321
7	0.547034	0.529787	0.513158	0.497123
8	0.501866	0.483824	0.466507	0.449885
9	0.460428	0.441848	0.424098	0.407136
10	0.422411	0.403514	0.385543	0.368449
11	0.387533	0.368506	0.350494	0.333438
12	0.355535	0.336535	0.318631	0.301754
13	0.326179	0.307338	0.289664	0.273080
14	0.299246	0.280674	0.263331	0.247132
15	0.274538	0.256323	0.239392	0.223648
16	0.251870	0.234085	0.217629	0.202397
17	0.231073	0.213777	0.197845	0.183164
18	0.211994	0.195230	0.179859	0.165760
19	0.194490	0.178292	0.163508	0.150009
20	0.178431	0.162824	0.148644	0.135755
21	0.163698	0.148697	0.135131	0.122855
22	0.150182	0.135797	0.122846	0.111181
23	0.137781	0.124015	0.111678	0.100616
24	0.126405	0.113256	0.101526	0.091055
25	0.115968	0.103430	0.092296	0.082403

Appendix 19: Relativity table

Leasehold values as a proportion of freehold value

Lease Length Remaining (Years)	2002 – Enfranchisable	Lease Length Remaining (Years)	2002 – Enfranchisable
125	98.1%	72	89.7%
99	97.6%	71	89.4%
98	97.4%	70	89.1%
97	97.1%	69	88.7%
96	96.9%	68	88.3%
95	96.6%	67	88.0%
94	96.3%	66	87.6%
93	96.1%	65	87.2%
92	95.8%	64	86.8%
91	95.5%	63	86.4%
90	95.3%	62	86.0%
89	95.0%	61	85.6%
88	94.7%	60	85.2%
87	94.4%	59	84.8%
86	94.1%	58	84.4%
85	93.9%	57	84.0%
84	93.6%	56	83.5%
83	93.3%	55	83.1%
82	93.0%	54	82.6%
81	92.7%	53	82.2%
80	92.4%	52	81.7%
79	92.0%	51	81.2%
78	91.7%	50	80.7%
77	91.4%	49	80.2%
76	91.1%	48	79.7%
75	90.8%	47	79.2%
74	90.4%	46	78.7%
73	90.1%	45	78.1%

Lease Length Remaining (Years)	2002 – Enfranchisable	Lease Length Remaining (Years)	2002 – Enfranchisable
44	77.6%	24	62.6%
43	77.0%	23	61.5%
42	76.4%	22	60.4%
41	75.8%	21	59.3%
40	75.2%	20	58.0%
39	74.6%	19	56.8%
38	73.9%	18	55.4%
37	73.3%	17	54.0%
36	72.6%	16	52.5%
35	71.9%	15	50.9%
34	71.2%	14	49.2%
33	70.4%	13	47.4%
32	69.7%	12	45.4%
31	68.9%	11	43.2%
30	68.1%	10	40.9%
29	67.2%	9	38.3%
28	66.4%	8	35.4%
27	65.5%	7	32.1%
26	64.5%	6	28.2%
25	63.6%	5	23.7%

Source: Savills Research 2003

(Savills Research stated in 2006 that important Lands Tribunal decisions might require a revision of the relativity table.)

Appendix 20: Sample valuation

The following is a sample valuation of a 90-year lease extension, using the formula provided in the Leasehold Reform, Housing and Urban Development Act 1993, as amended by the Commonhold and Leasehold Reform Act 2002. In many blocks of flats, the cost of the share of the building freehold is effectively the same as the cost of a 90-year lease extension.

Information on property:

Property:	Flat 1, Acacia Mansions, Long Road, London W11
Years left on lease:	70
Ground rent per annum:	£100

Values:

Market value of flat with 70 years on lease:	£440,000
Estimated value of lease as percentage of expected value with the freehold:	88%
Expected market value of flat with 90 years added to existing 70 years:	£495,000
Expected freehold market value of flat:	£500,000
Yield:	6%

Calculation of value of 90-year lease extension:

Diminution in value of freeholder's interest

Loss of ground rent			£100	
x years purchase	70 years @ 6.00%		16.38454	£1,638

Diminution in value of freeholder's interest

Reversion	Freehold value		£500,000		
	x present value £1	70 years @ 6.00%	0.016927	£8,464	
				£10,102	
Less					
Future interest	Freehold value		£500,000		
	x present value £1	160 years @ 6.00%	8.93396	£45	
	Total value of landlord's interests			**£10,057**	

Marriage value

Extended lease value		£495,000
Landlord's future interest value		£45
		£495,045

Less

Landlord's present interest	£10,057		
Existing lease			
(S110(4) HA 1996 amendment)	£440,000		
		£450,057	
Marriage value		£44,988	
Landlord's portion	@ 50%		**£22,494**
Total compensation payable for lease extension			**£32,551**

Sample valuation provided by Mark Wilson MRICS, myleasehold.com

Appendix 21: Sample of Leasehold Valuation Tribunal Decisions

Date	Address	Type of LVT Case	Years Left on Lease	Tenant Valuation	Landlord Valuation	LVT Decision	Yield Rate
12/09/2005	Flats 9–81 (Odd numbers only) Burns Drive, Hemel Hempstead, Hertfordshire HR1 2EP	Collective enfranchisement	68	£66,000	£201,637	£108,365	9%
18/10/2005	62 Mallaby Close, Shirley, Solihull, West Midlands B90 2PW	Lease extension	68	£4,532	£6,000	£4,567	7.50%
27/10/2005	54 and 54a Burnbury Road, London SW12 0EL	Lease extension	77	£9,600	£22,250	£12,585	8%
31/10/2005	16 Dugdale Hill Lane, Potters Bar, Herts EN6 2DW	Lease extension	57	£11,000	£20,758	£13,170	9%
31/10/2005	Hillside Court, 409 Finchley Road, London NW3 6HQ	Collective enfranchisement	71	£387,000	£731,067	£521,670	7.25%
02/11/2005	59 Truro Road, London N22 8EH	Collective enfranchisement	79	£5,090	£13,137	£10,400	8%
15/11/2005	43 Rednall Drive, Sutton Coldfield, West Midlands B75 5LG	Lease extension	58	£6,774	£13,211	£8,586	7%
22/11/2005	Flat 3, 29 Evelyn Gardens, London SW7 4AQ	Lease extension	44	£95,000	£131,145	£110,270	5.50%
24/11/2005	1 Cropthorne Court, Calthorpe Road, Edgbaston, Birmingham, West Midlands B15 1QP	Lease extension	25	£36,594	£44,059	£39,189	7%
07/12/2005	887a Oxford Road, Reading, Berkshire RG30 6TR	Lease extension	80	£360	£5,000	£360	7.50%

Date	Address	Type of LVT Case	Years Left on Lease	Tenant Valuation	Landlord Valuation	LVT Decision	Yield Rate
13/01/2006	Falstaff Court, Guild Street, Stratford upon Avon, Warwickshire CV37 6RB	Collective enfranchisement	65	£80,100	£218,668	£153,361	7%
31/01/2006	Third Floor, 8–10 Nile Street, London N1 7RF	Lease extension	42	£18,419	£90,061	£71,323	7.50%
01/02/2006	Raffles House, Brampton Grove, London NW4 7AT	Collective enfranchisement	60	£1,270,900	£1,708,424	£1,462,007	6.50%
08/02/2006	67 Grafton Road, London W3 6PF	Collective enfranchisement	79	£6,175	£15,500	£13,310	7%
16/02/2006	27 Woodside Court, Woodside Road, Portswood, Southampton SO1 2AP	Lease extension	64	£2,196	£9,600	£2,196	10%
10/03/2006	Hartley Court, 84 Woodstock Road; Oxford OX2 7PF	Collective enfranchisement	66	£325,500	£489,000	£384,840	7.50%

Appendix 22: OC2 Form

SPECIMEN

Application for official copies of documents only	**Land Registry** **OC2**

Land Registry _____ Office

The correct title number must be quoted. Use one form per title. If you need more room than is provided for in a panel, use continuation sheet CS and attach to this form.

1. Administrative area and postcode if known

2. Title number

3. Property description *Please give a full property description.*

4. Payment of fee *Place "X" in the appropriate box.*

☐ The Land Registry fee of £ [   ] accompanies this application.

☐ Debit the Credit Account mentioned in panel 5 with the appropriate fee payable under the current Land Registration Fee Order.

For official use only

Impression of fees

5. The application has been lodged by:
Land Registry Key No. (if appropriate)
Name
Address/DX No.

Reference
E-mail

Telephone No.	Fax No.

6. If the official copies are to be sent to anyone other than the applicant in panel 5, please supply the name and address of the person to whom they should be sent.

Reference

Appendix 22: OC2 Form (continued)

SPECIMEN

7.	I apply for official copies of the documents listed below

Documents which are referred to in the register of the above title
Applications specifying "All", "Any", etc., will be rejected.

Nature of document	Date of document	Title number under which it is filed	No. of copies

Documents which are not referred to in the register
Please supply as much detail as possible.

Nature of document	Date of document, if known	No. of copies

8. Signature of applicant _____ Date _____

© Crown copyright (ref: LR/HQ/Internet) 10/03

Appendix 23: Form 10 for the appointment of the founding directors and secretary

SPECIMEN

Companies House
— for the record —

Please complete in typescript,
or in bold black capitals.
CHFP000

Notes on completion appear on final page

First directors and secretary and intended situation of registered office

10

Company Name in full

Proposed Registered Office

(PO Box numbers only, are not acceptable)

Post town

County / Region — Postcode

If the memorandum is delivered by an agent for the subscriber(s) of the memorandum mark the box opposite and give the agent's name and address.

Agent's Name

Address

Post town

County / Region — Postcode

Number of continuation sheets attached

You do not have to give any contact information in the box opposite but if you do, it will help Companies House to contact you if there is a query on the form. The contact information that you give will be visible to searchers of the public record.

Tel

DX number — DX exchange

Companies House receipt date barcode

This form has been provided free of charge by Companies House.

10/03

When you have completed and signed the form please send it to the Registrar of Companies at:
Companies House, Crown Way, Cardiff, CF14 3UZ — **DX 33050 Cardiff**
for companies registered in England and Wales — **or**
Companies House, 37 Castle Terrace, Edinburgh, EH1 2EB — **DX 235 Edinburgh**
for companies registered in Scotland — **or LP - 4 Edinburgh 2**

Reproduced with the permission of Companies House

Appendix 23: Form 10 for the appointment of the founding directors and secretary (continued)

SPECIMEN

Company Secretary (see notes 1-5)

	Company name	
NAME	*Style / Title	*Honours etc
* Voluntary details	Forename(s)	
	Surname	
	Previous forename(s)	
	Previous surname(s)	

†† Tick this box if the address shown is a service address for the beneficiary of a Confidentiality Order granted under section 723B of the Companies Act 1985 otherwise, give your usual residential address. In the case of a corporation or Scottish firm, give the registered or principal office address.

Address ††	
Post town	
County / Region	Postcode
Country	

I consent to act as secretary of the company named on page 1

Consent signature | **Date**

Directors (see notes 1-5)

Please list directors in alphabetical order

NAME	*Style / Title	*Honours etc
	Forename(s)	
	Surname	
	Previous forename(s)	
	Previous surname(s)	

†† Tick this box if the address shown is a service address for the beneficiary of a Confidentiality Order granted under section 723B of the Companies Act 1985 otherwise, give your usual residential address. In the case of a corporation or Scottish firm, give the registered or principal office address.

Address ††	
Post town	
County / Region	Postcode
Country	

Day Month Year

Date of birth | **Nationality**

Business occupation

Other directorships

I consent to act as director of the company named on page 1

Consent signature | **Date**

Reproduced with the permission of Companies House

Appendix 23: Form 10 for the appointment of the founding directors and secretary (continued)

SPECIMEN

Directors (see notes 1-5)

Please list directors in alphabetical order

NAME	*Style / Title	*Honours etc
* Voluntary details	Forename(s)	
	Surname	
	Previous forename(s)	
	Previous surname(s)	

†† Tick this box if the address shown is a service address for the beneficiary of a Confidentiality Order granted under section 723B of the Companies Act 1985 otherwise, give your usual residential address. In the case of a corporation or Scottish firm, give the registered or principal office address.

Address ††	
Post town	
County / Region	Postcode
Country	

Day   Month   Year

Date of birth		Nationality

Business occupation	
Other directorships	

I consent to act as director of the company named on page 1

Consent signature		Date

This section must be signed by either an agent on behalf of all subscribers or the subscribers (i.e those who signed as members on the memorandum of association).

Signed		Date	
Signed		Date	
Signed		Date	
Signed		Date	
Signed		Date	
Signed		Date	
Signed		Date	

Reproduced with the permission of Companies House

Appendix 24: Form 288c for the change in contact details of a director

SPECIMEN

Companies House
for the record

Please complete in typescript,
or in bold black capitals.

CHFP000

288c

CHANGE OF PARTICULARS for director
or secretary (NOT for appointment (use Form 288a) or resignation (use Form 288b))

Company Number

Company Name in full

Changes of particulars form
Complete in all cases

Date of change of particulars | Day | Month | Year

Name — *Style / Title* — *Honours etc*

Forename(s)

Surname

† Date of Birth | Day | Month | Year

Change of name (enter new name) Forename(s)

Surname

Change of usual residential address ††
(enter new address)

†† Tick this box if the address shown is a service address for the beneficiary of a Confidentiality Order granted under the provisions of section 723B of the Companies Act 1985

Post town

County / Region — Postcode

Country

Other change (please specify)

A serving director, secretary etc must sign the form below.

* Voluntary details.
† Directors only.
**Delete as appropriate.

Signed — **Date**

(** director / secretary / administrator / administrative receiver / receiver manager / receiver)

You do not have to give any contact information in the box opposite but if you do, it will help Companies House to contact you if there is a query on the form. The contact information that you give will be visible to searchers of the public record.

Tel

DX number — DX exchange

Companies House receipt date barcode

This form has been provided free of charge by Companies House.

10/03

When you have completed and signed the form please send it to the Registrar of Companies at:
Companies House, Crown Way, Cardiff, CF14 3UZ — DX 33050 Cardiff
for companies registered in England and Wales — **or**
Companies House, 37 Castle Terrace, Edinburgh, EH1 2EB — DX 235 Edinburgh
for companies registered in Scotland — or LP - 4 Edinburgh 2

Reproduced with the permission of Companies House

Appendix 25: Form 288a for the appointment of a director or secretary

SPECIMEN

Companies House
— for the record —

Please complete in typescript,
or in bold black capitals.

CHFP000

288a

APPOINTMENT of director or secretary
(NOT for resignation (use Form 288b) or change
of particulars (use Form 288c))

Company Number

Company Name in full

	Day Month Year		Day Month Year
Date of appointment		†Date of Birth	

Appointment form
Notes on completion appear on reverse.

Appointment as director — as secretary — Please mark the appropriate box. If appointment is as a director and secretary mark both boxes.

NAME
*Style / Title
†Honours etc
Forename(s)
Surname
Previous Forename(s) — Previous Surname(s)

†† Tick this box if the address shown is a service address for the beneficiary of a Confidentiality Order granted under the provisions of section 723B of the Companies Act 1985

†† Usual residential address
Post town — Postcode
County / Region — Country
†Nationality — †Business occupation
†Other directorships (additional space overleaf)

I consent to act as ** director / secretary of the above named company

Consent signature — **Date**

* Voluntary details.
† Directors only.
**Delete as appropriate

A director, secretary etc must sign the form below.

Signed — **Date**

(**a director / secretary / administrator / administrative receiver / receiver manager / receiver)

You do not have to give any contact information in the box opposite but if you do, it will help Companies House to contact you if there is a query on the form. The contact information that you give will be visible to searchers of the public record.

Tel

DX number — DX exchange

Companies House receipt date barcode

This form has been provided free of charge by Companies House.

10/03

When you have completed and signed the form please send it to the Registrar of Companies at:
Companies House, Crown Way, Cardiff, CF14 3UZ DX 33050 Cardiff
for companies registered in England and Wales or
Companies House, 37 Castle Terrace, Edinburgh, EH1 2EB DX 235 Edinburgh
for companies registered in Scotland or LP - 4 Edinburgh 2

Reproduced with the permission of Companies House

Appendix 25: Form 288a for the appointment of a director or secretary (continued)

SPECIMEN

Company Number

† Directors only.   †Other directorships

NOTES

Show the full forenames, NOT INITIALS. If the director or secretary is a corporation or Scottish firm, show the name on surname line and registered or principal office on the usual residential line.

Give previous forenames or surname(s) except:
- for a married woman, the name by which she was known before marriage need not be given.
- for names not used since the age of 18 or for at least 20 years

A peer or individual known by a title may state the title instead of or in addition to the forenames and surname and need not give the name by which that person was known before he or she adopted the title or succeeded to it.

Other directorships.

Give the name of every company incorporated in Great Britain of which the person concerned is a director or has been a director at any time in the past five years.

You may exclude a company which either is, or at all times during the past five years when the person concerned was a director, was
- dormant
- a parent company which wholly owned the company making the return, or
- another wholly owned subsidiary of the same parent company.

Reproduced with the permission of Companies House

Appendix 26: Form 288b for termination of director or secretary

SPECIMEN

Companies House
——— *for the record* ———

Please complete in typescript,
or in bold black capitals.
CHFP000

288b

Terminating appointment as director or secretary
(NOT for appointment (use Form 288a) or change of particulars (use Form 288c))

Company Number

Company Name in full

	Day	Month	Year
Date of termination of appointment			

as director   as secretary

Please mark the appropriate box. If terminating appointment as a director and secretary mark both boxes.

NAME   *Style / Title   *Honours etc

Please insert details as previously notified to Companies House.

Forename(s)

Surname

	Day	Month	Year
†Date of Birth			

A serving director, secretary etc must sign the form below.

Signed   **Date**

* Voluntary details.
† Directors only.
** Delete as appropriate

(** serving director / secretary / administrator / administrative receiver / receiver manager / receiver)

You do not have to give any contact information in the box opposite but if you do, it will help Companies House to contact you if there is a query on the form. The contact information that you give will be visible to searchers of the public record.

Tel

DX number   DX exchange

Companies House receipt date barcode

This form has been provided free of charge by Companies House.

10/03

When you have completed and signed the form please send it to the Registrar of Companies at:
Companies House, Crown Way, Cardiff, CF14 3UZ   **DX 33050 Cardiff**
for companies registered in England and Wales   **or**
Companies House, 37 Castle Terrace, Edinburgh, EH1 2EB   **DX 235 Edinburgh**
for companies registered in Scotland   **or LP - 4 Edinburgh 2**

Reproduced with the permission of Companies House

Glossary

Absent landlord	A landlord the whereabouts of whom are not known to the leaseholders of the property.
Appurtenant property	A garage, outhouse, garden, yard, courtyard or other property outside the building, as referred to in Enfranchisement Notices.
Assured tenancy	A tenancy where the tenant has security of tenure and other rights under Part I of the Housing Act 1988.
Collective enfranchisement	See *enfranchisement, collective.*
Common parts	The parts of the building used by all residents, such as the front entrance and lobby, common staircase and common hallways.
Commonhold	A type of property ownership that took effect in 2004 that allows freehold ownership of individual flats, houses and non-residential units within a building or estate. Possession by commonhold, which is an alternative to the leasehold system, is not limited by time as with a lease.
Counter Notice	See *Section 21 Notice.*
Covenant	A legally-binding promise, as referred to in leases.
Demised	The grant of a leasehold interest, as referred to in leases.
Demised premises	The flat or house that is the subject of the lease.

Discount rate	The rate, also known as the yield, that is applied to calculate the present value of the future ground rent income stream and the present value of the reversion that the landlord will lose when forced to sell a freehold through an enfranchisement, similar to a compound interest rate.
Enfranchisement, collective	The process by which leaseholders collectively compel the landlord to sell to them the freehold of their building at a fair price in a statutory timeframe.
Enfranchisement, individual	The process by which a leaseholder compels his landlord to sell a 90-year lease extension at a fair price in a statutory timeframe.
Enfranchisement Notice	See *Section 13 Notice*.
Freeholder	The holder of the freehold interest of a property, usually the landlord.
Head leaseholder	The owner of a superior lease to that held by ordinary leaseholders, but which is not the freehold. This is also known as the party that holds an intermediate interest in a property.
Housing association	An organisation, body of trustees or a company that provides or manages housing and that does not operate for a profit. A registered housing association means an association that is registered with the Housing Corporation.
Initial Notice	See *Section 13 Notice*.
Intermediate interest	A middle-level ownership title in a property which is above the level of ordinary leaseholders and below the freeholder. This is also referred to as a 'head lease'.
Landlord	The immediate superior property owner above the leaseholders, from whom the leaseholders can seek a lease extension. The landlord is usually the freeholder.

Leaseback	A 999-year lease with a 'peppercorn' or zero ground rent that the nominee purchaser must agree to grant to the freeholder at the time of an enfranchisement for any flats in the building that are owned by the freeholder.
Lessee	Tenant or leaseholder.
Lessor	Landlord (usually the freeholder).
Marriage value	The additional value created in a flat or house by 'marrying' or combining the freehold and leasehold interests. The two interests are combined when the leaseholders buy the freehold of the building or, on an individual basis, a leaseholder secures a lease extension for his flat of 90 years or more.
Nominee purchaser	The person, company or other entity that buys the freehold of a building in an enfranchisement, on behalf of the participating leaseholders.
Peppercorn	Zero ground rent. Also known as 'peppercorn rent'.
Protected and statutory tenancies	Tenancies that have security of tenure and rent regulation under the Rent Act 1977. Where a protected tenancy comes to an end by a Notice to Quit, the tenant becomes a statutory tenant provided he is residing in the premises.
Public sector landlord	A landlord, such as a local authority, new town corporation or others defined in the Housing Act 1985, Section 1972.
Resident landlord	A freeholder or a member of his family who occupies as his only or principal home a flat in a building that is not a purpose-built block.
Resident management company	A company owned by residents who collectively own the freehold of their building or intend to buy the building. Also known as an RMC.
Reversion	The ownership interest in a flat or house that will return to the landlord (freeholder) at the end of the term of the lease.

Reversioner	The freeholder or landlord.
Right to manage company	A company set up and owned by residents that has the right to manage the building. Also known as an RTM company.
Section 5 Notice	The notice that must be served by a landlord wishing to sell the freehold of a building and to offer the right of first refusal to qualifying residents. (Refers to the relevant section of the Landlord and Tenant Act 1987.)
Section 6 Notice	The notice that must be served on the landlord by leaseholders that wish to buy their building freehold through the right of first refusal, after they have received a Section 5 Notice from the landlord. (Refers to the relevant section of the Landlord and Tenant Act 1987.)
Section 13 Notice	The initial notice served by leaseholders on a landlord informing him of their intention to collectively enfranchise the freehold of the building. Also known as the Enfranchisement Notice or the Initial Notice. (Refers to the relevant section of the Leasehold Reform, Housing and Urban Development Act 1993.)
Section 18 Notice	The notice that must be served by the nominee purchaser on a landlord in a collective enfranchisement if agreement is reached with a non-participant to join in the enfranchisement process. (Refers to the relevant section of the Leasehold Reform, Housing and Urban Development Act 1993.)
Section 21 Notice	The Counter Notice served by the landlord on the leaseholders after the landlord receives from the leaseholders a Section 13 Notice informing him of their intention to collectively enfranchise the freehold of the building. (Refers to the relevant section of the Leasehold Reform, Housing and Urban Development Act 1993.)

Secure tenancy	A tenancy or a licence that carries security of tenure, the right to buy and other legal rights under the Housing Act 1985. Many secure tenants are tenants of a local authority. Registered housing associations were able to create secure lets before January 1989. Since January 1989, most new lets by housing associations are on assured tenancies.
Tenant	A person or entity that holds a tenancy, including a leasehold, of a flat or house and thus has identified rights to occupy and use the property.
Tenant's interest	The value that a leaseholder is considered to hold in his leasehold property.
Term	The number of years granted by the lease, such as 99 years.
Underlease	The leasehold title held by the head leaseholder, below the freehold and above the ordinary leaseholders.
Unit	A flat.
Yield	See *discount rate*.

Index

This index covers all parts of the text. An 'f.' after a page number indicates a figure, or figure and text; a 'g.' indicates a glossary entry; a 't.' indicates a table, or table and text.